We Will Be Free

Memoirs of an East Prussian Survivor

Ulrich Karl Thomas

Copyright © 2015 Ulrich Karl Thomas

All rights reserved.

ISBN-13: 978-1516967490
ISBN-10: 1516967496

DEDICATION

For all my fellow Königsbergers
who did not live to tell the story

*"And you shall know the truth,
And the truth shall make you free."*
John 8:32

CONTENTS

	Acknowledgment	i
1	Bridges of Königsberg	1
2	Nitwits from the Lomse	15
3	Where've all the Flowers Gone?	35
4	Bits of Amber	51
5	A Soldier at Heart	67
6	Night of Broken Glass	83
7	First Gunner	103
8	The Herring Division	123
9	Everything Passes	143
10	To the Victor go the Spoils	175
	Epilogue	201
	Poem (Heimweh/Longing)	202
	About the Author	204

ACKNOWLEDGMENT

My daughter, Mary Ann (Thomas) Kassian, spent countless hours weaving the bits and pieces together, searching for and finding missing details and historical facts. She deserves credit for spurring me on to write, and for diligently forging the manuscript into the story you are about to read.

1 | BRIDGES OF KÖNIGSBERG

If I close my eyes I can still smell the distinct odor of the river, feel the dampness of the cool breeze, and hear the bustle of activity—Tugs chugging and straining to pull their loads. The penetrating whistle of steam ships. Smoke stacks belching out bursts of hissing steam. Drawbridges groaning as they swung on massive joints. The crash of heavy metallic doors closing off cargo holds. The high-pitched buzz of sawmills. The rumble and grind of machinery. The distant clatter of railway cars. The shouts of longshoremen and street vendors. The clap and jangle of horses pulling carts. The squawk of gulls overhead. I lived in the heart of Königsberg, and I could literally hear the city's pulse.

Königsberg was a magnificent metropolis near the Baltic Sea. A massive lake, which we called '*Das Frische Haff*,' was situated beside the Sea, separated only by a narrow strip of land. A massive storm in the ninth century fortuitously smashed a channel through the land, creating direct access to the sheltered, calm lake waters. This was a perfect situation for docking ships. Königsberg soon became part of the Hanseatic League, a late-medieval association of merchants, and later became the most important seaport in the Kingdom of Prussia.

In the late 1800s a channel was dredged through the Haff and up the River Pregel. By the time I was born in 1925, the Pregel bustled with sea traffic. It had a massive outer harbor with six huge bays carved into its banks. The inner harbor stretched inland more than 6 kilometers, well past the heart of Königsberg. Ships were docked all along the river at various factories and warehouses.

The protected position of its harbor made Königsberg the most important commercial city in the east part of Germany. It exported wheat, and other farm products, timber, hemp, furs, and many manufactured goods. There were huge shipyards, several dry docks of immense capacity, farm machinery, locomotive, rail car factories, and the largest grain elevator in all of Europe.

The city had a beautiful historical center which boasted striking Gothic architecture. Its most prominent landmark was the King's Castle, built in the mid-13th century. It was the seat of the Grand Masters of the Teutonic Knights and the Dukes of Prussia. It contained the *Schloßkirche*, or Palace Church (14th century), where Prussian kings were crowned. It also contained the grandiose *Moscowiter-Saal*, one of the largest halls in the German Reich, and a museum of Prussian history. Adjacent to the Museum of Antiquity was the spectacular "Amber Hall," whose walls were covered with large tiles of amber from the Baltic Sea.

The King's Castle and Palace Church

Dozens of notable writers, artists, mathematicians, and philosophers claimed Königsberg as their birthplace. Its most famous philosopher, Immanuel Kant, lived there all his life. He was appointed to a chair in metaphysics at the University of Königsberg, where he published his influential "Critique of Pure Reason." The famous Kant Library was located right next door to one of the high schools I attended. The internationally renowned Academy of Art on *Königsstraße* (King Street) boasted a collection of works by Italian and early Dutch masters. Statues of several Prussian kings graced the ornate *Königstor* (King's Gate).

And then there was the magnificent Grand Exchange, with fine views of the harbor from the staircase. The offices of the famous Royal Amber factory were located along *Bahnhofsstraße* ("Railway Street"). There was also an observatory, established by the astronomer Friedrich Bessel, a botanical garden, a zoological museum, and a fantastic zoo (which was definitely a popular place for kids). Two large theatres attracted star performers from all over Europe. Altogether, there were some 730 historical and cultural monuments and buildings in the city, which at the time I was born had a population of around 350,000.

I tell you all this so that you can grasp the beauty, grace, culture, and historical significance of the place I called home. Königsberg was to Germany what the city of Paris is to France, and the city of London is to Britain. I want you to get a glimpse of what this incredible Lady was like before she was vengefully and tragically ravaged.

And I must not forget to tell you about her bridges . . . The city is famous for its bridges, and specifically for posing a mathematical puzzle dubbed "The Seven Bridges of Königsberg." You see, the metropolis is built around the River Pregel, which flows through Königsberg in two arms. Two islands are situated in the middle of the city, where the two arms of the river join. I lived on the larger of those two islands. Originally there were seven bridges that joined the two river banks to the two islands, including a bridge between the islands.

'Die Holzbrücke' was the shortest way to the heart of the city from the 'Lomse'

Residents enjoyed taking walks and passing over the bridges that laced together the heart of Königsberg. But over the years, a controversy arose. Someone posed a challenge for walkers to find a way to cross all seven bridges without crossing a bridge twice. The islands could not be reached by any route other than the bridges, and every bridge had to be crossed completely; one could not walk halfway onto the bridge and then turn around and later cross the other half from the other side. It was an interesting challenge. No one could find a way to do it!

The problem came to the attention of a famous Swiss mathematician named Leonhard Euler. In 1735, Euler presented the solution to the problem before the Russian Academy. He explained why crossing all seven bridges without crossing a bridge twice was mathematically impossible. One could not sequentially traverse through an even number of inter-connected terminal points with an odd number of connections. While solving this problem, he developed a new mathematical field called Graph Theory, which is of fundamental importance to the modern-day networks between computers and the internet itself. So the next time you send an email, remember that the bridges of my hometown had something to do with it!

I guess that Euler's study must have spurred Königsberg to build more bridges, because when I was a kid, eight bridges crossed between the river banks and the islands at strategic spots. These were massive draw bridges that provided passage for the ships and stopped all street traffic when raised. A ninth bridge provided for both vehicle and train traffic. It was the longest of its kind in all of Europe as it swung out of the way for ships to pass. Two more bridges should be mentioned, of which one was exclusively for pedestrians and bicycles, spanning not the river but the lower of the two lakes in the city. The other bridge across the river was only for trains.

With numerous bridges, endless riverbanks, meadows, swamps, marshes, ponds, inlets, sandy hills, remnants of fortresses and wall-fortifications, my corner of Königsberg was a delight for children to play and explore. Yes, and sometimes get into trouble. A landfill for construction debris, demolition projects and refuse from the amber factory was often the target for our exploits. More about that later.

Trees graced several streets in the heart of the city. One broad street had a double row of trees down the middle. A schoolmate lived on that street, which had the impressive name: *Kurfürstendamm*; a *Kurfürst* is an appointed representative of the King or *Kaiser* (Emperor). The name suited the area. The street was lined with modern apartment blocks with fancy balconies. It's where the more affluent folks lived. Today, we would call the buildings walk-ups. To my knowledge, none of the apartments in the city, not even the tallest ones, had an elevator. Only major stores and office buildings could boast of such a convenience. A schoolmate, whose family name was Lindemann, lived on *Kurfürstendamm* Street. His mother kept his father's millwork shop going after he died, and they were quite well to do. She owned an automobile and gave me a ride in it on one occasion. Was I ever impressed! It was my only ride in an automobile until 1951.

Another memory I have of *Kurfürstendamm* Street is of numerous balconies being decorated with reeds and bulrushes when Jewish families celebrated the Feast of Tabernacles. Königsberg was home to one third of East Prussia's 13,000 Jews. It was a multi-cultural center, rich with diverse historical and cultural traditions, and religious beliefs.

The first Jewish synagogue was built in 1680 around the Königsberg castle. Eventually, the Jewish community built a new synagogue on *Schnülingsdamm* Street called the Jewish Congregation of Königsberg. It was near my elementary school, just across a plaza, called "*Der Judenmarkt*"—the Jew's Market. Some liberal members split off from this orthodox congregation and founded the *Israelite Synagogal Congregation of Adass Jisroel*. They built a modern synagogue less than a block from our home on Lomse Island. As a child, I never really gave much thought to the Jewish synagogues and customs. The Jews were just part of the colorful mosaic of all the different types of people that inhabited my bustling city.

My daily path to middle school took me down by the port through the Fish Market. It was an open air market, about half a mile long on a broad street along the waterfront. A building, smack in the middle and towards the end of the street had public toilets. Similar facilities were located at strategic places throughout the city.

The Fish Market was in operation every day all year long, except Sundays and major holidays. Some fishing boats moored along the waterfront of the market all day to sell their wares. Other boats docked briefly in the early morning to unload their catch to be sold by other vendors.

I remember it vividly. The fish would squirm in the wooden boxes, their tails flailing, mouth and gills opening and closing, in other words, very much alive. So alive, that sometimes one or even more jumped out of the box, and much to our delight, made their escape by splashing into the river. But most of the time, the vendors quickly apprehended them and threw them back into confinement, stacking another box on top to prevent the slippery offenders from attempting another jail break. The boxes were then loaded onto hand drawn carts, so the vendors could sell their fish throughout the city.

A continuous row of buildings lined the other side of the street. It was tightly packed like building blocks, as most city blocks were. Only the odd narrow passageway, just wide enough to squeeze a cart through, provided connection to the next street.

At the end of one such passage was the well-known, and often crowded 'Cheese Corner'. I don't think I have ever seen a larger variety of cheese. And the great thing about it, was that the vendors would always give us samples to taste. There was no haggling over price there. Every purchase was carefully weighed and wrapped. I could smell the cheese long before I reached the corner. I loved the smell and loved eating the cheese even more.

Without exception, every building along the Fish Market had a store of some kind situated at street level. The upper floors were used for residences, offices, or warehouse space. Our family doctor had his office near the edge of the market, close to the bridge.

A large variety of fish were sold in the market: cod, flounders, pipefish, pike, herring, stickleback, sprat, sardines, smelt, and eels— every kind of species indigenous to the Baltic Sea. Some stores specialized in selling one particular type of fish, while others carried a broad range of products. Certain vendors specialized in a specific method of preservation, such as salted, pickled or smoked.

The stores at street level were unique in another way. The storefronts most often had counters running along their entire width. A hinged canopy was propped open during the day to reveal the seller's goods and to provide protection from sun, rain, or snow. There were no standard store hours, per se. When the shuttered canopies were up, it was a sign that the vendor was open for business. A solid door at the side of the counter provided access to the inside of the store, while a larger recessed doorway provided stairway access to the upper levels of the building.

Barrels of herring, curing in brine, dotted the sidewalk in front of numerous storefronts. The price was clearly marked on the side of the barrels with chalk. Prices were as low as two cents and ranged up to 15 cents for one herring. You had to dip your hand in the barrel to pick out your purchase. The barrels were never more than half empty, as the fish were constantly replenished. They lay out there all day in the open barrel, and were only covered for the night or when the store was closed.

Smoked flounders and eels were prominently displayed on counters. We called the thinner smoked eels, "shoelaces." The larger ones dangled from tall racks, often with fat dripping from their tails.

Smoked sprats came in wooden boxes with secured lids. But at least a box or two would be open for display, and for customers who only wanted to buy a few of the small oily fish. Sprats weren't sold by weight. You had to ask for a handful, or a row or two, if you didn't want an entire box. If you lingered and could not or would not make up your mind, you might be offered a sprat to taste. Your purchase was always wrapped up in old newspapers. It was wise to negotiate beforehand, since the price would be much steeper if you had already committed to buy.

But the most interesting thing, and what the market was best known for, was the fisher-women. They occupied the center strip of the street, sitting back-to-back with stacks of crates by their sides. The uppermost crates were open to display the fish they had for sale.

A small space to allow for foot traffic separated each cluster of four fisher-women from the next. When no customers were at their stands, the women chattered endlessly with each other in Low German (*Platt Deutch*). I would often hear the familiar rumble of their colorful rural slang. My mom could speak Low German. She had picked the dialect up as a girl, from my grandfather. I could understand

A Fisher-Woman selling her wares

it, and do a pretty good imitation, but didn't have much opportunity to use it, so never became fluent.

The fisher-women positioned themselves down the center of the Fish Market come rain or shine, heat or cold. They put up huge umbrellas, which provided them some protection from the elements. All of them wore skirts that were gathered at the waist and extremely wide and long. Most of them also wore bonnet-like head coverings or hats with broad rims. In the winter, they draped cape-like blankets across their shoulders and backs, and kept their hands in fur muffs, which hung around their necks from strings. They also placed pots with smoldering charcoal briquettes under their wide skirts, to keep their feet and legs warm.

Fisher-women sold larger varieties of fish by the piece and smaller varieties by volume. They set their prices arbitrarily, often depending on their mood and their opinion of the buyer. But basically, their prices depended on the type, size, freshness or supply of fish. . . and it declined as the day progressed. How much you paid depended largely on your approach and bargaining skill. The fisher-women would feel cheated if a customer did not haggle. I sometimes heard the bargaining turn into a boisterous shouting match. It was quite comical.

Fisher-women were known for their colorful vocabulary and short tempers. Since most of them spoke only Low German, dealing with them was quite an experience. No passer-by was spared their clamorous, animated, heavily accented invitation to buy their "superior product" and "the freshest on the market anywhere." The fish were fresh indeed and needed to be clubbed on the head once or twice before they could be wrapped up.

If you were not quite convinced of their claims of freshness, they would press the gills open to show you. If you still dared to voice your concern, you could expect to be pelted with fish, not only from that specific woman but from those around her listening in. All one needed to set them off was to insult the quality of their goods, and then you would have to dodge flying fish coming from every direction. As boys we would try to set them off by shouting: "Your fish stink!" and then run.

Fresh (live) eel for sale on the Fish Market were always kept in covered containers, as they were killed in front of you before they were wrapped. It was often hard to pick "your" eel as they were a squirming mass in the container, trying to get out. You brought the freshly-killed eel home to fry. But even though you cleaned and cut it up, some pieces, especially the tail, would still squirm and jump up and down in the pan. "Blue eel," that is eel cooked in water rather than in a pan, would not cause that reaction. But whether fried, cooked, or smoked, eels were so tasty!

The Fish Market used wooden containers of three different sizes and supposedly uniform volume for measuring fish. I always wondered if the measuring boxes truly were uniform in size. Anchovies, smelt, oyster and a larger kind of smelt-like fish were measured and sold like that. To fill the containers, the vendors just scooped the fish into them with their hands.

One had to be vigilant as the fisher-women had different ways of getting ahead. A favorite technique of theirs was to conveniently forget to keep their stubby, bunched fingers out of the container of fish when filling it.

The Cabbage Market, the general market at the far end of the Fish Market, also sold many goods by volume. There, and at markets and stores throughout the rest of the city, vendors used two standard sizes of boxes, which were simply called "a measure" and a "half-measure." The half-measure was about 3 inches high and maybe 6 inches square. The full-measure, as the names imply, was roughly twice that size.

The Cabbage Market only operated during the summer. The booths were draped with bundles of dried herbs, straw flowers, brooms (whisks made of birch branches), and braids of garlic.

Dry beans, peas or lintels and other dry goods were sold by measure. The vendors used metal scoops to heap the goods in whichever measure of box the customer requested. They levelled the measure by drawing a stick across the rim, and then emptied the purchase into the customer's bag. (Yes, we thought of the environment before the Green Environmentalists were even born. You never went to the market without your own bags!)

It was a different story with onions. They weren't levelled. The containers were filled to the brim and then heaped up until the last onion rolled down off the top of the pile. I don't know why, but that was just the way it was.

Some stuff was actually sold by weight. The weights sat in a row in their respective holes in wooden blocks. They had little knobs on top so the merchant could pick them out and place them on the balance. To achieve the requested quantity, several different weights were often needed.

And then there was the famous *"Königsberger Klopse"*—a Prussian specialty of meatballs in white sauce with capers, which is still made today in some specialty restaurants in Kaliningrad and present-day Germany. Barb and Ernie's Restaurant in Edmonton serve them on special occasions. We called them *Saure Klopse* (sour meatballs.) If you're interested, you can find some recipes on the internet.

The Kohl Markt (Cabbage Market)

Most days I used the same route to go to school. But every day there was something unique and interesting to see; like dredges at work, pile drivers pounding new bollards, or divers with shiny diving helmets, rubber suits and heavy lead-soled boots. I loved to watch the divers. Two men would pump air in a steady rhythm, and another would help the diver put on his helmet and secure the glass front. The helpers made gestures with their fingers and tugged on the line for communication when the diver was in the water. We would watch the bubbles rise when the diver worked under water, to see how far he had ventured away from the diving platform. I was fascinated by how they needed help to move in those cumbersome suits—and how, when they came up out of the water, the glass front of their helmets were opened before the helpers stopped pumping air.

Every once in a while, spectators gathered to watch the water police pull an unfortunate casualty out of the river. With many streets or sidewalks extending right to the water's edge, one had to be alert. Heavy steel bollards allowed ships or barges to be tied up for mooring right at the water's edge. A careless person or a drunk might fall in, as there were railings only at sparse intervals, to allow unimpeded access for docking ships.

It was impossible to escape the smell of 'harbor' near the river. It was a pungent blend of bunker oil and ageing fish. The same smell permeated the air when we visited the fisherman's wharf in Los Angeles some years ago. It took me back to the familiar aroma of my childhood.

We could always detect a change in weather or shift in wind by the smell of our river. The outer harbor had a terribly foul odor. When the wind carried that smell in to the city, we knew that all kinds of dying fish would be floating belly up on the surface of the water the next day. The wind would cause the river to slow down, and would sometimes even reverse the flow, depriving the fish of oxygen. When that happened, it was feast day for seabirds.

For a young boy, Königsberg was an extremely colorful and exciting place to live. I didn't understand at the time that this was due in large part to its past and ongoing role in world politics. Historically, Königsberg was a naval and military fortress of the first order. Old fortifications, dating back to the time of the Teutonic Knights, were still evident. The fortifications consisted of an inner wall, connected to an outlying system of walls, and twelve detached forts, of which six were on the right and six on the left bank of the Pregel. Between them lay two great forts and ramparts.

We often played on the remnants of the old fortification—sandy hills—which we called "der Wall." The top of the *Wall* served as a high vantage point from which we could see the traffic on both arms of the River. The old moat was overgrown with bulrushes, it was a wonderful place to play hide and seek. While chasing our playmates, we would occasionally stumble upon lovers who had gone to the *Wall* hoping for privacy in the dense bulrushes. If there had been actual fortified buildings on the island Lomse, they had long since vanished.

In the fall, Mom, my sister, and I went to part of the former fortification, called das *Friedländer Tor* (Gate) to pick rosehips. It was near the old arm of the River. A major road intersected the old fortification. The earth over the massive brick gate was overgrown with wild roses. We harvested the rosehips to make jam. The rosehips were large and fleshy, but it was quite a job to remove the seeds from the fleshy part. I'm sure that none of you can guess what the seeds were good for. Try putting a hairy kernel on under your shirt on your back. No itch powder can do a better job!

As I said, Königsberg played an important role in world politics. In the early 1800s, it was a center for political resistance against Napoleon Bonaparte. In 1871, Königsberg's King Wilhelm I defeated Napoleon III in the Prussian-Franco war. Due in large part to the ongoing conflict with the Napoleonic Empire, Wilhelm succeeded in convincing 25 independent German states to join together under his leadership to form a unified German Empire.

World War 1 began in 1914, less than fifty years later, when the Archduke Ferdinand of the Austro-Hungarian Empire was assassinated. Austria invaded Serbia, whom they blamed for the assassination. Russia mobilized against Austria in support of their ally Serbia. This caused Germany to mobilize against Russia in support of their ally, Austria. The chain of events soon drew all the world's economic powers into two opposing alliances: the Allies—the British Empire, the Russian Empire, America, the French Empire, Belgium, and Italy, versus the Central Powers—the Austro-Hungarian Empire, the German Empire, the Ottoman Empire, and Bulgaria.

More than 9 million soldiers and 7 million civilians died as a result of the war. It was one of the deadliest conflicts in history. Following the defeat of the Central Powers, the Allied victors were in no mood to be charitable to the defeated nations. France was particularly bitter against Germany, and vindictively wanted the German Empire brought to its knees.

The Treaty of Versailles did just that. The most humiliating portion of the treaty was the "guilt clause," which forced Germany to admit blame for a war it did not start. Military clauses forced Germany to disarm, severely restricting the size of its army and navy, and disallowing it from having an air force. Reparation clauses forced Germans to financially repay the world for all the damage it caused. These reparations were assessed at 132 billion Deutschmarks (roughly equivalent to $442 billion US in 2015), a staggering sum that would be paid back in German gold, commodities, resources, ships, securities, and on-going reparation payments from citizens. Territorial clauses stripped Germany of 25,000 square miles of territory and 7 million occupants. The treaty unilaterally gave the province of West Prussia to Poland, creating the Polish Corridor and giving Poland land-access to the Baltic Sea, and the harbor Gdingen, where the bulk of Germany's shipyards were located.

Königsberg and East Prussia were thus separated from the rest of Germany. The Treaty of Versailles literally cut Germany in two. I remember how anxious my parents were when they had to travel across the Corridor to get to my Grandpa Thomas' fiftieth wedding anniversary. The Poles were notorious for making it difficult for Germans to travel back and forth. It was insulting that Germans had to virtually beg to travel across land that had once belonged to them.

Controversial even today, scholars often argue that the excessively punitive terms of the treaty supported the rise of the Nazis and the Third Reich in the 1930's, which in turn led to the outbreak of World War II. Nowhere were the effects of the Treaty of Versailles more keenly felt than in my hometown.

The resentment was general and open; as was a nearly unbearable feeling of impotence. In school our teachers talked openly about the injustice done to Germany—that we had been unjustly blamed, stripped of colonies, robbed of lands, robbed of the rich coal mines of the Saar, and humiliated by our separation from the rest of Germany. We were taught how the Treaty had severely handicapped the economic development of Königsberg and the rest of East Prussia.

A political time bomb ticked away during the years of my childhood. As I spent my boyhood playing along the banks of the Pregel, Hitler's nationalist sentiment and ideology began to gain momentum. *"Mein Kampf"* was widely distributed and eventually adopted as the Bible of virtually every one in public life. About 10 million copies of the book were sold and distributed as required reading for every employee of the state.

I had no inkling that a book published the year I was born would bring about such drastic change. . . and that the city I loved would, in a few short years, become such a bastion of Nazi philosophy.

Seven Bridges:

1. Grüne Brüke (Green Bridge)
2. Köttel Brüke
3. Kaiser Brüke (King's Bridge)
4. Honig Brüke (Honey Bridge)
5. Krämer Brüke (Shopkeeper Bridge)
6. Schmiede Brüke (Blacksmith Bridge)
7. Holz Brüke (Wood Bridge)

My Neighborhood:

A. Our Apartment
B. Kartofelhändler (Potato Man)
C. Lumpenspeicher (Rag Warehouse)
D. Drahtspeicher (Wire Warehouse)
E. Tischlerei (Millwork Shop)
F. Wohnhaus (Apartment)
G. Tor (Gate to Jewish Property)
H. Schmiede & Schenke (Pub & Blacksmith)
I. Speicher (More Warehouses)
J. Synagoge & Waisenhaus (Synagogue & Orphanage)
K. Fischmarkt (Fish Market)
L. Kant Memorial
M. Der Dom (Cathedral)
N. Gemüsemarkt (Produce Market)
O. Baptisten Gemeinde Klapperwiese
   (Baptist Church)
P. Hundegatt (Riverfront Warehouse Area)

2 | NITWITS FROM THE LOMSE

We were a family of six: Mom and Dad, one younger brother and two younger sisters and I. We lived on the larger of the two islands, *die Lomse*, connected to the city by three of the "Bridges of Königsberg." I remember the fire that caused us to move there. I was between two and three years old when fire in one of the suites forced us out and all the other tenants of the two upper floors also. I don't remember seeing fire, but I do remember the panic and commotion on the stairway, and my dad racing to carry me down to the lowest floor. I remember him handing me to a lady in one of the lowest suites. I can still envision the open doorway and the dark, dark hallway beyond.

Our island was about 3 and a half kilometers long and a little more than 1 kilometer wide at the widest spot. Less than a tenth of the land on the island was developed. All residential buildings in our area had multiple stories. Some had tailor shops, barbers or cobblers at street level. There were several small businesses: grocery stores, a butcher shop, a store that sold only milk and eggs, a couple of bakeries, a stationary store, a blacksmith shop, a pub, a co-op and a few other small outlets.

More than half of the buildings were non-residential: high warehouses, sheds with storage yards along the waterfront. There were some small ship related repair facilities, a factory where margarine was produced and one where coffee was roasted. The new modern Jewish Synagogue and a Lutheran Church (*Kreuzkirche*) were also located on our island.

There were a few dingy tenement buildings, which gave the entire area a bad reputation. So although the island was comprised of neighborhoods with various names, it was generally known by a small neighborhood named *Lomse*. People who lived anywhere on the island were called, "*Dummer von der Lomse*," which could be translated as, "Nitwits from the Lomse," or "Hillbillies from the Lomse."

Two apartment blocks at the far end of our street could be compared to the "The Projects" of modern-day New York. Though they didn't have the type of problems with crime or drugs as the New York projects, they certainly were the place where the poor and underprivileged lived. Many people who lived there spoke only Low German. The children kept to themselves. Even on the way to elementary school, they formed their own group, and didn't socialize with others.

We lived in a six-story tenement building with 20 suites. After coming in the front entry of our building, you turned right to go up the stairs. All the stairs between levels went up on that side. On each level, a wide landing snaked all the way around the building and led to the stairs going up to the level above. Sloped windows over the stairs let light in during the day.

The entrances to the toilets were located across from the stairwells. One door on each side gave access to two side-by-side toilets, which were partitioned with a stubby door for privacy. There was no light and no water in those toilets. It was almost like an outhouse, only somehow—I'm not exactly sure how—the waste ended up in the sewer. Maybe it was by gravity. A ventilation shaft between the two sets of toilets on each floor went all the way through the roof. You could feel the cold draft on your bottom when you sat down in the winter. Needless to say, in the summer you would not spend any extra time in there because of the horrible stench. Toilet paper had not come on the market yet. We had to use cut-up newspaper to do our wiping. The newspaper was cut into squares and kept in a dispenser—a wire contraption that was fastened to the wall. It worked like a giant safety pin, pinning in about 1 ½ inches of tightly packed squares.

Newspaper was used for many other purposes too. The most noteworthy for me, was for cleaning our cast iron frying pan. I still have trouble cleaning a frying pan in the sink, and am tempted to revert to using paper.

Newspaper had other uses too. In winter, we would wrap several layers around our socks to keep our feet warm. If our boots got wet, we stuffed them full of newspaper to absorb the moisture and help them dry out. That same paper was then reused to polish our shoes, and after that, was repurposed as kindling to start fires. Nothing was wasted. Especially not precious pieces of paper.

The tenants in our building were responsible for keeping all common areas clean. The more expensive places had cleaning ladies to do that. But since ours was a lower budget building, my sister and I had to take on that chore—especially when mom was working. That meant that every four weeks we had to clean the stairway and the landing—scrub them, if necessary, polish the wooden spindles and handrails, and wipe down the door casings. The tenants on the ground floor had to keep their floor and outside steps clean. They were also responsible to lock the entrance doors at 10 o'clock in the evening.

There were four suites on each floor—and hence a four week cleaning rotation. But there were other common areas used for storage, laundry, and carpet-cleaning, that also needed to be cleaned periodically.

The uppermost floor of the six-story building contained a bank of locked storage units. A large, open space on either side provided room for drying laundry. Each suite was assigned a specific laundry-drying day.

A stairway led from the top floor onto the flat roof. There was a carpet rack located up there. Vacuum cleaners had not yet been invented. To get their carpets clean, people would sling them over an outdoor rack and use a cane to beat the dust out. We used the rack in the summer, but in wintertime, we spread our carpet out face-down on the fresh snow and beat it horizontally. It got far cleaner that way. In my mind, I can still hear the '*Teppichklopfer*' (carpet-beater) whizzing through the air. It was an intricate instrument, made of several strands of slender, woven cane. Oddly enough, the canes used for beating carpets were thinner than the ones the teachers used at school to give misbehaving pupils "a caning."

Besides the storage on the upper floor, tenants were also assigned a padlocked storage space in the basement. Everything possible was stored there: coal, firewood, carrots, potatoes, preserves, a vat with sauerkraut, beets, turnips and other such commodities. We stored preserves of all kinds on the shelves, together with bottles of blueberries, which we had gathered during the summer in a forest at the edge of the city.

It was always damp down in the basement. One could tell the water-level of the river by checking the covered sump in the floor. Large rats with webbed feet occasionally showed up in the building, and would boldly confront you, especially if you cornered or startled them. I had one such encounter on the stairway leading up to the second floor. The rats would make a hissing sound when they felt threatened, and would bite you, if your legs were bare. They somehow got in from the river, where rats were plentiful. Maybe it was through the sump.

Dad would try to keep the rats out of our space in the basement. He would hollow out a turnip, let the shell dry and fill it with a mixture of plaster of Paris and lots of sugar to entice the rats. The rats would eat the mixture and then die when the plaster hardened in their digestive systems. We would leave the dead rat or rats laying there for a day or two, so the other rats would get the message, and stay away for a while.

Nowadays I'm sure someone would alarm the "Humane Society" and charge us with cruelty to helpless animals. But we didn't think it cruel. It was a matter of health and safety to try to keep the rat population under control and our goods from being eaten by the rodents.

A steel grating on the first floor allowed light and air to filter down into the basement. A number of barrels sat on the floor below the grating. That's where we deposited our garbage or stuff for recycling. Specific barrels were allocated for different items: one for glass, one for ashes, and another for aluminum foil, empty toothpaste tubes, and foil wrappers from cigarette packs or chocolate bars went in the aluminum barrel. Some cheeses also came in foil wrappers and some other stuff like creams or ointment came in aluminum tubes. Plastic, as we know it today, was not yet in use. At that time, the gramophone was in its infancy with Bakelite plastic records, which broke easily.

Everything that could be recycled was recycled. Germans were very resourceful and careful not to waste anything that could be repaired or reused. Kitchen scraps, like potatoes and vegetable peels, were placed into one barrel, which was regularly picked up by a farmer to feed to his pigs. Even ashes were put in a special covered container. It took two burly men with wide carrying straps over their shoulders to haul those heavy barrels up the stairs for collection.

To get to our cellar area, we had to make our way around these barrels of garbage. Since there was no electricity in the cellar, and no light coming in except through the steel grating, we carried a lighted kerosene lamp. If we had to stay longer, we lit a carbide lamp. That lamp gave a more intense light and didn't give off any fumes, but took a little longer to get going.

Those carbide lamps could also be attached to the front of your bicycle for riding at night. Police would give a ticket to anyone riding the bike without a light at night. We had dynamo driven bicycle lights but they were hard on the tires and it took more effort to pedal, so we preferred the carbide lamps.

Most of our streetlights were fired by natural gas. Whenever the flame on these lamps became uneven or dim from residue build-up, a new burner had to be screwed in. A *'Laternenputzer'* (lantern cleaner) would make the rounds on a bicycle each evening to light the streetlamps which had failed to ignite automatically when the gas was turned on. The glass window at the front of his carbide lamp allowed easy access to the flame. He had a long extendable pole with some kind of a wick on the end, which he would light from his lamp. He would then reach up to light the street lamp. His lamp was a lot larger than the carbide lamps we carried on our bikes.

The *Laternenputzer*, as the name implies, also had to keep the lenses of the street lights clean. My friend Hans in Germany, who also grew up on the Lomse, told me that the boys in his immediate neighborhood got such a kick out of watching the *Laternenputzer*, that they shinnied up the poles to snuff out the flame, to make sure he had plenty of lamps to light.

I've never seen any carbide lamps in Canada. They required a lot of maintenance and were extremely dangerous when neglected. They consisted of an upper water container with a needle valve at the bottom. The lower container held carbide pieces around a perforated stem. Both parts were tightly screwed together with a gasket to stop gas from escaping. Acetylene gas was produced when water reacted with the calcium-carbide pieces. The needle valve regulated or shut off the flow of water. The amount of water being released determined how much gas was produced, which in turn regulated the brightness of the flame. Too much water could overpower the capacity of the burner and the lamp could explode. Bottled acetylene gas and oxygen are still used for cutting and welding of steel.

HinterLomse is one street over from VorderLomse, the street we lived on.

Each suite in our building consisted of three rooms: a bedroom, a living room and a kitchen. The bedroom had two double beds with a clothing wardrobe in between. Mom and Dad slept on one bed. We three children slept on the other, with our baby brother Hans Dieter, in a small crib nearby. Only an open archway separated the bedroom from the living room.

Nitwits from the Lomse

Two elderly sisters lived in an identical suite below ours. They made ends meet by operating a mangle to press laundry. It filled their bedroom space and we could hear when it was in use. (My grandfather had access to an even larger community mangle that was housed in a dedicated building and could be used free of charge.) To use the mangle in our building, we paid the elderly sisters by the hour, which was about as long as it took us to press a basket of laundry. My mother would go in with a basket filled to overflowing with washed laundry, but once she had neatly pressed and folded all the items, they filled only about a quarter of it.

The mangle was about 9 feet long, 5 feet wide and 6 feet tall. It required about another 4 feet of clearance at each end. Its heavy hardwood frame and platform remained stationary. The moving parts primarily consisted of a heavy box that rolled back and forth over rollers, which were wound up tight with laundry and placed underneath. The weight of the moving box is what got the wrinkles out.

This mangle is similar to, but smaller than the one operated by the sisters in our building.

It was hard to crank the large cast iron flywheel to engage the sprocket and get the mangle going, because the box was filled with large rocks, and tough to budge. When it was moving, a rhythmic clicking sound could be heard as the sprocket wheeled around the cogs above. The cogs were situated between two metal bars that were attached to the ends of the box with a metal frame. The clicking would stop with a thud when the operator lowered a lever on either end of the frame. Doing that forced one end of the box up so a roller with pressed clothing could be removed from the platform and replaced with one that contained wrinkled laundry.

A large table for rolling up laundry stood across from the mangle. It had a shallow trough at one end. Extra rollers were stored on a shelf underneath. The rollers were made of beech or birch and were about four inches in diameter and three feet long with knobs on each end. Long strips of unbleached linen cloth were secured between the knobs. When loaded with laundry, they looked like massive ancient scrolls.

To load a roller with laundry we'd place it in the trough and spread the attached strip of linen over the table. Starting at the side closest to the roller, we'd lay the laundry out. If the laundry was too dry we'd sprinkle it with water from a container that looked like a large salt shaker attached to a long handle. After placing and smoothing out our clothing on the linen, we'd wind it up around the wooden roller as tight as possible. More laundry was placed on the linen sheet and rolled up until the end of the sheet was reached.

We then placed the loaded roller in the mangle to be pressed. Usually a roll had to be taken out, tightened, and replaced at least once during the process. You also had to make sure to place them at a right angle, otherwise the knob would catch on the frame. Whenever that happened, we'd have to raise the box, rearrange and straighten the laundry, reposition the roller, and start over. As you can tell, getting your laundry pressed was a massive and laborious undertaking!

We weren't allowed near the mangle when we were smaller. It was just too dangerous. We were lucky if mother let us watch the process from the end of the table. Some children lost fingers when their hands came too close to a heavy moving roller, or caught them between the moving box and the frame. That's how Uncle Kurt lost part of his ring finger.

I was happy when I heard the click-click-click and thud of the mangle because it meant money was coming in for our neighbors. The ladies charged a lower price to customers who wanted to operate the mangle themselves, and slightly more for customers who wanted them to press the laundry for them.

I will spare you all the details of doing laundry, hoping that you can imagine the amount of effort it took. I will just say that doing laundry took my mom several days of hard work. It involved washing, boiling, scrubbing, rinsing, 'bluing' (final rinse in water with blue dye added to make things look extra white), hanging clothes to dry, and then pressing them in the mangle afterwards. But I would like to mention one more thing essential to doing laundry; the laundry soap.

Laundry soap was an amber-colored paste that contained white granules. We purchased it at the grocer's in bulk, out of a barrel, and took it home wrapped in wax paper. The soap was rubbed directly onto dirty clothing, which was vigorously rubbed on a scrub board. The scrubbed laundry was then boiled in a large kettle, rinsed and "blued." The slippery soap concoction had a unique odor that I can remember to this day. Mom kept the unused soap in a closed metal container to keep it from drying out. It was also a remedy for extremely dirty hands.

As I am thinking about the laundry soap, another household cleaner comes to mind—soda crystals. The crystals were added to the wash water to soften it and break grease down. But we boys sometimes used them for a different purpose. The fact that they looked virtually identical to candied sugar led us to use them for more mischievous ends.

Candied sugar was quite popular, and came in either white or brown big lumps. The cheaper kind often had little bits of string embedded, around which the crystals had formed. When a playmate noticed you sucking on something, they would assume that it was candied sugar and would ask for a piece to share. It was easy to play a trick on someone by offering them a piece of crystallized cleaning soda out of your pocket, which looked just like the white candied sugar. You watched their reaction when they put it in their mouth, laughed when they spit it out, and ran away fast if they got mad.

The living room in our suite had two tall windows facing west, and another window of the same size in the kitchen. Each had a pair of lower windows, which opened outward and a fixed window on top. Thick frost would form on the windows in the winter. To minimize the draft, we placed long rolls of fabric against the crack on the bottom. These tubes were sewn of brightly colored fabric and stuffed with cotton or rags. My mom then placed little tufts of cotton on top of the rolls to imitate the snowflakes we were trying to keep out. On extremely cold days the frost build-up was thick. When the weather warmed up, the frost melted, and we removed the rolls.

The window sills were wide with a built-in shallow trough, which caught condensation, and channeled it through a little tube into a removable container beneath. That little box had to be emptied often when the weather warmed up and the ice on the windows melted. But the sills were ideal places for growing plants, and like most people, mom took full advantage of that.

Mom also stored large glass jars on the kitchen window sill. Rollmops, pickled herring and jars with fried fish in vinegar would sit there curing, or in different stages of consumption. We mostly purchased a kind of large smelt. Since the vinegar softened the bones, we consumed the fish whole— head, tail, innards and all. Or, we downed them after they came out of the frying pan all crisp and crunchy.

We ate a lot of fish. I remember eating only a few meat dishes during my childhood. From time to time we ate a soupy hash made from the lung of beef, fried uncured bacon, fried liver with onions, or meatballs in a sweet and sour sauce.(*Saure Klopse* or *Königsberger Klopse*) We also ate Turkey from time to time.

Bacon was purchased at the butcher. He would cut it to the customer's instruction from a slab, taken from a rack, where sides of beef or pork hung in different stages of use. This was not smoked bacon. We had ours sliced ½ to ¾ inch thick with the skin left on. Mother would fry the bacon in the cast iron frying pan, with lots of chopped onions. We would heap a mound of mashed potatoes onto our plates, make a depression in the middle, and fill it with the sizzling fat and onions. I would munch on a slice of crisp bacon, placed on the side of the potato mound, a bite at a time, with the bacon skin sometimes presenting a challenge. My mouth still waters when I think of that.

We had a massive wooden table with brass casters in the middle of the living/dining room. Someone gave the table to us. We loved it, because it could be expanded much longer than the room would allow. We often played house under the table by draping blankets and letting them hang down on every side.

But the most important fixture in our suite was a built-in clay tile oven in the corner of our living room, our *"Kachelofen."* The oven was typical for homes of that era. I remember when our first oven was torn down and replaced by a new one. The old one had been very tall, almost to the ceiling, made from glazed green tiles with a few decorative tiles with a round embossed pattern and an ornate crown gracing the top. The old oven also had a niche on the wider side with cast-iron doors, which was an ideal place to cook rice, roast apples, and keep the teakettle warm.

There was a firebox on the narrow side of the oven. It had a very heavy cast iron door which was screwed shut for a tight seal. A slider on the bottom of the door regulated the airflow. A tray below the fire grating collected ashes and had to be emptied every day in winter.

We usually started a fire in mid-morning with kindling and wood pieces, and coal or brown coal briquettes placed on top. When that was burning well, we placed coke on the flames. (Not the kind that you drink in bottles.) Coke is a solid fuel that looks like a grey, porous rock. The coke and coal combination made for a hotter fire. The oven would give off heat long after the fire was out.

Our first Kachelofen was bigger than this one. It reached almost all the way to the ceiling.

We closed the door of our *Kachelofen* and allowed just enough air in through a slider in the door to keep the fire going throughout the day. If we didn't let enough air in, the fire died, and we had to scrape out the crystallized residue of coke and coal. Using the coke meant that very little ash was left behind. That meant fewer trips to the basement to empty the ash box into a barrel.

Mom didn't like it when that old oven was demolished. It was a messy affair and took several weeks before the new one was finished. The new one wasn't nearly as tall or as nice. The clay tiles were plain white. Rounded corners were the only embellishment. The cast-iron doors were also much plainer and smaller. The niche had no doors and was much smaller than the old one. Though it wasn't as attractive, the potters, as we called them, assured mom that it would be just as efficient as the old one.

I would watch the workmen any free minute I had, fascinated how the firebricks were laid up, the oven door installed, tiles and mortar mixed, tiles cut and the joints grouted. I don't remember how long it took mom to clean up after they left. She expressed hope that she would never have to go through that again, saying that she had enough mess to clean after the unavoidable periodic re-lining of the fire chamber of such an oven.

Our kitchen stove was on the other side of the oven wall. I really don't know what to call that contraption. Cook stove? Oven? Range? It was made of brick, firebricks, clay, and glazed tiles and had cast iron doors. The top was also made of cast iron and covered the entire cook stove. It was a little lower than our ranges now and measured about 6' long and 3' wide.

This stove had two fire boxes on opposite ends—one for cooking and the other for baking or roasting. The entire top surface was made out of heavy iron. The cook stove had four 'burners', all of the same basic size. The 'burners' had a cup shaped center piece surrounded with a lip and a handle the so the burner could be lifted out. Around that were four rings, about one inch wide for a total size of about twelve inches. The cook could remove these individual rings to control the heat from the open fire underneath, or to suit the size of the pot. Some pots could be partially hung down into the fire by removing the right number of rings. There was also a removable plate the size of a medium cookie sheet. Mom could place a standard size cast iron pan in there to cook a pot roast or casserole.

The fire door and the door in front of the ash pan were at the narrow end of the stove. Next to the doors was a built-in hook to hang the poker, which was also used to lift out the different rings and pull the ash pan out. We stored the fire wood and coal bucket in an open space between the stove and wall.

If you search the net for "*Kachelherd*" you might get a picture, though I could not find one like ours. Most pictures showed a two tiered "Herd", ours was flat. The oven for roasting or baking was near the door entering the kitchen. If the door to the oven was open, you couldn't get in to the kitchen. That was very convenient to keep unwanted visitors out, or to lock out siblings.

I remember only a few times when that oven was used other than for Christmas baking. Baking at Christmas was a big affair with all children involved. Mom engaged us in forming different cookies from regular and chocolate colored dough, creating spiral, striped or checkered patterns. We also used a variety of cookie cutters. We had to chop nuts and almonds for topping since we seldom used store-bought trimmings.

Mom made cakes occasionally, but never baked them in our oven. The cakes were taken to our baker with a nametag stuck into the dough. He wanted to know what kind of dough it was, whether it needed time to rise or not. Mom baked mostly '*Streuselkuchen*' which used yeast rather than baking powder. '*Streusel*' is the topping (crumbs), made from butter, flour and white or brown sugar, strewn as evenly as possible on top of the flattened dough in the pan. The baker would charge us a few pennies to bake our cakes, and would only do the baking after he finished his own baking, about mid-morning.

I remember trying to pick crumbs off the sometimes-still warm cake, when I was sent to fetch it home. Of course I tried not to be found out, and picked only here and there with great care, and was very concerned when a bigger lump came off. It was a treat to eat what little cake was stuck to the name tag when it was pulled out before the cake was cut to be served on Sunday.

We had a cast iron vat at the end of the oven by the door. It was recessed into the oven, but was removable and had a two-part lid. It was designed to keep water hot when fire was in the oven and for filling and ladling out hot water. But since we mostly used the other end of the big oven, the water was only warm enough to do the dishes or wash up with. It had to be refilled from the tap with a pitcher. We also had to descale it once in a while.

During the war, as heating materials were rationed more and more, a 'Burn-Hex' was introduced. It was a box of welded heavy gauge sheet metal about 14" square with a small door on one side, and metal drawer underneath to catch the ash. It had a stubby stove pipe-like projection at the bottom. A grating separated the fire chamber from the ash box and the draft could only be regulated by moving the ash drawer ever so slightly in or out. The Burn-Hex was placed into the burner hole of the main stove. Although it took very little to heat that thing up, the heat was hard to control and only one pot or two very small ones would fit on top. "The Hex is hexed" was the common saying. It did save fuel, but it ruined many a pot and, if not watchfully attended, produced that unmistakable scorched flavor in your food.

A heavy cast iron sink was fastened to the wall in the kitchen. The sink was coated on the inside with white enamel, and had little holes for drainage. It had a brass faucet and only ran cold water. The faucet was quite high—we could easily fit a pail under it, even if we rested the pail on the rim of the basin. The basin itself was half-round, like a 1/4 section of a pumpkin, about 14" wide and maybe two feet off the floor. I mention that because my dad fainted once and gashed his head on the edge of the sink when he fell.

One of the earliest memories of our home on the Lomse has to do with an imposed ritual, which made absolutely no sense to me . . . . Not then and not now. Our floors were made of tongue and grooved boards from a native coniferous tree, similar to spruce but harder. The boards were about six inches wide and unfinished. Custom dictated that every Saturday the floor had to be scrubbed until white. Then, and perhaps to enhance the whiteness, white sand had to be sprinkled on the scrubbed floor and be swept up a short time after.

I remember having to go to a barge with a small pail to buy the sand. The barge was moored across from the synagogue, not too far away. A pile of pure, white, grainy sand was stored in the hold of a barge. I had to walk up the plank leading onto the walkway around the hold, where a man filled my pail. Thankfully all that stopped. The next norm in fashion dictated that the floors now 'had' to be painted. I remember sitting on the floor to help dad fill in all the cracks between the floor boards to prepare them. I still remember the unforgettable odor of the paint, and how the fumes made my eyes water. It must have made a profound impression on me, because I also have a clear picture of the paint can in my mind. The label read "Mahogany Sigella Floor Enamel," and was decorated with a drawing of a parakeet perched on a rainbow. The floor was undoubtedly painted a few more times after that, because the color somehow changed— but I remember only that first time.

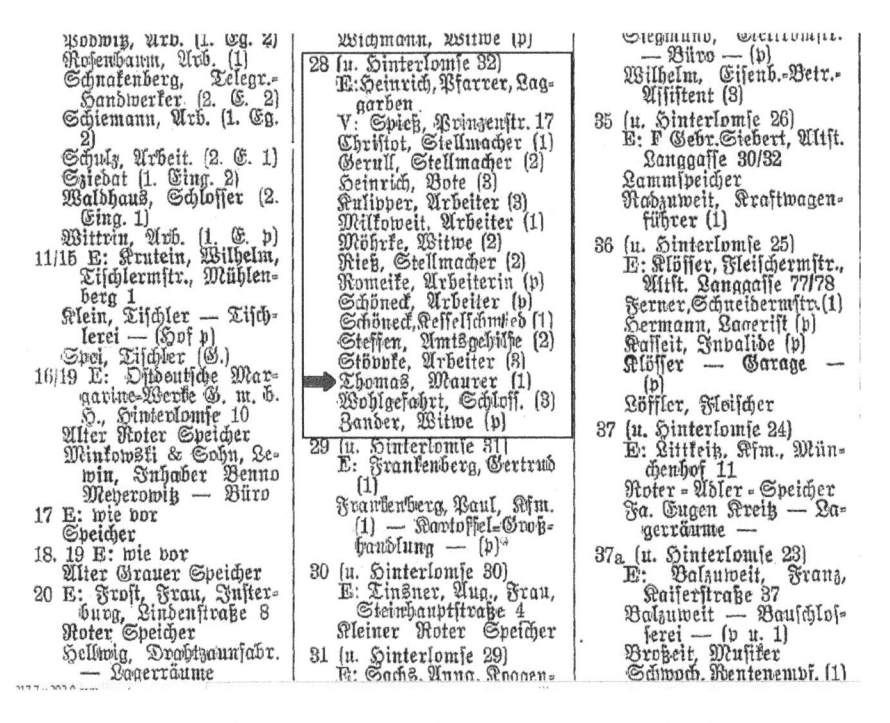

The above list, taken from a 1935 census of Königsberg, shows who lived on our street. Number 28 was the number of our building. The simple census notes only our last name (Thomas), that my Dad was a bricklayer (Maurer), and that we lived on the first floor of the building (1).

The windows in our suite opened individually, but had no screens. There was a hook to secure them in open position, and a locking mechanism to fasten them shut. Yet even with the windows closed the street noise would filter through. That didn't bother us, because it would let us know what was going on in the street below. We could hear vendors peddling their wares from carts they pulled around, the clanging of horse's hoofs and the noise from metal rims of the wagon wheels bobbing across the cobblestones, "*Katzenköpfe*" is the German term. Sometimes we heard happy singing, or even the noisy fighting from the apartment across the street from us.

When any of us kids in the neighborhood heard a particular couple argue we would open a window or go out into the street to take advantage of the hilarious and inevitable outcome. The lady was bald and always wore a wig. We did not know her name, she was simply known in the neighborhood as "*die Perücksche*" (the wig-wearer). Without fail, at some point during the argument, her husband would grab her wig, and toss it out the window— only to be caught by a 'lucky' kid, who was waiting on the street to catch it. The winner would triumphantly run around with his trophy until the man showed up to reclaim it. When the other kids shouted, "Here he comes", the kid would drop the wig for the man to retrieve. But the show wasn't over until the pair emerged from their suite, she with her wig in place, and headed down to the pub, arm-in-arm, to reconcile and make up. If we were allowed to stay out long enough, we would also see the couple stagger back from the pub. They would walk arm in arm on wobbly feet, in unison zigzagging across the street while trying to belt out a popular song. Of course, they had to stop frequently to catch their breath or, with wild gestures to correct one another's lyrics. Given their drunken state, I have no idea how they made it up the stairs to their suite.

Two other people living in that apartment building piqued our curiosity. A man who lived on an upper floor had a large St. Bernard dog. He would harness the dog to a little cart, to which a massive drum was fastened. The dog would pull the cart and the drum down the street. I suspect the man played in the Salvation Army band. But we lost sight of him early on.

Another man, known to us only as '*der Lumpensammler*' (rag collector), lived at street level. He always gave in to our begging. We didn't beg for money or food, as was common in those days. When we knocked on his door, he knew that we had come to beg for buttons.

We played various games with the buttons. One game involved feeding a strong thread through opposite holes on the button to create a closed loop by tying a knot on the ends of the thread. Sticking a finger in each end of the loop with the button in between, we would twist the thread by twirling it in circular motion. When the thread was sufficiently wound, we would move the fingers in and out ever so lightly to keep the button spinning. We would sit in a group and compete with each other to see who could produce the best sound or who could keep the button spinning the longest.

The metal buttons with holes in them were the best—the kind that were crimped together at the outer edge. They "sung" the best; producing a high pitched hum or whistle. Part of the fun was that it was impossible to tell from looking at the buttons what sound they would produce.

The *Lumpensammler* made his living by collecting and selling rags. His living room was stacked full with different piles of rags. He would remove all the buttons, zippers, snaps, and hooks, sort the rags, and sell the different bundles to the 'Rag Warehouse' on the corner.

That warehouse was where the neighborhood '*Katzenmutter*' (cat lady) regularly fed anchovies or small sardines to an ever increasing motley army of cats. She went to the fish market at the end of day and begged for the unsold remnants. It was a feeding frenzy when she appeared, as the cats lunged at the fish and each other. The regular feeding caused the multiplication of wild cats, but likely also led to a decrease in the number of neighborhood mice and rats.

The warehouse across the street from the rag warehouse must have been the favored haunt for the cats, as it was the storage place of raw products for the margarine factory and, no doubt, the main attraction for rats and mice.

Gypsies, chimney sweeps, beggars, knife and scissor grinders, and all kinds of street vendors were part of growing up in our neighborhood. Gypsies were the most colorful characters, and as a group, the ones we were warned to be the most wary of. They would stop on the street at several places with their heavily laden one-horse wagons, which served as both their living quarters and workshop. Some of the wagons looked like the chuck wagons you'd see at the stampede. Others were built of wood— with windows, curtains, flower boxes and all, painted in bright colors.

They would go door to door to offer their services. You never knew when they were going to come. They just showed up unannounced. Some gypsies mended pots. You had to be on guard to get the same pot back, as they had a reputation for trying to pull the wool over your eyes and switch a cheaper pot out for the one you gave them to fix. Others sold different kinds of lace or head scarves, some offered to read your palm and tell the future from the lines in your hand.

They would ask plenty for their services. One had to be a determined haggler to resist their bartering. They always backed up their prices with some clever sob story. Our neighbor lady was excellent at dealing with them. Mom asked for her help whenever she couldn't get rid of them. That neighbor lady had a colorful vocabulary that would make even a sailor blush and could rebuff even the most persistent gypsy peddler.

The gypsies travelled in caravans. When they came to town, they set up camp on a large space east of us, on the other side of the river. During the day they spread over the city, in the evening, they parked their wagons in a huge circle with the horses tied up toward the outside. They left an opening, so city people could enter the circle and join their revelry. A lot of people flocked to the evening campfire to listen to the fiddling, the singing, and to watch the gypsies dance in their colorful outfits. The gypsies didn't charge for folks to join them, but placed little pots in several places to collect donations. It was strange in a way, since they had no hesitation to openly beg when they came to your neighborhood.

The chimney sweep was another regular in the neighborhood. In the winter you could always tell where he had been because of the black foot prints in the snow. His face was all black from soot with only his eyes and a small slit of his lips distinguishable. He had a long pouch slung over one shoulder, hanging down his front and back, with a curved metal scraper hooked on the pouch. Over his other shoulder he carried a coil of wire rope, a large round stiff brush with a weight attached, and several smaller brushes. He wore a tall top hat that seemed to be glued to his head—the same type of hat worn by the sweeps in Mary Poppins and Oliver Twist. He'd stop by the neighborhood a day ahead of time and shout up the stairwell to let residents know that he'd be in the area the next day. The neighbors would make sure you knew that the chimney would be cleaned, because if you failed to close the shutter of your stove and oven, the soot would come through and mess up your place.

The sweep stood on the chimney ledge, high up above the buildings. He chose the right size of brush and plunged it up and down the chimney flue several times to scrape out the soot. Then he clambered down to the door at the foot of the chimney in the basement, and used the curved scraper to scoop the soot into his pouch. The soot was black as black could be. It was said that he sold it for some purpose—perhaps for medicinal purposes, since in those days black creosote was used in antiseptics, astringents, and laxatives.

Another man that frequented our neighborhood was the scissor and knife grinder. He'd set up his portable grinding shop close to the entrance of an apartment block. With a loud voice he called out and made his presence known, so that people would have their knives or scissors ready for him when he knocked at their door. His grindstone, polishing wheel, and wire brush were mounted on top of a wheeled box-like contraption. His tools were stored underneath. He pumped a treadle to turn the sharpening stones. We loved to watch the sparks fly as he sharpened the edge of a dull knife or meat cleaver. He would take scissors apart for sharpening. Just how he managed to return everything to the right owner remains a puzzle to me, as he did not seem to tag or put any markings on them.

Our street-smart neighbor lady, Mrs. Milkoweit—the neighbor who knew how to handle gypsies—taught us to be wise to the tricks of the professional beggars too. She showed us how the beggars made swindler marks

(*Bettlerzinken*) on door casings, way down low, where they wouldn't be noticed. The markings let their fellow beggars know which begging approach they had successfully used at that home.

For example, one symbol indicated a religious approach while another showed that they had used a feigned illness or tragedy. The marking also indicated what kind of a response the beggar had encountered—whether their approach had resulted in money or food. If the markings were painted over or scratched out the beggars would have to start all over again. Few people were aware that the beggars made those marks. In fact, they keep on making them to this day. Robbers have now developed their own '*Zinken*'. Deciphered by the police, they are sometimes able to catch burglars in the act and can advise people how to secure their property.

EXAMPLES OF SWINDLER MARKS

Symbol	Meaning	Symbol	Meaning	Symbol	Meaning
	OVERNIGHT ACCOMODATION POSSIBLE		WARNING FIERCE DOG		HERE THEY GIVE NOTHING
	RESIDENT LIVES ALONE		DOG		HERE THEY GIVE FOOD
	OLD PEOPLE		CAREFUL DON'T PROMISE ANYTHING		HERE THEY GIVE MONEY
	NO MAN IN THE HOUSE		POLICE LIVE HERE		HERE THEY PAY FOR WORK
	ONLY WOMEN IN THE HOUSE		LEAVE QUICKLY		ACTING SICK PAYS OFF
	ACTING RELIGIOUS PAYS OFF		HERE THEY GIVE SOMETHING		CAREFUL YOU'LL GET A BEATING

We appreciated having Frau Milkoweit as a neighbor. Not only did she help us with the gypsies and beggars, but her husband worked at the plant where coal was converted to gas. The workers got to share the by-product of this process—coke—which was fantastic for increasing the efficiency of the *Kachelofen*. The Mikloweits would share part of their large entitlement of coke with us. Coke was not for sale on the residential market yet, so we were very fortunate to get it from them.

They also let us in on a good and cheap source of firewood. Near Herr Milkoweit's work place was a factory which produced wooden spools for thread. Workers used hole-saw drills to core cylinders from 2 or 3 inch slabs of birch. Automatic lathes turned these cylinders into spools. The spools were taken to the yarn factory, where they were wrapped with sewing thread.

The birch remnants looked like Swiss cheese. They were packaged together with damaged cores and spools and sold for pennies a sack. We stored up a lot of this discarded wood to burn for the winter. The bags had the added benefit of providing plenty of shapes and cylinders of wood for us to build toys and play with.

I have to take you back to the other side of the street to where the rag man lived. There was a space of about eighty feet between his apartment and the next building, which housed the pub and blacksmith shop. That distance was filled with a high plastered masonry fence and a huge wrought iron gate. That gate provided entrance to the back of the Jewish property. That property, including the Synagogue and their other buildings, took up about a city block's length along the Lindenstrasse.

Whenever we saw the Jewish orphans playing soccer in that space, we would clamber over the gate to join the game. Over time, we got to know some of those kids by name and viewed them as our friends. Getting over the gate was no easy feat. The brick walls and columns on either end were topped with cement-embedded protruding glass shards. The walls were at least sixteen inches thick and ten feet high. The gate itself was at least ten feet high at the top of the arch. The vertical ends had spear-like cast iron points. The structure was definitely designed to keep people out! It was frowned upon for us to play with the Jewish kids, both by people on our street and by the supervising Jewish teacher. I'm not sure why . . . it may have been due to their fear of us injuring ourselves climbing that treacherous gate.

Our street was paved with cobblestones. *Katzenköpfe* (cat's heads) was the fitting German name for that type of stone pavement. I remember when those stones were ripped out and replaced with smoother paving stones. There was a raised sidewalk all along our side, except in front of the building next door. That building was lower and had two sets of large doors to allow horses and wagons to drive in to load and unload potatoes. The owners of the potato business had a son about my age, who was deaf and mute. I was told that he fell off a cart as a youngster and lost his hearing as a result. They lived above their warehouse. The only contact I ever had with the boy was when he occasionally drove a cart down the street and waived his hand in greeting.

The cobblestone also extended up to the warehouses and yards on the other side of the street. This was so that wagons could be pulled right up to the doors. A raised stone slab formed a step at the entrance to the apartment across the street and at two or three other apartments at the far end of the street. A shallow depression in the street channeled rainwater into a sewer grate.

Almost all warehouses in our city were several stories high, with a hoist projecting from the peak of the roof. A few hoists were still operated by hand through pulleys and a rope running inside the warehouse through all the floors. There were double doors on each floor under the hoist. This facilitated loading and unloading right from wagons unto each floor of the building.

Nitwits from the Lomse

From our kitchen window we had a clear view of the warehouse on the other side of the street, which handled chain link fence material. Sometimes the workers spread fencing mesh out on the street to measure and achieve the required length. I often watched them join pieces of fence mesh together by twisting the corkscrew-like wire links through the end of both sections.

The blacksmith shop was down the street at the back of a warehouse. Dad had his stone tools stretched, tempered and sharpened there. The front of the warehouse was home to the neighborhood pub. It was the gathering place for locals. My Dad could not tolerate alcohol in any form. Even a glass of beer, if drunk too fast, would make him violently ill. But in summertime, we would enjoy a popular cool non-alcoholic drink, called *"Schorle,"* from the pub. It tasted a bit like liquorish or root beer, but not as sweet.

A typical street of warehouses.

All the women in the apartments were attuned to the clicking of horse's hooves and would look out of their windows for the inevitable dropping of apples—the apples that horses push out of their rear ends, that is. The women would drop whatever they were doing, and race to the street to be first to scoop up the manure. They'd sweep every bit of it onto a dustpan with a stiff hand-broom. Mixed with water, the horse manure made prized fertilizer for the many plants and flowers which graced the wide windowsills of most homes.

For a young boy, living on the Lomse was one great adventure. Outsiders may have viewed us as disadvantaged, but we certainly didn't share that sentiment. We thought ourselves privileged to live there. The island provided an endless variety of smells, sights, interesting people, and never a shortage of things to do. I was as happy and content as a child could be. It was only from time to time that I sensed the tension in the world of grown-ups.

It was not uncommon to see people on the street handing out political leaflets and invitations to political rallies. The demonstrations and marches were accompanied by "runners" on the sidewalks, who besides handing out leaflets, often accosted people who didn't pay attention or show due respect for their political flags. The runners would knock the hats off of men who dared to show indifference, and brashly "get in their faces." (To take ones hat off was a common sign of respect when a funeral, religious procession, or flag passed by.) The forced obeisance heightened when the "Brown Shirts" appeared in greater numbers. Brown Shirts was the nickname for Adolf Hitler's private army, which were officially called *Sturm Abteilung* (Storm Contingent) or the SA. They were men who took a prominent role in organized marches and rallies. They protected the gatherings of the NSDAP (Nazi party) from disruptions from the Social Democrats and Communists. The Brown Shirts disrupted the meetings of political opponents, and openly intimidated and terrorized anyone who they viewed as a threat.

Sometimes the aftermath of street fights were all too visible when clashes between opposing alliances and political convictions boiled over. Mom would try to keep me away from the demonstrations, but it was impossible to be unaware of them, since most of them took place on the Lindenstrasse Weidendamm, just one street over from where we lived, where the Jewish synagogue was the most prominent building. That street was wide, allowing columns of protesters to march in opposing directions. They tried to outdo each other with the noise created from each group's marching band or boisterous singing.

Our next door neighbor, Mr. Milkoweit, had communist leanings, having been part of a union with that philosophy. I overheard Mom and another neighbor talk about it. There was a strong element of Communism in a neighboring district, and the constant threat of a Communist take-over. I remember clashes with street fights, and banner and night-torch marches by opposing parties. I could hear the noise of the political demonstrations from my room, and see the glow of the torches illuminating the street.

From time to time I would see groups or individuals wearing red armbands with a black swastika on a white circle. More and more young people began to proudly wear a diamond-shaped pin on their jackets. The pin also had a black swastika in a white circle on a bright red enameled background. It was the badge of a new organization called "Youth for Hitler."

My mom seemed to take a far greater interest in politics than my dad. She often engaged in political discussions with neighbors. Whenever Herr Prange came for dinner, political events would be assessed according to their relevance to the Bible.

Herr Prange was a single gentleman from our church who had a club foot, and walked with a marked limp. He made a living by selling Bibles and Christian books door to door. Since he lived in a residence for single men, and rarely had the benefit of a home-cooked meal, mom regularly invited him over for Sunday dinner. Herr Prange followed politics closely, and shared my mom's opinion of the role of Jews in God's plan. He was keenly sensitive to the subtle stirring of hatred against the Jews, that was beginning to show up in the media. He and my mom were alarmed when they noticed that the Jews were being publically slandered, and put down.

The political situation was becoming increasingly volatile. The Treaty of Versailles was such a sore point. It popped up in almost every conversation. Perhaps the separation from the "Reich" (what was left of the old Germany) was more intensely felt in everyday life in our province of East Prussia.

Germans viewed the terms imposed by the treaty as blatantly unfair . . . especially the guilt and reparation clauses. From our perspective, Germany was drawn into the conflict through a political alliance we had with the Austro-Hungarian Empire. We did not initiate hostilities. The fact that Europe was a political powder keg was certainly not the exclusive fault of the German people.

I didn't know much about politics, but I knew that the adults were worried about the threat of Communism, and extremely bitter about the forced admittance of blame and the heavy economic burden placed on our country. Germans could barely support their families, yet saw a significant portion of their hard-earned wages go toward "reparation payments." We even had a term for it: the "*Weidergutmachung*" –a negative term which literally means "Pay-back, Make it Right." The word sarcastically referred to the fact that our country was blamed, shamed, and disdained. We were the bad guys. Everything was our fault. In the eyes of the international community, Germans owed the world a debt we could never hope to repay. It is no wonder, really, that Hitler's stirring of National Pride, his rejection of the Treaty of Versailles, and his stance against Communism fell on increasingly sympathetic ears.

3 | WHERE HAVE ALL THE FLOWERS GONE?

My first day of school was a big event. Every first grader received a "Zuckertüte" (sugar bag), a long cone shaped cardboard container decorated with coloured foil and full of candies and other goodies. Those long containers came in different sizes, the average was about 2 feet long with a 6 inch diameter opening at the top. A broad, lacy paper around the top, tied with a ribbon, kept all the goodies from falling out.

Each student posed with their *Zuckertüte* for their school photo. Box cameras had been introduced by that time, and some people owned one, but mostly, photographs were still taken by professional photographers.

New students also got a pack with which to carry their books and school supplies. The box-like contraptions were called "*Ranzen.*" The better ones were made out of leather. The rest were made of a cardboard-like but very stiff material to imitate the leather ones. *Ranzen* came in various colors. They were about 16 inches wide, 12 inches high, and perhaps 3 inches thick. The narrow straps were made out of leather. These were quite uncomfortable on your shoulders, and chafed your skin in the summer heat. The only thing that *Ranzen* had in common with a modern-day backpack was that they were slung on a student's back.

The *Ranzen* often needed to be replaced during a child's early years of elementary school, as their smooth surface made them an ideal substitute for a toboggan. In wintertime, we used them to slide on the fresh snow at every opportunity. But there was a lot of explaining to do when we arrived home with big rips in the surface, or with contents that had broken after we hit a bump.

A first grader's *Ranzen* inevitably contained a slate chalkboard-like tablet, an eighth of an inch thick, and about the size of a legal sheet of paper. That's what we learned to write on. The frame had a hole on one of the shorter edges, to which a couple of sponges were attached with string. The sponges served as erasers. First graders were easily recognized by the colorful sponges dangling and bouncing from the back of their *Ranzen*. It was a big no-no to keep the sponges inside. The moist, porous eraser might get moldy, or accidentally erase your homework.

We usually carried two slate tablets—one for drawing and the other one for math and writing. The drawing slate was blank. The slate for math and writing had red or blue squares permanently etched on one side and straight lines for writing etched on the other. I must also explain that the tablets were machined smooth. Their matt surfaces could easily be scratched. That sometimes happened inadvertently when a hard particle was embedded in your "pencil." You could purchase a special abrasive stick to rub out the scratches, but if the gauges were too deep, you'd have to purchase a new tablet.

Our 'pencils' were about as thick as drinking straws and were made of soft slate. They were light gray in color but left white marks on the tablet. Instead of being encased with wood, like modern-day pencils, the slate stick was wrapped with paper. The paper had to be peeled back, and you had to rotate the pencil in your hand constantly as you wrote, as the edge wore down. The slate was likely similar to what we call soapstone. Welders still use flat soapstone markers because those marks aren't affected by heat.

Needless to say, those writing utensils didn't last long in the hands of a first grader. They often broke from pushing down on them too hard in an effort to write letters between the lines or from putting numbers in the little squares. But we used even the stubby pieces until too much of the paper was removed, and oil from our skin rendered them useless.

I learned Gothic handwriting first. With the sharp corners in the letters, it was probably the easiest script for little hands to manage. In grade 3 or 4 we had to switch to what was called *Sütterlien*. The whole population was urged to adopt the new script. It looked strange at first with all the curves and turns. But then, shortly after starting high school, just when we had mastered it, *Sütterlien* script was declared obsolete. Everyone had to switch to what we called "Latin script" and with few exceptions, is comparable to the cursive script used in most Western countries today. I still write the letter 'r' the way I learned it then in the Latin cursive.

One of our teachers in high school was very fond of the old Gothic handwriting and encouraged us to retain it. He gave us extra marks when we used that script in assignments and it measured up to his standards. In my mind I can still hear him say: "Light on the upstroke. Heavy on the down stroke. Extra pressure on the end!" The "extra pressure on the end" produced a little flair at the tail-end of each letter. Of course it could only be done with pen and ink and a special nib. We used a wide array of nibs in our pen holders. Glossy black ink was used for calligraphy, as opposed to the ordinary type of ink that we had in the inkwell on our desks.

This is my handwriting, illustrating how I was taught to write the alphabet in Latin Script

 Fountain pens grew in popularity, but caused all kinds of problems when the tiny balloon that held the ink came off, or when the ink froze in your briefcase in the winter. The fountain pens that had a piston to suck the ink into a small internal reservoir were not as prone to accidental spillage, but also had to be kept from freezing.

 A small group of us children from the Lomse walked to elementary school together in the mornings. The group grew larger as we were joined by more and more children walking that direction. When we reached our destination, the mixed group split into boys and girls. All schools at the time were segregated by gender. Mine was a large school of about 400 boys. There were at least that many girls at my sister's school next door.

 The school yard was not paved but made of solidly packed-down and levelled slag. It was surprisingly good for play. No matter what the weather—snow, rain or shine—the surface never got soft or muddy. We definitely ended up with skinned and bleeding knees, though. But they were taken in stride, and not deemed worthy of bothering the school-nurse with.

The grounds of the boys' and girls' schools were only separated by a chain link fence, so recess was a noisy affair. In spite of being a bit crowded, there was enough room to kick a ball around, which someone always did. The only trouble came when the boy's ball landed on the girl's side, or the girl's ball came flying our way. You can imagine how the rivalry erupted when that happened!

I have a vivid memory of that school basement. We had to line up in a rather dark hallway for food distribution. The funds for that came from the United States. We called it the Quaker feeding. It consisted of a bun and a small bottle of white or chocolate milk. I looked forward to that handout. The process didn't take very long. Class by class we were shuffled through the basement in orderly fashion. The buns seemed to be baked individually and were quite different from what you could buy in the store. They didn't have a hard crust but a brown glossy top. They tasted really good. But what really impressed me was the milk. I was amazed that the milk and chocolate milk, stored on the wire racks, came in such small bottles. At home, we picked up our milk in a can from the store in our neighborhood, where it was ladled out from a large metal milk can, which had two sturdy metal handles for lifting, and the lid attached to one of them with a chain. The lids would be taken off only when needed, to keep flies out.

The color painted on the lids of those cans would identify the type of milk it held. The milk store sold whole milk, buttermilk and skimmed milk, cream, butter and eggs. We called skimmed milk, "blue" milk, due to its pale, watery color. Pasteurized milk was also sold from one of the large cans but people were slow to accept and reluctant to buy it. We had no refrigeration, so milk had to be purchased fresh daily.

Our milk can was made out of aluminum and held about 2 liters. It had a tight fitting lid on a somewhat smaller neck. The handle, which folded out of the way, had a wooden grip for easier carrying. Most of the time, we could only afford fat reduced milk. I don't remember us ever buying chocolate milk.

Winters in Königsberg could get very cold. I clearly remember one such day. My hands got so cold on my way to school that I stopped in the middle of the bridge and refused to carry on. I was crying and the other children clustered around to coax me on. They had a hard time to convince me that not moving would simply make matters worse. By not moving my feet would get colder and hurt even more than my hands.

That bridge, the Kaiserbrücke (Emperor Bridge), is connected with other strong memories. The street went uphill for two or three blocks on one side of the bridge and then descended on the other side. The elevation reduced the number of times the bridge had to be opened, since the height allowed smaller ships to pass underneath. There were low lying buildings on the far side of the Kaiser bridge. One of the buildings had a large yard. That's where a military field kitchen was stationed. It opened every day to feed the needy.

We Will Be Free

During the bad years, I often had to go there to get food. We used a large lidded pot with a carrying handle to get whatever was served up that day. I remember the pea soup and dried prune soup with dumplings. I don't know if it was my favorite, but I think of that military field kitchen every time I eat pea soup. I'm grateful how it helped provide for us during the years when we had little.

After the First World War, there was a steady increase of inflation to a point where money was worthless. I vaguely remember dad coming home after a week's work with a briefcase full of money and mom running to the store to find out if it was enough to pay the accumulated grocery bill. I don't know how the grocer managed. A lot of people relied on his willingness to extend credit on the promise to pay as soon as possible. He kept a record in a little book. There were no receipts and no signatures, but complete trust on both sides.

And then there was no work.

After the Wall Street Crash of 1929, the US called in its loans to Germany, and the German economy collapsed. The world was hit by the "Dirty Thirties." And in Germany, the situation was particularly dire. My dad became one of the millions unemployed, without any hope of paid employment in the foreseeable future. He would ride a bike out into the country with a bag of tools on his back in search of work. He hoped to find someone for whom he could work for in exchange for food. Sometimes, he would be gone all week only to return home empty-handed. When Uncle Hans made the rare trip into the city with his horse and wagon filled with a load of potatoes or other stuff to sell, he would drop off a sack of potatoes or turnips for us. It was a long trip—18 to 20 hours. My mother was always so grateful when he came.

With God's help, through the kindness of Uncle Hans and especially of the Jewish families Mom worked for, we survived. I don't think we children realized how badly off we were. I do not remember being starved. But I do remember that Mom would give instructions to us about what we could eat, how to get supper started after school, and when to go to the soup kitchen.

My parents must have already been near the point of despair when a diphtheria outbreak hit Königsberg. It escalated their pain and suffering to an unbearable level. Dora had just returned from a hospital stay after a bout of pneumonia when the rest of us children got sick—me, Lotte, who was about four years old, and my baby brother Hans, who was about one and a half. I must have been in grade three at the time. I have no recollection of Dora's hospital stay, and only mention it because my mom surmised that it was the medication in Dora's system that prevented her from catching diphtheria along with the rest of us.

Mom panicked when we started burning up with fever. Dad hurried to summon our family doctor to our bedside. He was also a member of our church. It was much easier to personally go get the doctor than to find somebody who had a telephone. The Doctor examined us on our beds. Of my baby brother Hans's examination I have no recollection. I only remember my younger sister Lotte immediately being sent to the hospital. I saw Dad rush out with Lotte bundled in blankets in his arms to carry her to the *Krankenhaus der Barmherzigkeit*, (Hospital of Mercy), where I ended up just days later in the same fashion. Ambulances were probably around. I remember hearing the term "*Krankenwagen*," but I don't remember seeing one until much later.

The last picture of us, taken before the diphtheria outbreak. Hans was just over a year old, and was not in the photo.

That was the last I saw of Lotte and Hans. Hundreds of children died from diphtheria that year. I was sick in the hospital for a long time and remember the struggle to breathe and swallow. It was prior to the practice of intravenous feeding, so the nurses tried to make me drink milk or chocolate milk to keep me from dehydrating. Each time I tried to drink it, the milk promptly came back up through my mouth and nose. To this day I have an aversion to drinking milk. I know it's all in my head, but I struggle not to gag every time the smell of milk even comes remotely close to my nose.

When I got home from the hospital, everything seemed strange. Lotte was gone. Hans was gone. The house was hushed and quiet. The windows seemed crooked. The doorways looked narrower at the bottom than on the top. The floor did not seem level. Everything was lopsided and out of proportion. At times, the whole room seemed to spin. That changed back to normal after a while. But in school, when I finally got there, the teacher often poked me with a pool-cue-like pointer to wake me when I nodded off. I didn't have the energy and stamina of a normal third grader.

The extended illness and loss of my brother and sister affected me in other ways. I became extremely shy and withdrawn. So much so, that my sister Dora had to come along to speak for me when Mom sent us to get something from the corner grocery store. One time, when Dora was not along, I stood alone in a dark corner of the store for what seemed like an eternity, while one customer after another walked up to the counter to be served. I simply could not muster up the courage to go up to the counter and speak to the storekeeper. Little by little those things improved and turned back to normal too. But mom never recovered. She grieved for her dead children. From that time on, a thick mantle of sadness covered her. I missed her smiles and laughter. She was never quite the same again.

The Hospital of Mercy, where my sister and brother died.

The Castle Pond Promenade

Almost every Sunday we walked to the cemetery, which took about an hour one way. It was a leisurely walk along the lower lake. We called the wide path around the lower lake 'The Promenade'. There was also a wide path along the larger upper lake. We would watch the row boats, which could be rented for an hourly rate at several places along the shore. I think mom found the peaceful walk comforting because we were never in a hurry to get to our destination.

The cemetery was the most modern one in the city. It was known as "The Crematorium" because it was the only burial facility that also performed cremations. It had an impressive building in the middle that was a light color, with pillars that looked rather like the Whitehouse in Washington, only smaller. The surrounding cemetery was divided into several sections. There was the children's section, a family section, a military section, a section for single graves, and a section for cremated remains. Each area also had a large number of variously-sized private, secluded plots. Those higher-priced plots were surrounded by evergreen hedges, with only a small opening for access from the public foot path. Some had elaborate tombstones or even statues.

The plot we never failed to visit in the children's section had a large statue of Jesus, hewn of white marble. It had letters chiseled into the base below His outstretched arms, saying: "*Lasset die Kindlein zu mir kommen.*" ("Let the Children come to Me.") There was a small grave in that plot, completely blanketed in rich, green ground cover. It was undoubtedly the resting place for a child from a wealthy family, whose parents had felt as helpless against the assault of death as my parents and the other families in the city had.

Lotte and Hans' graves weren't in a private cove, and weren't nearly as elaborate as the one with the Jesus statue. They didn't have tombstones—only a few graves in our part of the cemetary did. Their graves stood side-by-side separated only by a small space between the two little mounds. The mounds were covered with evergreen groundcover, and had a strip of soil for plants at the head of the grave. Mom filled the space with bright purple and white pansies. Every week she would carefully water, weed and fertilize the flowers. The plots were marked with a metal sign, bearing the grave number. No names, just numbers. I can still envision the ornate shape of the markers, but I can't remember the numbers of my brother and sister's graves.

On our walk home we saw swans glide up to the grassy shore, hoping to be fed. It was fascinating to watch how they gracefully slid through the water, sometimes with little ones sheltered between their cupped up wings, as if to shelter them from harm. It's not that the young swans couldn't swim. We often saw them swim behind their parents, single-file, with the precision of a military formation. Maybe the mother swan just wanted the assurance that all her young ones were safe and accounted for. I wonder if the swans made my mother think about Hans and Lotte, and the tragic fact that she was unable to protect her young swans. Death had snatched two of them away—right from under her wings.

Spring and summer passed. The pansies bowed their heads and lost their blooms. The home of the swans froze over. And life went on. The stillness of gliding swans was replaced with music from loudspeakers and the merriment of skaters on the frozen lake.

The *Schloßteich*, surrounded by the Promenade, was the most prominent skating place in Königsberg. The City maintained all surfaces and kept them free of snow, and charged users a few pennies entrance fee for this service. Skaters used a boathouse as a place to put on their skates and warm up. Very few people had skates with the blades attached to the boot—as is common now. The skate blades were detachable, and were fastened to winter boots with clamps and straps, like the old roller skates.

The lake ice was divided for different uses: the center oval was designated for use by members of the figure skating club. Around that was the general area for skating. That's where we had the most fun. Spontaneously, the kids and grown-ups would form a long row of skaters that we called a *"Schlange"* (snake). We hung on to each other and skated in rhythm as fast as possible, weaving from side to side, often catapulting the skaters on the end of the line into the snow bank. The speed skating oval was often open to the public. I was a fairly fast speed skater. I enjoyed the rhythm of the movement and harbored a secret wish to own a pair of speed skates. There was also an area for figure skating and one for ice hockey—though hockey wasn't a popular sport.

People from the Lomse would also skate on the ice of a large meadow, which would flood when the river ran high and froze in the winter. But after a heavy snowfall it was usually not possible to skate there. Few people were willing to clear a large enough area. Because there were no buildings or trees to provide a windbreak, it was prone to drifting. The lack of shelter was also a deterrent, because there was no place to warm up when you got cold.

I will have to weave in some more stories about life in the city, whose greatest source of vitality came from the river Pregel. As I mentioned earlier, we lived only a block away from the Holtzbrüke Bridge and the northern arm of the Pregel. It was quite a spectacle when the icebreaker came through in wintertime. The temperature dipped to minus 30 for a few weeks almost every year, and the ice got thick quickly. The icebreaker would ram its bow up onto the ice with full force. The ice would first crack, then in slow motion, the bow would go down, and large chunks of ice would shoot out on each side, with water spraying and steam billowing everywhere. The vessel then backed up, churning water in its wake, and repeated the ramming operation over and over again. A much heavier icebreaker plied the waters between the outer harbor and the open sea. The noise of icebreakers was deafening and hard to describe. It was a clash between powerful, determined manmade engines, and the river's stubborn resistance to their harsh interruption of its seasonal slumber.

Only large motorized boats or steamers could get through the ice floes in wintertime. Barges, moored all along the banks of the river, were immobilized, and vulnerable to being damaged from the pressure of the ice. To relieve the pressure, workers cut a small channel around each barge. First, they used a special axe to chop a hole through the thick ice. The ice was more than a foot thick most of the time, so it took some time and skill to make a hole large enough to accommodate the ice-saw.

View of the Holtzbrüke Bridge closed, with the Fish Market in the background

The ice-saw was weighted at the bottom so it could cut through the ice on the down-stroke assisted by gravity. Two men, one on each side of the horizontal handle, heaved the saw up and down and cut a channel about a foot wide around the barge, leaving a narrow strip of ice directly beside the barge to stand on. They lifted the blocks of ice out of the water and piled them up around the trench like a barricade. They would have made excellent building blocks for a snow fort! But unfortunately, the blocks froze to the surface almost as soon as the workers put them down.

The Holzbrücke was the bridge closest to us. It was the one I had to cross to go to middle school. It was located on Lindenstrasse/ Weidendamm Street, near the Jewish Synagogue and orphanage. It was called *Holzbrücke*, Wood Bridge, even though the wood had long been replaced by steel and concrete. The bridge was the narrowest one on the navigable part of the Pregel. Its limited width made it challenging for large ships to pass. It took two tug boats, one at the bow and another at the stern, to steer the larger vessels past the bridge on their way to the plywood factory, pulp mill or other businesses upstream.

Two men manually cranked up the wings of the bridge. They then positioned themselves on either side of the opening on the piers. The men dipped large rope balls, into the water and held them up against the side of the piers, to help the ship pass through the opening undamaged. The balls were woven from sisal rope and stuffed with coarse fiber. Often the fit was so tight that the intense friction would cause steam and smoke to come from the water-soaked balls. After their cargo was unloaded, the ships would ride higher and the fit was not quite as tight on their return trip back down the river and out to sea.

The Holzbrücke wasn't raised for every vessel. Tugs and smaller boats had smoke stacks which could be flipped back to pass underneath. Some boys made a game of trying to spit into the opening of those smoke stacks as they passed under the bridge, but that could literally backfire on you, as the smoke billowed out unpredictably, and with some force. Racing across the bridge for a second attempt made it even more likely that an erupting cloud of smoke would send more than your spittle back.

Our street ran parallel to the Lindenstrasse/Weidendamm and intersected on our end with the edge of the river. There, steps led down to a floating platform, where a water taxi made regular stops during the summer. It also served as the diving platform for the neighborhood boys. That is, as long as we didn't spot the boat of the water police tied up at the Holzbrücke nearby. Swimming was actually "verboten" in that part of the river and for several kilometers upstream. Some boys told us of the paddling they'd received from the water police after they got caught swimming there. We were not unaware of the dangers. A boy from the apartment block next to ours lost his life when he got too close to the propeller of a tug boat. But who could resist a quick dip on a hot day when the water was practically right at your door?

The Holtzbrüke Bridge on Lindenstrasse/Weidendamm Street. Our street was a block over to the left, just outside the edge of the photo. The water-taxi station, which we used as a diving platform, can be seen under the far left-hand side of the bridge.

We got a kick out of teasing the men, who, with long grappling hooks propelled the barges along from bollard to bollard. They walked on the perimeter of their barges, and moved them with their feet, by pulling or pushing off the bollards with their grappling hooks. It was hard work when they had to propel the barges against the flow of the river.

We would swim up to a barge and use the compulsory safety rope or cable running from bow to stern to hoist ourselves up unto the deck. If the barge lay low in the water, we could clamber up without the aid of the rope. Some men would react to our appearance with shouting or cursing, others obviously did not mind. Laughing, we would jump off, and dive underneath for a repeat performance on the other side. It was great fun! But it was foolhardy. I misjudged the distance once, and panicked when I felt the bottom of the barge on my back.

I learned another, even more painful lesson, from a similar event. On my first approach to one particular barge, I reached to grab hold of the metal cable. I didn't notice that it was frayed, probably from water corrosion. The individual strands of metal stuck out like quills on a porcupine. When the pain hit, I reflexively grabbed on to the metal cable even harder and with both hands. Fearful of getting hurt even worse, I didn't immediately let go. When I got home, my mom had to painstakingly pick rusty bits of steel cable out of my bloodied, swollen palms. I heal fast, but don't necessary learn fast. I was finally convinced that the "no swimming" restriction made sense. I don't think I ever swam in that arm of the river again.

Swimming was allowed upstream of the final bridge on the wide, southern arm of the river. There, the water traffic was minimal. And on warm summer days, it was well worth the long walk. Königsberg had several open air facilities for swimming in the city, with water slides, diving boards and change rooms, even a sandy beach, but the entrance fee was 10c a day. Who in his right mind would pay when you could swim in the river for free?

We gladly forsook the water slide and diving boards for the great adventures the river afforded. The city pool facilities couldn't compare to the excitement of the timber floats. Small tugs constantly pulled timber floats to the mills situated on the far side of the river. Often, the floats simply drifted down the river. Some drifting floats had makeshift huts on them. They were manned by rafters, who guided the floats downstream for days. The floats moved slowly and were an open invitation to board. We jumped on and off and teased the men on the rafts in the same way we teased the ones on the river barges. But we never attempted to dive under the floes and swim from one side to the other. We knew that was far too dangerous.

Different kinds of log floes were lined up along 'our' side of the river waiting to be processed by the mill. Some were a jumbled mass of logs, kept together by a barrier around the perimeter. The barrier was formed by the outer logs being laid end to end and held together with a heavy wire. These floes were unpredictable and we stayed away from them.

Then, there were what we called the "piano floes". They were made of logs laid neatly side by side like a keyboard, and kept in place with a heavy wire stapled to the end of every log. It was such fun to run across the logs as they bobbed up and down. If they were in the water for some time, they lost some of their buoyancy and you had to run fast to avoid landing in the water or having your foot slip in between. When we got tired of swimming, we could watch workers feed logs into the mill. Or, we would search for a big chunk of thick bark so we could carve our own little boats, equip them with paper sails, and set them afloat.

Several rowing clubs had their boathouses on the far bank of the river . Rowers would often glide by in their sleek rowboats—the kind you see in racing regattas. I was probably less than 10 years old at the time. Little did I know that in just a few years, I would get to row a boat like that in high school as part of the rowing team.

The hardship of the Great Depression provided Hitler the political opportunity he was looking for. The number of unemployed was astronomical. People were starving. Political extremists rioted on the streets. Not only were we burdened by reparation payments to the victors of World War I, we were also threatened by unemployment, hyperinflation, political chaos, and a possible Communist takeover.

In the midst of the crisis, people looked for someone to blame—and for a solution. Hitler offered it to them. The success of the NSDAP in the elections grew. The number of their seats in the *Reichstag* (Parliament) rose from 12 in 1928 to 230 in July 1932. Nevertheless, three elections in 1932 failed to result in a majority government. In an attempt to keep the country from descending into chaos, the conservative German National People's Party (DNVP) formed a coalition government with the NSDAP and appointed Hitler as Chancellor.

1933 was a pivotal year. Hitler was appointed Chancellor of the coalition in January. In March, the Reichstag passed the Enabling Act, which allowed him to exercise dictatorial power. In April, Hitler set up the Gestapo. In May, he banned trade unions. In July, he banned opposing political parties. In October, he withdrew Germany from the League of Nations. In November, he made the para-military swear allegiance to him. In just one year, Hitler's rise to power was complete. The *Hansaring* was renamed *Adolf Hitler Strasse* to mark the emergence of the New Regime. I missed all those important political events. 1933 was the year that diphtheria ravaged my family.

But I do remember the first 'plebiscite' under Hitler in 1935. People were asked if the small but coal-rich province of the Saar should again become part of Germany, as it was given to the French as part of the Versailles Treaty. The propaganda machine was fully employed. Political posters were plastered on all public notice boards. There were speeches at street corners and in school rooms by guest political speakers. When the big day came, every adult who voted affirmative was given a silver coated lapel pin with the German word for yes—"*Ya!*" (Yes!) It seemed to me that everyone wore that pin for weeks afterward. The Saarland became part of the German Reich again. It was the first positive thing that had happened to Germany in a very long time.

It took a while for our family to recover economically from the depression, even after dad started to work again. Funeral costs and accumulated grocery bills had to be repaid. Mom kept working and my sister and I helped by doing the chores around the house so our family could meet our obligations and get back on our feet again. God's provision was evident in many ways during that troublesome time. My mother was very talented at embroidery. She picked up some work embroidering graduation caps for the University in Königsberg. The caps were brimless, and made out of red velvet with a tassel attached to the top—similar to "Shriners" caps. With fine gold threads of various textures, mom embroidered the name of the graduate and the emblem of the faculty on the side of the cap, and a band of laurels around the rim.

She also kept house for two Jewish families, who lived just two blocks east of us. They sometimes sent groceries home with her, and gave us clothing and toys to play with. The head of one of the families was a surveying engineer. Through mom he gave me stacks of technical books and some surveying and drafting instruments before they left the country. That gift, I think, sparked my interest to pursue the same career. All that changed, of course, with the unforeseen turn of events that took place not many years thereafter.

Things had definitely improved. My dad found steady employment. He had to work outside the city frequently, but was well paid. Mom stayed with those two Jewish families out of gratitude for their support during the bad years. I remember them leaving the country before the persecution of the Jews set in. I think they trusted mom enough to let her in on their plans to leave secretly. They left most of their belongings behind. She was sad when they left and saw their departure as a foreboding of bad things to come. Mom got a new job in the harbor area after the Jewish family left. She worked there cleaning the office, until the destruction of the city in 1944.

Many other Jewish families also read the political situation correctly. The most famous Jew that left Königsberg at that time was songwriter Max Colpert, who wrote, "Where have all the Flowers Gone?" It took several years before I realized just how lucky they were to have left when they did. I remembered the general unease among the students, during my first year in high school, when some of my Jewish schoolmates didn't show up at school anymore. One of them sent a postcard afterwards, saying that they had settled in Ecuador. The card was addressed to the school, the teacher showed it to us and read the greeting.

Hitler's ideology was becoming increasingly prominent. (On a side note, the term 'Nazi' was not used in Germany until after the war, and then only in a derogatory way.) Somewhere along the way, schools decided that students had to study and memorize portions of Hitler's manifesto, *"Mein Kampf."* To this day, when somebody abruptly makes a career change and/or enters politics, I mockingly recite Hitler's words: *"Und ich beschloß ein Politiker zu werden"* (And I made up my mind to become a politician!). When Imperial Japan signed an Anti-Communist Pact with Germany we had to study Japanese culture and history.

By the time I hit high school, Hitler's propaganda machine was in overdrive. We were so inundated with politically-correct messages that we had gotten used to it. Virtually everything was politicized. Even everyday activities. Movie houses had to run a short government clip called, The *"Die Deutsche Wochenschau"* (The German Weekly Newsreel), prior to the featured film. Some clips featured nostalgic reviews of Hitler's rise to power, or rebroadcast his political speeches. They had titles like *"Der Sieg des Glaubens"* (Victory of Faith), *"Tag der Feiheit"* (Day of Feedom), *"Triumph des Willens"* (Triumph of the Will), and "Hitler's *Aufruf an das deutsche Volk"* (Appeal to the German People). Other films, like *"Hitlerjunge Quex"* (*Hitler Youth Quex*) and "S.A. Mann Brand" (*Brownshirt Brand*) were quasi documentaries and recruitment pieces to get people to support and join the groups of the new regime. Some, like *"Das Erbe"* (The Inheritance) and *"Glückskinder"* (The Blessed Children) were blatant propaganda pieces, supporting euthanasia, sterilization, and the pursuit of a pure Aryan race. Others like: *"Der Ewige Jude"* (The Eternal Jew), *"Juden ohne Maske"* (The Jews Unmasked),and 'Jude Süß' (*Jew Sweet*), railed against Jews and were designed to incite hatred toward them.

Political messages and anthems constantly blared from the radio. The newspapers were forced to promote the government's point of view and policies. Most of my friends and I just shrugged it off. It made no difference whether we agreed or disagreed with the politically-correct drivel.

I must say, that the common people were very careful to differentiate between the various political entities. Members of the NSDAP (National Socialist Workers Party) were dubbed *"Parteibonzen."* (Party Bigwigs). We were also careful to distinguish between "SS" and "Waffen SS." Members of the latter group were often forced to serve in that unit, while the former served voluntarily.

Laws were passed, banning marriage between Jewish and non-Jewish Germans, forbidding young German women to work for Jewish households, depriving Jews of German citizenship, and ordering Jews discharged from service in the German army. Groups like the boy scouts, girl guides, and other youth organizations were abolished or absorbed by the state controlled "Youth for Hitler." The leaders made sure that all sports and all other activities were accompanied with generous helpings of propaganda. By about 1937, it was obligatory for every child over 10 years old to attend *Das Jungvolk*, the younger version of Youth for Hitler. Repeated non-attendance had to be reported to the police.

These developments indicated that all was not well. Nevertheless a positive mood filled the air. Hitler's regime was producing national pride, stability, and economic growth. The feelings of shame and impotence imposed by the Treaty of Versailles were being replaced with a determination to hold our heads high and work together for a better future. Hitler brought about many positive changes and instilled optimism in our hearts. The Depression, both economically and emotionally, was starting to feel like a distant bad dream. None of us imagined that a man who inspired such hope would soon bring about a nightmare far darker than the one from which we were just awakening.

4 | BITS OF AMBER

My mother, Maria Marquardt, was the oldest of four sisters. She was born on May 31, 1892 on a large farm, Adlig Pohren, a rural community, that by 1936 had burgeoned to a population of 208. Adlig Pohren was located a few kilometers north of the nearest city, Bladiau, and about 60 kilometers southwest of Königsberg. It was one of several similar large farming operations in the area. My mother could name at least six. All of the operations were managed by one administrator and owned by the Schichau family, who were also the owners and operators of several shipbuilding plants, including a massive one in Königsberg.

Mom's dad, my "Opa" (Grandfather) Marquardt, was the farm's *Glöckner*. Literally, *Glöckner* means one who rings the bell as an assignment. That very fact implies authority, but I don't know what exactly the profession entailed. On one of my visits to his house, Opa showed me the bell tower. It was an open wooden structure, comparable to the wooden windmill towers on the prairies. When the *Glöckner* rang the bell each morning, all the farm workers, who had finished their assignment the previous day, were to gather at the foot of the tower for directions. That's about all I know about a *Glöckner's* responsibilities.

My sister and I felt apprehensive whenever we went to visit Opa. We dreaded the long walk from the nearest train station to his home. We counted off the distance using the whitewashed stone markers along the way. Every tenth stone had a white number painted on the background of a black circle, indicating the distance to the next town. We would run ahead and sit on the next white stone to rest until the others caught up. The landscape was monotonous. I can't remember trees along the road, nor can I remember ever encountering another person.

I think that our reluctance to visit Opa can be attributed to the shadow of family conflict that unconsciously weighed on our young psyches. The woman we knew as "Oma" was disdainfully referred to by my aunts as "that woman." Their biological mother had died when they were in their early or mid-teens and they greatly resented their father's new wife. To my knowledge, Dora and I were the only two of Opa's grandchildren that ever went out to the farm to visit.

Opa and Oma lived in a duplex-type retirement house, which the landowner provided for his workers when they reached 70 or 75 years of age. If I remember correctly, there were two of these duplexes located next to each other. A natural spring behind their house was the source of drinking water for the community. The spring had been capped, but water continuously gushed out of a steel pipe. It came out with so much pressure that the surrounding air seemed to vibrate. The force made fetching water a tricky business. Your pail would go flying if you tried to catch the full stream. You had to catch just a tiny edge of it with the lip of your pail, and even then, it would fill fast and was hard to hang on to.

Opa carried the water home in two wooden pails hanging from chains, which were attached to each end of a carrying yoke he placed across his shoulders. The yoke had a carved-out area in the middle, to make it more comfortable around the neck. A similar carrying instrument was used in the Königsberg harbor to load and unload barges.

They had a large garden in front of their house, just across a narrow road. Opa kept busy in the garden work shed, repairing various farm implements such as the field-worker's wooden rakes, whose tines often broke and needed replacing. Wire baskets were widely used on the farm, and when in need of repair, they would also be mended by Opa's magic touch.

He had rigged himself up a home-made carving bench. The bench had a foot pedal that, when depressed, would close a clamp. The clamp held his project firmly in place. He could sit comfortably; straddling the bench with his knees, depressing the pedal with his foot. That left both hands free to manipulate his tools. He'd release the foot pedal often, to quickly swap or re-position his project. I was astonished at how fast he worked. I once saw him produce an axe handle out of a chunk of wood in what seemed like no time at all! Nothing appeared to be beyond the range of his expertise—from wooden ladles to handles for scythes, sharpening axes, shovels or scythes. Naturally, he had a great array of tools in his shed; including a huge hand-cranked grinding stone, and a water trough to keep the massive stone wet.

Opa restored the dulled edges of the worker's scythes with a special hammer and small anvil. The anvil was secured to a stubby section of a tree trunk, which was large enough for Opa to sit on. There, he'd balance the scythe on his knees guiding it across the anvil and hammer away to give it a keener edge. The final razor-edged sharpness was achieved by using a whetstone. Every cutter would carry one of them to re-sharpen in the field when needed.

Opa smoked a pipe, for which he grew and cured his own tobacco. The government had set a limit for the number of tobacco plants individuals were allowed to grow, so he made good and sure that he reached the maximum each year. His long beard was stained with tobacco. His outer garments also had stains that marked his pipe's habitual resting place.

For smoking outdoors, Opa used a short pipe, which sort of rested on his upper chest. He had no teeth left in his mouth, so he couldn't clamp down on the pipe the way a smoker normally would. He overcame this handicap in his own ingenious way by placing a rubber gasket from the porcelain closures of beer bottles at the end of the pipe's mouth piece. The gaskets were about the size of a Canadian Loonie with a hole in the middle. By keeping his lips closed around the gasket, and puffing out the other side of his mouth, he managed just fine.

There were only two rooms in Opa and Oma's home. A curtain separated their bedroom from the main room. A trap door in front of their bed gave them access to a root cellar. Since they had no electricity, most of the light in the main room came from the open fire in the hearth. During the day, some light came in through the only window. But because of the large overhang on the roof, it was always extremely dim in there. A kerosene lamp hung from the ceiling, though I do not recall it ever being lit. Metal holders, from days-gone-by, were still fastened to the wall; from when pitch-laden wood slivers were used for light instead of candles.

A chain hanging down from the large chimney provided a way to suspend pots or frying pans above the fire in the open hearth. That's how they cooked. The frying pan was huge and had three loops that Oma connected to the hanging chain. The pot had a heavy lid, which, of course, had to be removed to stir whatever was cooking. I remember biting on bits of charcoal when eating scrambled eggs. And the pea soup tasted like smoke. Every barbeque brings memories of Oma's cooking.

Opa ascribed his good health and vitality to his daily sip of rye. After supper each evening, he'd sit in his rocking chair in the corner next to the fireplace smoking his pipe. He kept his box of tobacco on a ledge that extended out from the hearth. The intricately carved tobacco box was an example of his fine handiwork. Opa did a lot of wood carving. I remember a beautiful mirror frame he carved for my Aunt Minna that hung in the entrance to her house. A pipe cabinet hanging on the wall of his duplex was also proof of his skill.

A large pipe cabinet hung adjacent to the fireplace. It displayed several pipe heads and a variety of mouth pieces behind a carved-wood, glass-paneled door. There were several different sizes of pipes. All the heads were made of porcelain, adorned with intricate pictures, and topped with filigreed silver lids. The largest one had some kind of a silver knob at the bottom of the head, so that it could rest on the floor. Opa would stuff tobacco into it, attach the mouth piece to several tubes he had connected to the porcelain head. With the pipe resting on the floor, he would light it from the fireplace with one of the sticks sitting in a container in the nearest corner. After the pipe was lit to his satisfaction, he'd stomp on the stick to extinguish the flame and put the remnant back into the container to be reused until it became too short. There was no danger of the floor catching fire. It was made of solidly packed smooth clay. He closed the lid of the pipe with his foot after he lit it.

Moles had multiplied in that area and their burrows became a hazard for farm animals. To contain the problem, the government offered to pay a bounty for the moles at 50 cents a tail. The trapper could keep the rest. Opa caught, skinned, and tanned so many moles that he was able to get two fur coats made for my older cousins. It was quite an accomplishment; because each pelt was only about the size of half a sheet of paper.

As I mentioned, my Opa had four daughters. Three of them—my mom, Aunt Bertha, and Aunt Anna—lived in Königsberg. Aunt Anna was the baby of the family. She belonged to the Sisters of Mercy, a Protestant fraternity of nurses. After Hitler came to power, Aunt Anna resigned from that fraternity and joined an order of nurses that had political leanings. Because she was unmarried, lived in a small apartment, and worked shifts, Dora and I didn't see much of her, and didn't get to know her well. So I can't tell you much about her.

Opa's second-oldest daughter, Aunt Bertha, was married to Paul Hellwig, a master tailor who specialized in dress uniforms for military officers. They had two daughters, Ursela and Erika, who were quite a bit older than me. I saw them often, but the age difference meant that we weren't playmates, and had only a basic knowledge of each other's lives.

Uncle Paul's family lived north-east of us, on *Rippenstraße* (Rib Street), in a neighborhood called *Roßgarten* (Horse Garden). It was about a 45 minute walk from the Lomse. We would cross through the stone-paved yard of Königsberg's impressive Catholic Church as a shortcut to get there. Except for the commercial zone along the main street, all the structures in Paul and Bertha's neighborhood were residential apartments, five to eight stories high. Things seemed a lot more cramped there than on the Lomse. Not only were the buildings higher, but there were no trees. Although the streets teemed with people, the area seemed dull to me. You couldn't feel the pulse of the river there. No ship whistles. No harbor smell. No street vendors peddling wares.

Uncle Paul and Aunt Bertha lived on the ground floor. They used one room of their apartment for Paul's tailor shop. His massive work table was pushed up against a window, which faced a very small yard. Not much light came through. Bolts of *feldgrau* (field-grey) and *steingrau* (stone-grey) wool sat on the shelf, along with skeins of fancy "Russia" braid, metallic embroidery thread, whip cord, several colors of trim and piping, ornate shoulder-straps

(*Schulterklappen*), shoulderboards (*Schulterstücke*), scissors, tailor's chalk, pins, dressmaker "hams" and all the other necessary supplies for constructing *Waffenröcke* (Military Dress) uniforms. Uncle's current work-in-progress was modeled by the mannequin that stood on guard next to the table.

Uncle would tailor-make each thigh-length, eight button *feldgrau* tunic, and customize it to display the officer's branch and rank. He piped or underlaid the shoulder-straps and collar patches in the officer's *Waffenfarbe*, a color code which identified the branch of service to which he belonged: white for infantry, red for artillery, rose for Panzer troops, and yellow for cavalry. *Waffenfarbe* piping also edged the collar, cuffs, front closure, and elaborate scalloped rear vent. Trousers were *steingrau*, with the outer seams piped in *Waffenfarbe*. Fancy loops of braid (aiguillette) draped from the officer's right shoulder epaulet to the sternum of his tunic. His medals, decorations, and ribbons were displayed side by side on the left breast. On the other side, above the right breast pocket, was the visual acknowledgement of the new National Socialist reality: the *Wehrmachtsadler* Eagle, clutching the swastika in its claws. The uniforms were striking, but I couldn't imagine myself ever wearing one. Being in the army wasn't on the list of things I wanted to do.

I was impressed by the ever ready huge iron. It was connected to the gas line with a rubber hose, lit in the morning, and was kept at a hot working temperature all day. Uncle had a container with yellow powder on the table. It was some kind of fabric glue. Sprinkled on fabric, the iron would activate the glue. Sometimes several layers were bonded together, one on top of the other.

A pair of knee-length pants pops into mind, which uncle had made for me from army fabric. They were the style of pants that boys commonly wore back then, but fancier, with "all the bells and whistles." Uncle made allowance for growth by making the hem extra wide. The trouble was, the stiffness of the fabric, compounded by the wide hem, rubbed my skin raw. Even a short walk caused agony. The perfect fit, extra deep pockets and even a watch pocket and chain anchor could not compensate for the sores those pants created. Needless to say, I only wore them when visiting him. Thankfully I outgrew those pants fast.

Uncle Paul and Aunt Bertha had a fancy modern flush toilet. I was fascinated with how you pulled on a porcelain-handled chain to make the water rush down into the bowl from a tank up on the wall. It sure was a lot nicer than our set up! They also seemed to eat fancier food. It was at aunt Berta's that I ate asparagus with grated cheese and browned butter for the first time.

Opa travelled to Königsberg at least once a year to visit "his girls." On one such occasion, I accompanied him to Aunt Bertha's house. We were walking down one of the busy retail streets near the heart of the city when Opa had to clear his nose. In good old country fashion, he held the right side of his nose closed, and cleared his left nostril with gusto. His repeat performance on the other side left a big gob of snot running down a storefront window. I was so embarrassed that I wanted to vanish.

Aunt Minna was the only daughter who didn't live in Königsberg. She lived in Schalben, near Warnicken—by the Baltic Sea, with her husband, Hans. Uncle Hans was a trained cattleman (*Schweizer*) and a certified beekeeper *(Imker)*. He held a position as an *Instman* on a large farming operation. The closest corresponding English term would be husbandman. Hans' main responsibility was to care for the farm livestock by feeding, herding, breeding, and milking them twice a day by hand. He was also responsible for a team of four horses. Tante Minna took over the chore of milking when uncle was drafted.

Hans and Minna's only son, Herbert, was older than me. So Dora and I didn't have any cousins our age to play with. Herbert left home to start a live-in apprenticeship right after elementary school, when he was only 14 years old. He took up the blacksmith trade and became so skilled at it that he was hired by the horse racing stable in Königsberg.

Dora and I spent all of our school holidays at Uncle Hans and Aunt's Minna's. My mom would often accompany us on the hour and a half train ride(That train stopped at every small hamlet!) to Schalben, and visit for a while before heading back home. Mom thought we'd have a far better time on the farm during breaks than at home, alone and bored while she worked (Not to mention us getting into trouble!). She was right. Dora and I had great fun at Aunt and Uncle's place. We took part in their daily routines, and they did a lot of special things with us too! I think they enjoyed having us just as much as we enjoyed being there.

Their house looked like a fairy tale cottage. It had thick, white-washed walls and a dense thatched roof made of reeds. The reeds needed to be repaired or replenished at times. Uncle harvested them in the winter from the frozen marshes and ponds by cutting them down with a scythe just above ice level. The edge of the roof was about two feet thick, and layer upon layer rose up to a peak, where a unique cap crowned the top.

Superstition had it that lightning would not strike where storks nested. People tried to get them to build nests on their roofs by mounting an old wagon wheel on their roof or chimney. If you could get a pair of storks to move in, the same pair would come back and nest year after year. And the nest would be taken over by one of their offspring, when the parents were too old to make the trip. Uncle didn't have storks on top of his house, but he did have two pairs on the barns—one on the cow barn, and another on the horse barn across the way.

Uncle's house had two stories. Compared to Opa's shanty and our apartment, it was a spacious affair. The bedrooms were on the upper floor, accessed by a set of stairs from the entry. There was a "smoker" next to the stairs on the upper floor, which was part of the chimney. It was of great interest to me. It looked like the chimney had been enlarged to contain all kinds of bars with hooks. Aunt Minna hung meat or sausages on these hooks to smoke. How my eyes watered when I tried to look down the dark chimney after my aunt opened the doors to the smoker to take some bacon out! I must have been quite small then, because I could hardly peek over the bottom ledge. Part of the chimney extended into the bedrooms and kept the upstairs bedrooms warm during the winter.

The large kitchen had a milk separator and butter churn bolted to a bench along one wall. The oven was similar to ours at home but even larger. The tiles were brown and there was a huge firebox and a cavernous space to store firewood. But I mostly remember the barrel in the far corner. It had a cover of sackcloth and my aunt was the only person allowed to peek underneath. That's where a hen, or sometimes a duck, incubated her chicks.

One year, there were little piglets penned up in a box, sitting on a bench near the stove. Their mother had birthed a very large litter, and couldn't feed all of them, so they had to be bottle fed. That was quite a chore—especially when they got a little bigger. It wasn't the feeding that caused us problems, but their incessant squeals and squirms and attempts to wiggle free after they were satisfied.

We hauled water from a large pump across from the house. Without fail, I would get my little finger caught between the handle and housing when operating it. There was a round weight on the handle that was designed to help give extra push on the down stroke, but the handle was tough for little hands to hold onto. The weight gave some extra oomph, alright; I lost a fingernail several times over the years by not holding the handle in the right place. Would I ever learn? It was the same year after year. Despite my resolve not to repeat the painful experience, I'd go to pump water and Bam!—the blood oozed out from under my fingernail again.

Uncle looked after Holstein cattle, the white ones with the distinctive black spots. He had about a hundred head in the herd. After the grain had been harvested, Uncle would let the cattle pasture on clover, which grew out on the fields as a second crop. In the morning, he would herd the cattle and horses out to feed on the sweet greens. In the afternoon, his trained dog helped round them up again, to keep them from overindulging. There was one cow who must have stuffed herself full, because she bloated up very badly and collapsed.

Uncle always carried along a little wooden box for such an emergency. The box contained what we called a *"Trikar"* and several brass ferrules, tubes with a wide flange on one end. The *Trikar* was like an awl with a stubby point and a round shaft. Uncle would slip a ferrule over the shaft and punch the instrument into the rump or side of the cow, where the bloating was most pronounced. When he pulled the awl out, the small brass ferrule remained, and kept the wound open, so the excess gas could escape. Most of the time, this procedure solved the problem, and the cow experienced no lasting ill effects after the ferrule was removed. I remember only one time, when Uncle got to a cow too late, that the cow died and had to be destroyed.

Uncle kept several hives of bees in the garden next to the house. The whole bee-keeping process amazed me. A removable panel at the back of the hive allowed us to peer through the glass and observe and monitor the activity inside. In response to what was happening in the hive, Uncle would put metal sliders with notches over the flight holes. That would allow only the smaller worker bees in and out, facilitate the slaughter of returning drones, or prevent a queen from leaving with a swarm of followers.

Many times he would put his ears close to the hive. He said that he could hear when a new queen was ready to take off at daylight with a swarm of followers. If this was the case, he told my Aunt to be on guard the next day, ready for action. When the cloud of bees emerged from the hive, she was supposed to fill a spray pump with water from a barrel nearby, and quickly spray water into the air. This tricked the bees into thinking it was raining, and discouraged them from flying too far. Most of the time, it worked. After the swarm had settled in a nearby tree or shrub, Aunty sent us to call my uncle to gather the clump of bees.

For that chore, Uncle used what he called, "a catcher hive." It was a container made of an old straw hive, with a strap on the bottom, and a removable lid on top. With a goose wing he had saved from butchering, Uncle would quickly scoop the mass of bees into the open end, pop the lid on, set it down, and take cover. It wasn't long before he knew if he had successfully recaptured the Queen. If she was in the Catcher Hive, the bees that remained outside the hive would frantically buzz around it, attempting to join her. If not, they would reorganize around the Queen and fly away.

During peak honey season, Uncle installed middle walls into the hives. He told me that the middle wall was the most 'labor intense' for the bees. The pre-embossed hex shapes on the wax mimicked the bottom of honeycomb. It sped up the formation of the comb and encouraged the bees to concentrate on honey production. Uncle let me help cut the wax pieces to the right size. Then, he carefully melted them into the thin, evenly spaced wires that stretched from the top to the bottom of the frames. In a good year, it took the bees about four weeks to finish their work. Uncle would remove the honey laden frames and replace them with empty ones. A hand-cranked centrifuge helped us extract the honey from the tiny wax cells after the wax covering was removed from the cells. Uncle had a tool for that. It was like part of a small comb but with longer tines and was made out of metal with a wooden handle. A giant fork with sharp points, might be a better description.

There was so much to learn and try in regard to the bees alone, not to mention the herding of ducks, geese and turkeys. Chickens did their own thing. Except for scattering grain on the ground for them to eat, they didn't need much attention. The only exception was if we heard a loud cackle coming from any direction other than the chicken coop. The cackle betrayed the fact that a chicken had illegally dropped an egg. It was our signal to set out and search for its misdeed.

Ducks and geese were good followers—at least in the morning, when you led them down to the fenced- in area of the creek to swim. Getting them back home for the night was another story. They weren't nearly as mindful then. Unhurried, they constantly stopped to nibble on a sprig of grass or to investigate an interesting looking object. The ducks were the worst. They waddled along leisurely, and seemed to have a great need to gather and consult with one another along the way. They bobbed their heads, wagged their tails, and chattered intensely, like a bunch of old women at a coffee shop nattering about the latest juicy scandal. To break up their gossip session, you'd have to take a run at them, and shoo them by waving your arms, or threaten to poke them with a stick.

Turkeys required by far the most attention and care to bring them to maturity. Even the mature birds seemed to be too dumb to take care of themselves. My Aunt had a long list of strict instructions for looking after them. At the top of the list: "Never allow them to get soaked in the rain! At the slightest sprinkle take them to a shelter!" Another thing she was particular about was the turkeys' diet. She sent Dora and me out to gather a certain kind of nettle, which she mixed with finely-chopped hard boiled eggs and softened barley. The turkeys ate this mixture until they were about half grown. After that, we could feed them various types of grain. But apparently that wasn't tasty enough for them. They seemed particularly intent on stealing the pig's food—boiled potatoes mixed with bran.

One year a gander took up residence in uncle's yard as a self-appointed watchdog. He would only let members of the household enter. Everyone else got attacked. On one occasion, he unleashed his fury on me. He lunged at me with his neck outstretched close to the ground, tongue hissing, wings wide open. I froze. But that didn't stop him. He was out for blood! I screamed as he bit my legs to punish my unwelcome intrusion. I was finally rescued by my aunt, who heard the big commotion from the house. Uncle later told me to teach a beast like that a lesson by grabbing him by the neck and spinning him around a few times before letting go. I am not sure if I tried his advice, but I was never bitten again.

We got a kick out of teasing a certain male turkey that was particularly sensitive to our insults. We'd sneak up and "gobble, gobble" at him a few times. That's all it took to set him off. His face would deepen to various shades of purple. He'd puff himself up as big as possible, and angrily strut around in circles with his wings dragging on the ground. The feathers on his wings were worn straight like being cut with scissors , where he dragged them across the ground, when blustering. His head would jerk back and forth as he screamed out an incessant, piercing "GOBBLE! GOBBLE!!!" in response to our taunt. It always took quite a while before he settled down.

My sister and I never got bored of life around the farm. Some things, though, seemed to fascinate me more than her. She had a great dislike for some of the distinct farm smells. That kept her from visiting the dairy, where cheese was produced. She would never go to the next building, where the pigs were kept. The two buildings were in close proximity because the pigs were fed with some of the by-products from making cheese.

It just sprang to my mind how uncle nearly lost his life there. The liquid manure from the pigs flowed through a pipe into a reservoir next to the building. The reservoir was a brick lined pit in the ground. From there, the manure was pumped into tanks on horse drawn carts to be spread on fields for fertilizer. When uncle stepped on a plank covering the pit, the plank gave way, and uncle fell into the toxic sludge. He surely would have drowned, had the pit been full. Someone heard the commotion, grabbed a ladder and rescued him. Uncle had to leave his clothes behind and drove home, covered with a frock he borrowed from one of the workers. If you're familiar with the smell of pig's manure, you will know that exposure to the fumes alone can kill you. After scrubbing down, uncle was fine, but extremely careful around that pit from then on.

Uncle was also engaged by the dairy '*zum Ferkel beschneiden*', that is, to castrate male piglets, a practice used even today on piglets up to one week old. It prevents the meat of male pigs to take on a boar smell and flavor. Uncle used a straight razor for that purpose. He would hone the razor on a leather strap beforehand. He would keep the strap taut with one hand while flipping the razor rapidly up and down the length of the strap. He must have done that a thousand times. He was so fast that I could not see when he flipped the razor over its back edge with every stroke. Then he would test the razor for sharpness on the hairs of his forearm, and repeat the sharpening process if not satisfied.

He unloaded large cans of milk at the dairy twice a day, hauling them in from the milking out on the pasture. I was fascinated at how that milk was turned into "*Tilsiter*" Cheese. Uncle would frequently take a squished, broken or otherwise unsaleable cake of cheese home. Then it was time to feast on cheese with bread, not bread with cheese!

Speaking of which, my aunt would bake several loaves of rye bread every other week. The loaves were round and a good foot in diameter with a heavy crust. Did it ever taste good, especially when it was fresh out of the oven! If you were down to the end of the last loaf, you'd have to chew a little harder. I loved to eat that rye bread with lots of freshly churned butter and sliced radishes, with a sprinkling of salt—or plain, with a chunk of home-smoked bacon, sprinkled with pepper. I'd cut the bacon into bite-sized pieces, and savor each one as I popped it into my mouth while chewing on a bite of bread.

It was a special treat to ride on the top of the wagon when Uncle took in the harvest of grain. He allowed us to climb up to the very top, using the rope that tied down a pole to secure the load. The wagon was pulled by four horses. Uncle admonished us to hang on to the pole, as the top-heavy wagon swayed from side to side, and he didn't want us catapulted from our perch. It was better than a carnival ride! We stayed up there until we reached the threshing machine, or a nearby stack of sheaves—which were sometimes piled even higher than the ones on which we sat. On longer trips, Uncle would sit on top of the pile with us. He'd guide the horses with a set of extra-long lines—one set for the back pair of horses, and another for the front pair, who were attached to the wooden tongue steering mechanism.

There was a blacksmith shop located in a house not far from Uncle's place. To me it looked like they forgot to put the front wall in that house when it was built. Since the shop was open to the street, I could watch the never-ending wonder of the blacksmiths plying their craft. The sparks flew as they hit or shaped the metal. And when they cooled the red hot iron in vats, the steam would hiss out in big billows. Most of the time, the blacksmiths worked on individual projects, but occasionally one would hold something on the anvil while the other pummeled it with a hammer. There was quite an array of tongs around the forge, which was in the middle of the cavernous room. A large metal hood over the forge funneled sparks and smoke up through the roof. All kinds of hammers sat on the floor near the anvil and lay on the edge of the hefty chunk of tree trunk, which kept the anvil in place. Many interesting things hung from the open beams. Everything in the shop—all of the implements, beams and open rafters—had the same charcoal hue. I was so proud when a blacksmith invited me to pull the bellow, and my efforts turned the embers red hot and the metal in the fire a bright yellow.

Bits of Amber

As fun as all the activity around the farm was, by far the best part of going to Aunt Minna and Uncle Hans' was our frequent excursions to the Baltic Sea. Getting there required a long but leisurely walk along a dirt road. A large patch of wild strawberries by the roadside provided a welcome break. We stuffed ourselves full of the sweet berries, and strung more onto long stalks of Timothy grass, to be eaten along the way, or relished at home with fresh farm cream.

We would stay at the beach most of the day, enjoying the pure white sand and the waves. An area with an expanse of shallow water was our favorite spot. The '*Krajebieters*', meaning crow-biters, lived just a few kilometers north. To augment their meagre food supply of fish, these men would catch migrating crows in nets and kill them with a swift bite to the neck. Then they'd pluck, cook, and pickle the crows in large earthenware pots, to be eaten in the winter, or when fishing was impossible. Tasting a bit like wild pigeon, the crows were prized as a delicacy by the locals. Giving a crow as a present was considered a special way of saying "thank you."

A Crow-Biter at work

At the end of their fishing ex-cursions, the fishermen hoisted their boats up onto the shore. They'd grunt and strain as they rotated a crude winch (consisting of a wooden spindle pierced with a long pole) to wind up the attached rope. Some boats were hauled up by brute manpower, without the assistance of a winch. The fishermen would mend their nets in the shade of their boats or in the cool of tree groves by the sea shore. Smoke boxes, with steel doors at the front and on top, were situated here and there. Some were even made of wood. The fishermen hung their freshly caught fish on steel rods, and placed them into a smoke box through the top doors. Pine cones were used as fuel. The smoke from the cones gave the fish a unique flavor. Huge piles of cones were stacked near the smokers for that purpose.

The homes of the fishermen were clustered in small groups. There were hardly enough to call the community a hamlet. Their houses, which were typical of the area, looked about the same as my Uncle's. Some roofs were decorated with an interesting weather vane. The same sort of vane graced the mast of every fishing boat. Each was unique: some very colorful and very intricate in design. The tradition stemmed back to the mid-1800s, when laws specified that each fisherman had to display a sign on his boat showing which fishing village it belonged to. Originally, the vanes consisted of a simple two-color design like a flag. But with time, fishermen began to add shapes of buildings, trees, lighthouse, churches and horses, creating highly stylized works of art.

We'd collect bits of amber that washed up on the sandy shore of the Baltic. Amber is fossilized tree resin (not sap), which since ancient times has been appreciated for its color and natural beauty. It's used as an ingredient in perfumes, as a healing agent in folk medicine, and as jewelry. The Baltic Sea abounds with amber, as the area was once covered by pine forests. Each fresh roll of waves offered up the chance that a nugget would be deposited at our feet—a beautiful gift from ages past. All we had to do was pick it up.

The best time to find amber was just after a storm, when the sea spit out a mat of seaweed across the length of the beach. We would roll up that mat like a blanket, and pick out the pieces caught in the tangled, smelly mess. On such days it was not uncommon to spot fishermen standing in the shallow waters with big nets, to 'fish' for amber as it floated in on the waves. They had an uncanny knack for knowing which floating weeds were likely to yield the greatest treasures, and only scooped the promising ones up into their nets.

People living close to the shore harvested the seaweed, not for the amber, but as fertilizer for their gardens. So we had to be there at just the right time, before all the seaweed was gone, in order to have success in our treasure hunt.

The government stipulated that pieces of amber larger than about a quarter had to be turned in. But most of what we found was smaller than that. It came in all different shapes and a great variety of colors—from dark golden brown to butterscotch to honey-colored to light yellow. Sometimes it had a rough surface. Other times the surface was smooth and glossy, polished to perfection by the waves. If you were really lucky, you'd find a piece that had an inclusion of an insect, or a piece of bark, or small pine needle. We always held our discovery up to the light and examined it carefully, to see if the sea had been kind enough to send us such a precious treasure.

One year, I used the amber I had collected to make a jewelry box for my sister. I mixed together a homemade paste of fine sawdust and glue. I fastened a mosaic of amber to the surface of a box with this sticky concoction, and then used a thicker mix to fill the spaces in between—much like grouting ceramic tiles. After the paste dried, I carefully stained it a contrasting color with a fine brush. My cousins in the city were impressed with Dora's jewelry box and asked if I would make one for each of them.

I made their boxes a little larger and of a different shape. But then I ran into a problem. I didn't have enough amber to finish their boxes. I only wanted to use small, flat pieces—not thicker ones. Neither Dora nor I wanted to totally deplete our collections, or part with our prized finds—pieces that had inclusions, or were a unique color or shape. And it would be a while before we'd have the opportunity to head back to the Baltic and collect more. I thought and thought about what to do at school that day. I knew my cousins were looking forward to their jewelry boxes, and didn't want to disappoint them. That's when I remembered the landfill on the Lomse—the place where the city garbage was dumped, and where the amber factory also got rid of its trash. It was not a general garbage dump, whet garbage, as we know it, was picked up from homes, as mentioned earlier, or dumped on city owned land for composting.

After school, I didn't waste any time. Mom wasn't home from work yet, so I ventured out without discussing the idea with her. I stuck a small garden shovel in my pocket to help me dig through the piles of debris. It wasn't long before I discovered a pile of amber factory debris. I found a promising spot and started to dig. To my delight, I soon hit 'pay-dirt'. Just as I had hoped for, there was a small, concentrated area full of rejects and broken pieces of amber. I quickly filled one pocket and half of the other. I wanted to make sure I had enough, so I knelt down to dig at another spot.

A sharp pain in my knee made me drop the shovel. I tried to jump up and nearly fainted. I had knelt on the sharp edge of a glazed clay tile. The gash was very deep. I don't remember how I got home. My mother was startled, upon her return, to find me surrounded by bloody bandages, desperately trying to patch myself up. Since my parents were not in a financial position to face medical bills, we decided not to get the cut stitched, but to let it heal on its own. It took a long time. In those days, you could go to the neighborhood druggist for a salve or advice, and only see a doctor when the druggist could not help. Yes, the boxes were eventually finished and Ursela and Erika appreciated them greatly. But I never did tell them of the mishap. I don't know how long they kept those boxes, but I have a large scar over my left kneecap as a lasting reminder.

I don't know whether the amber factory was owned by the government, but I know that the day mining operation for amber near my Uncle's farm was. As Hitler solidified his power and probably seized the factory, the factory became a major producer of all kinds of politically inspired products, and must have generated huge revenues.

One product, which I particularly remember, was a bright metal image of an unusual boat, mounted to a piece of polished amber. Those particular boats were only used in a small area, a little further north along the Baltic Sea, a narrow stretch of moving sand dunes, now known as the "Curonian Split." The proceeds were supposed to go to support the poor fishermen in this area, and to enable them to keep their unique way of life. I also remember a similar broach being offered in aid of an international agricultural fair, and another that promoted the Northern Railway serving the area north of Königsberg. (That was the railway we used to travel to Aunt Minna's.)

The government made constant appeals for citizens to donate. 'Volunteers' solicited money in exchange for trinkets such as pendants, broaches, pins, and even Christmas ornaments. The trinkets were made out of wood, metal, porcelain, glass, or pottery. Collections were made for Germans in Poland, for Germans in Czechoslovakia, for Germans in Hungary, for the poor, for the cold, for people engaged in "Home Industry." There were collections for anything and everything the government deemed to be a worthy cause. Begging, as such, was outlawed. And beggars, if caught, would end up in jail. Only the government was allowed to beg and pocket the proceeds.

In 1935, Hitler repudiated the military clauses of the Treaty of Versailles and reintroduced general conscription, with a one-year period of service. To the German people, he was a hero for standing up against the hated Treaty. The armed forces rapidly expanded. In 1933, there were 4,000 officers and 100,000 enlisted men. Three years later, that number had increased fivefold to over 20,000 officers and 500,000 enlisted men. The number of officers commissioned from the four *Kriegsschulen* (Officer Training Schools) had increased from 180 per year to over 3,000 per year.

Needless to say, Uncle Paul was busier than ever. He was hardly able to keep up with the demands of supplying dress uniforms for an ever increasing military. Military uniforms by far outnumbered civilian clothing at my cousin Ursula's wedding.

It was a pompous affair. Dora and I had to hold the heavy, monstrous train of Ursela's veil as she walked down the aisle. During the ceremony, I was supposed to straighten it out at one point, but jumped up too soon. Was I ever embarrassed! At the reception Dora and I had to give small speeches and recite a poem for our cousin. I don't remember the poem but it must have had something to do with cooking. I do remember the two wooden spoons I used as props during the recital.

Uncle Paul was proud that his daughters were both marrying military officers and gaining husbands who had such powerful and promising careers. Cousin Erica's fiancé was part of the "Condor Legion" fighting in Spain to help "Genralissimo Franco" gain control over the "Communist Usurpers." It was a unit composed of volunteers from the German Luftwaffe and

Ursela marries a German officer

Wehrmacht. They served with the Nationalists during the Spanish Civil War from 1936 to 1939. Erika's fiancé barely made it back in time for Ursela's wedding, and had to hurry back to his military duties in Spain right afterwards. He and Erika got married a year or two later when he returned.

Uncle sometimes seemed to question our attachment to the Baptist Church. He only attended church for weddings. He was extremely superstitious, as were many people in our area. Every New Year's Eve he practiced what in German is called "*Zinngießen*" (Tin Pouring). It was believed that important events could be foretold by this practice. In the last hour before the New Year, families would hold a cast iron ladle containing chunks of soldering tin in the fire until the chunks melted. In turn, each family member would pour some liquid metal into a large, flat-bottomed bowl of cold water. The patterns in the resulting lumps of metal were then examined and interpreted. Each person kept his or her lump as a sign of things to come.

My mother did not like that practice and was quick to point out the folly of it. I just thought the whole idea was silly. But Ursela and Erika bragged about the exciting futures their lumps of tin predicted. Hitler had promised peace and prosperity. My cousins' tin seemed to verify his claims. But for all the optimism it wasn't long until we discovered how wrong his promises— and their *Zinngießen*— really were.

5 | A SOLDIER AT HEART

Dad was born on May 16, 1889 in Hermannsfeld, a small village in the province Thuringa in central Germany.

I never met my Opa Thomas, Dad's dad, and what little I know about him and my paternal side of the family comes from bits and pieces I heard from people I met in Hermannsfeld after the war, and what we've patched together from records my sister acquired from the German Lutheran church.

"Thomas" isn't actually a German surname—it was a Christian name, popular in Scotland. Scots were renowned for their battlefield prowess and military expertise. They were well-versed in different types of warfare, weaponry, strategy, and organization, which made them ideal commanders and highly-sought after mercenary soldiers. One Scot rose to the rank of General in the Russian army and served several Tsars.

Another Scot, Johann Andreas Thomas, my Great-Great-Grandfather, was apparently hired by Tsar Alexander II to help the Russians fight against the French in the Napoleonic wars. We don't know when the Thomas clan settled in Russia. Verbal transmission says that they came from Scotland, part of the clan settling near Hamburg/Germany and others going to Russia to serve as mercenaries. Johann, my forebear, took part in the Battle of Leipzig (Battle of Nations), fighting in the Quadruple Alliance of Britain, Russia, Austria, and Prussia. The battle involved over 600,000 soldiers, making it the largest battle in Europe prior to World War I. Defeated, Napoleon was compelled to return to France.

Lutheran church records state that: "Johann Andreas Thomas, a Russian soldier, stayed behind in Hermannsfeld in 1813, date of birth unknown". That's all the information we have. It's unclear whether he stayed behind because he was injured, whether he was discarded by the retreating French as a Prisoner of War, whether he had completed his service-for-hire, had had enough of mercenary life, or because he fell in love with a local girl. Regardless, it was the Napoleonic Wars that brought the first Thomas to the vicinity and led to the establishment of a German line of Thomases in central Germany.

Johann married Margarethe Elisabetha Krell on January 17, 1830. Johann Kasper Thomas, my Great-Grandfather, was born in Hermannsfeld 1832, and his son, my Opa, Heinrich Gustov Thomas, was born in 1860. The villagers nicknamed him "Barbarossa," an Italian name meaning "red beard," because his beard was extremely long and reddish in colour.

Barbarossa was the name of a medieval German Roman Emperor and King, who fought in the Third Crusade, and who figures prominently in German folklore. According to legend, Barbarossa is not dead, but sleeps with his knights in a cave in Thuringia, Germany. His red beard has grown through the table at which he sits. The story promises that when the ravens cease to fly around the mountain he will awaken and restore Germany to its ancient greatness.

This German folklore was well-known, and a story of perpetual hope for the German people. Perhaps that is why the Emperor, Kaiser Wilhelm II, named his flagship pre-dreadnought battleship "The SMS Kaiser Barbarossa" in 1900. And why, in World War 2, Hitler dubbed Nazi Germany's invasion of the Soviet Union, "Operation Barbarossa." Opa Barbarossa, who was part-farmer and part-woodworker, probably reminded people of the folklore hero's larger-than-life aura. The villagers in Hermannsfeld told me that he could not escape detection in wintertime because of the long footprints he left behind in the snow. I inherited my long feet from him, and apparently some facial features too.

Opa Barbarossa married Auguste Fridolinde Seyd in 1883. Six years later, she gave birth to my dad. Opa must have been overjoyed to finally have a son, for he enlisted the support of several friends as godfathers and added their names to the name of his firstborn, as was the custom at the time. It resulted in the longest name I have ever heard:

Albin Albert Christian Christoph Gottlieb Max Thomas

Maybe Opa realized how much trouble it was to write out six names, because his second son only got two: Gottlieb Louis. Three daughters, whose names I don't know, and who I never met, were born later on.

My Uncle Gottlieb worked with Opa Barbarossa in the carpentry shop. He expanded the business and farmed the small and widely scattered pieces of land that Opa and he acquired. My dad, on the other hand, must have had the adventurous, mercenary blood of our ancestors running through his veins. He didn't want any part of the farm and started an apprenticeship in bricklaying. When World War I broke out in August 1914, he was among the first to volunteer.

Dad was a soldier in both world wars. He fought for the German Fourth Army Division in the infamous Battle of Passchendaele in 1917—also known as "the Battle of Mud," near Flanders Fields. During the 3 ½ month campaign, the area was saturated with the heaviest rain the region had seen in thirty years, effectively turning it into a swamp. Tanks got stuck and soldiers found movement very difficult. It was a horrific, costly battle for both sides. The British and Canadians lost 310,000 men and the Germans 260,000. Dad's battalion had to surrender when they ran out of ammunition. He ended up in a Canadian prisoner-of-war camp in Normandy. I forgot the name of the place.

Dad said that the German and Canadian soldiers had high regard for each other as fair, but fierce fighters. He had a great deal of respect for his captors. But somehow, he managed to escape from Prisoner of War camp and trek across France back to Germany. He arrived home quite some time after the war had ended. He did not talk very much about his experience. Actually, he didn't talk very much at the best of times. I do know that he was wounded—shot—several times. Seven times, if memory serves me right: five times in the First World War, and twice in the Second World War.

One bullet from the Battle of Passchendaele lodged close to his spine near a shoulder blade. The wound healed but the bullet stayed. Because of its proximity to the spine, the doctors feared complications from any efforts to remove it. Leaving it undisturbed was obviously a good decision, because the bullet eventually travelled several centimeters away from its original position, so it could finally be removed—twenty years after the fact. I remember him going to the hospital for the operation. The doctors gave him the bullet as a souvenir and dad made it into a pendant for his watch chain.

History books describe the horrors of front-line World War I trench warfare in lurid detail: the appalling suffering, the fear and monotony, the incessant artillery barrages, the rotting corpses, the mud, the damp, the cold, the rats and lice. The experience hardened the men, who went through it together, were forged into a *"Frontgemeinschaft"*—a front-line band of brothers. They were shocked when, after the war, the Treaty of Versailles restricted the German Army to 100,000 men, and a great number of them were suddenly de-mobilized. Paramilitary groups (*Freikorps*) formed to fill a need for the many soldiers who had suddenly lost their army "family," and who were left to deal with the emotional devastation of their country's loss and the horrors they had experienced on the front. My Dad joined the "*Stahlhelm*" (Steel Helmets) paramilitary, the largest organization of its kind.

I think my Dad missed the regimented life of a soldier. He and the other war veterans of the *Stahlhelm* regularly performed military drills in hopes of a return to former Army glory, re-emergence of a Kaiser, and re-establishment of the German Empire. They organized a housing program, and an employment service for their unemployed working-class members. I remember one Christmas when the *Stahlhelm* showered us with gifts.

Since he was athletic, Dad also joined a Christian fitness organization. The emblem on their flag was made up of four capital F's arranged in the form of a cross. The letters represented their motto, which were the German words for fresh, pious, happy, and free (*Frisch, Fromm, Fröhlich, Frei*). When hard times hit, dad could not afford the membership fee and had to quit. That group was later outlawed under Hitler's rule. The *Stahlhelm* however, continued, and was forced into Hitler's SA.

Dad was an excellent marksman. Whenever he could, he participated in shooting competitions, which were a traditional event at carnivals. Most times, his target was a small red dot on a stiff cardboard picture of a game animal— elk, deer or moose. The winner was the marksman that hit that dot or came closest to it. The names of the three top competitors were marked on the picture, and the winner got to take the target home. We had a lot of these cardboard trophy animals in our attic. Mom did not want them in the home.

Uncle Hans, Aunt Minna's husband, was an equally good marksman. It was always entertaining to watch the fierce competition between the two whenever we managed to go out there to visit them and attend a carnival event.

Dad's shooting skills were no doubt a result of his military training and service. But since he had been demobilized, he carried on where he left off in his training as a bricklayer. As was required by the trade guilds at that time, each new journeyman had to travel for several years to acquire new skills. He became proficient in intricate stucco work, stone masonry, and what we now call cribbing. In some areas of Germany, all form work and pouring of concrete was carried out by bricklayers.

I'm not exactly sure how Dad ended up in Königsberg. I know he travelled extensively throughout Germany while training as a Journeyman, even served a few month as a "deacon" in a home for handicapped boys, "The Bodelschwing Institution." I suspect he probably settled in Königsberg after meeting my mother. They married in December of 1924. My mother was his third wife. I know nothing about the first marriage; how or why it ended. No one talked about it. We had a wedding picture of his second marriage. All I know is that his second wife died in childbirth, and that his wife's parents, who had never approved of the marriage, took and raised the child. I remember Dad sending gifts for the child's birthday and other special occasions to somewhere in Thüringa. I'm not even sure if my step-sibling was a boy or a girl.

Dad was not the scholarly type, but it was obvious to me that he had the gift of teaching. He taught many men the tricks of the trade before their journeyman examinations. I remember them sitting around our table in the living room. With miniature bricks, the size of domino pieces, Dad would patiently show them how to lay certain "bonds" as they were called, as well as how to fashion corners, chimney tops, and arches; and how to master other elements of bricklaying.

He collected cigar boxes whenever he could get a hold of one. He would use the thick, heavy part of the cigar box to whittle contours for fancy plaster moldings. He also had several commercial molds for doing detailed decorative stucco work for fancier buildings. Sometimes he would prepare things at home for next day's work. He made a thick soup—a mixture of plaster-of-Paris, water, and a little bit of sugar—and poured it into the molds, ever so careful not to trap air in the mixture. The sugar slowed down the setting of the plaster.

The actual shaping of decorative stucco moldings was done on site. I sometimes had a chance to observe Dad do that when I went to his worksite to deliver his lunch. To shape them, he used a thicker mix of plaster with a higher proportion of sugar, to allow for more time to work it. Dad applied the mix with a trowel to where the molding was to go, draw the template he had prepared, or a standard metal one, across the wet plaster. With the edge of the trowel he carefully removed the excess or added more of the mix. The work had to proceed fast so the mixture wouldn't harden before it could be molded. Several applications of the mix were required for heavier or more intricate moldings. I tried my hand at it a few years ago, making plaster rings around two ceiling lights in our house here in Canada, just to see if I could remember how to do it.

I could tell that Dad took a lot of pride in his work. I think it appealed to the artistic side of his personality, as did music. Dad loved music! He played the trumpet in the Salvation Army band. That is, until bad times hit and he had to sell the trumpet. He later acquired a mouth-organ and played that often. Dad also sang in two choirs of the local Baptist Church where he and mom were members: the male choir and the mixed choir.

I have many memories associated with that church. The name of the church alone is worth mentioning: *Baptisten Gemeinde Klapperwiese*. The name would undoubtedly elicit a perplexed smile from German-speaking people because "*Klapper*" is mostly associated with the unpleasant sound of pots clanging. "Baptist Fellowship of Clanging Pots" would be an extremely odd name for a church! But in our area, the word *Klapper* also referred to the noise of storks clapping their beaks. The Church was named *Klapperwiese* because it was located near a former swampy meadow, where flocks of storks had congregated to feast on frogs.

The church building was massive, seating more than 2,000 people. But it was rather plain. It didn't boast gothic architecture like the Dom, fancy stained glass like the Catholic Church, or a splendid rounded dome like the Jewish Synagogue. Baptists don't believe in spending money on such things. They are much more pragmatic than that! Yet although it was unimpressive, the facility was definitely functional. Congregants entered the churchyard through a door in one wing of a monstrous double-sided wooden gate. The gate was flanked by houses on either side. These were owned by the church and provided accommodation for single men on one side and women on the other. That was where our club-footed friend, Herr Prange, lived.

There was a large Churchyard between the gate and the church doors—I'd say it spanned a distance of about 60 or 70 feet. Directly inside the church was a huge vestibule with pigeon-hole mailboxes where members received announcements and tracts and Christian periodicals for distribution. You could go up the stairs to the right or the left to get up to the balconies, or you could walk ahead through another set of doors to get into the main auditorium.

The auditorium had balconies on three sides. Two banks of pews were located in the center section of the upper floor, in front of a large pipe organ. Those seats were reserved for the 120-member choir. I often sat there, next to dad, as he sang tenor in the choir. I remember one time when two men had to tread the bellows for the organ because the mechanical system had failed. I was intrigued to see how much effort it took for those men to keep up with the demand for air when the organist was playing and how they hung on to a rail as they bobbed up and down on the pedal of the bellow. I don't think the organist purposely pulled out all the stops that day to make them sweat, but it sure seemed like he did.

Sunday school was for boys and girls up to 15 years old. Boys met on the side balconies and the girls met on the main floor. I remember one particular weekend when boys and girls of all ages gathered on the main floor for a special open session. A visiting teacher set up a flannel board on the platform just in front of the Baptismal tank. I had never seen a flannel board before. I wasn't exactly sure what it was. The teacher began to place colorful, cut-out felt-backed images on the board as he taught us the Matthew 13 story about the seeds and four different types of soil. I remember being amazed at how the pictures magically clung to the background—and I also remember how the Lord used that flannel graph story to tug on my heart.

Another meeting had a similar effect on me. Hans Bertram, author of the book "Flight into Hell," came to our church to give a series of talks. He was a German aviator pilot. In the early thirties, he and his co-pilot flew from

Cologne, Germany to Australia in their seaplane, "The Atlantis." While flying over the ocean, they were caught in a violent storm that pushed them miles off course and forced them to land on a rugged, remote coastline of Western Australia, in hostile aboriginal territory. After more than six weeks of wandering through the outback, friendly aboriginals finally found the two men, who by then, were close to death. Bertram recovered, but his co-pilot didn't. I was moved by Bertram's story—and so were others. Eventually a series of movies was produced about his dramatic ordeal.

Our Church sponsored all sorts of meetings and activities year-round. At Christmas, it gave every child a plate full of goodies. It was a large porcelain plate, like a large rimmed soup plate, that had 'Sunday School' and the year written in gold letters around the gold-edged flange. I looked forward to the Christmas celebration and the annual Sunday school picnic too, but the New Year Eve's celebration is what excited me the most—not for the singing or preaching, but for the 'fellowship' that followed. It was always a happy, festive occasion. A wealthy bakery owner provided an overabundance of "*Pfannkuchen*"—deep-fried, glazed, doughnut-type balls filled with jam. We were allowed to eat as many as we could. Though there was no limit, I could manage two at best.

On the long walk home we worked the calories off anyway—not that anybody cared about those things back then. Sparkling fireworks, the chorus of ships blasting their steam whistles, ringing church bells, and revelers throwing streamers down from the balconies shouting "Happy New Year," made our walk home even on the coldest of nights a joyful one. Yes. In those early years of my childhood the New Year always promised to be happy indeed!

One of my earliest memories, though somewhat hazy, is of me sitting on my dad's shoulder at an early air show. Königsberg had a rich aviation history and a lot of people would go to the shows. Stunt fliers performed amazing feats with planes like the Messerschmitt, or the aerobatic F2 Tiger. I vaguely remember a stuntman walking out on the wing of a bi-plane in flight. I also remember the highly decorated World War I flying ace, the great Udet, grabbing a hat off a pole while flying upside down in his U-12 Flamingo. He was arguably the most famous stunt pilot of his day. I can still remember the deafening roar of the engines and the excited cheers of the crowd.

Dad enjoyed those aviation events. Another "flying" activity he enjoyed was building and flying kites. I remember him taking me out to fly kites on the "*Fleischerwiese*" (butcher's meadow). On one particular day, the winds were just right. My mother sent my sister Dora along on the excursion and my younger sister too, in a pram. The year might have been 1930 or 1931, when I was five or six years old. My youngest brother wasn't born yet.

I held the kite up on tip toes as high as I could, and dad ran against the wind to get it up. It wasn't long until it soared high in the air. The dance of the kite's tail mesmerized me. I don't know why dad had to turn his attention away from the kite to attend to Dora, but for some reason he did. Since I was too young to manage the flying kite on my own, he tied the string to the pram. Big mistake! The wind took my baby sister on the ride of her life, bouncing her up and down in the pram as it careened across the bumpy field. I squealed when I saw it take off. My dad dropped Dora and went bolting after it as fast as he could. It was quite the sight, watching dad race across the field to catch up with a kite-powered pram! It definitely would have qualified for a "funniest home video" award, had we had video cameras in those days. After the excitement Dad was perhaps a bit winded, but I don't think my little sister or the rest of us were any worse for wear. But of course we didn't tell Mom. She didn't find out about the episode until much later, when it somehow came out in conversation—perhaps when we recounted the funny story to guests.

For several years, we rented a garden plot to grow vegetables. These plots were leased by the City and were located in various areas. One year, we looked after a plot for a family who had a long lease on it, and could not tend it themselves. After that, we leased or bought (I'm not sure which) a rather large garden plot near the outskirts of the city. We had a makeshift shed on that plot. I have vivid memories of digging a well there.

Dad had acquired a few sections of concrete pipe, about the size of a manhole section, but without rungs. With the first section positioned where he wanted the well, he dug the dirt out from the inside of the concrete pipe. Gravity caused it to sink down as the dirt was removed. Then, he placed another section of concrete pipe on top and dug the hole deeper. Section by section the pipes dropped down and the hole got deeper. We'd hoist the dirt up by pail, using a rope and pulley. I loved to play with the clay coming out of the hole. I formed all kinds of objects and creatures with it. I even experimented with various clay-sand combinations, to keep my creations from cracking when they dried and hardened.

I really enjoyed making things, so I was delighted when I got a fret-saw kit for Christmas. It contained tools and a bundle of blades, and several pieces of plywood with patterns marked on them. In the process of cutting out the first pattern I broke a few blades, but in any case, I was hooked! With my new tools (and better ones that I acquired along the way) I constructed several lampshades, ornamental jewelry boxes, and silhouette-like pictures. I even produced a few fancy wastebaskets. When I first started, I had to beg for the plywood from a cabinet maker in mom's church. Later my mom gave me money for patterns and materials. I also acquired parts to build a crystal radio, and tinkered around with low-voltage electrical gadgets.

I gave away most of my creations as gifts. But sometimes people, who saw them, liked them so much that they paid me to build one for them. The daughter of our neighbor was married to a wealthy merchant—she purchased some fancy wastebaskets, and so did mom's last employer.

My proudest accomplishment was a scale model of the battleship, "The Scharnhorst," built out of ¼ inch Finnish birch plywood. I bought the plans and materials myself. To make the hull I traced the pattern on the wood, cut out progressively larger layers, glued them together, and then filed, sanded and sanded the stack until it was smooth and shaped just like the hull of the real ship. It was not a complete hull, but a waterline model, which sat flat for easier display. The superstructure, turrets, guns, masts, and other parts of the deck also had to be cut out and smoothed into the right shape with sandpaper. I made the gun barrels out of wood dowels, and purchased some of the more intricate bits and pieces, like the cranes and lines, at the Hobby Shop. I drilled out the numerous portholes, and carefully painted the finished ship grey.

The SMS Scharnhorst

The Scharnhorst was one of the first battleships Hitler built in defiance of the Treaty of Versailles. It was a big event and great excitement for the entire city when it docked in our harbor. Dad took me to see it. We actually got to go on board the impressive ship! A band of marines played and the mood was electrifying. The ship was cause for much jubilation. It visibly demonstrated that Germany finally had enough guts to stand up against the humiliating and oppressive measures the world had unfairly imposed on us. It's difficult to express just how much this event meant. It buoyed up our spirits like the first spring day after a long, cold, dark winter, making us hope

A Soldier at Heart

that maybe—just maybe—the snow was going to melt and we'd feel the joy of sunshine once again. The Scharnhorst signaled that an end to the hated Treaty was in sight. It meant a lot to Germans. An awful lot!

I had another memorable visit to a special vessel when the *Schulshiff Gorch Fock* was in the harbor. It was a three mast training ship that complied with Treaty stipulations. That event may have preceded the battleship experience and it seems to me that the sailors wore white uniforms, whereas the Navy wore blue.

I also got to see the world's first designated cruise ship, the "*Wilhelm Gustloff*," when she was taking on passengers to visit the Norwegian fjords. That ship belonged to the fleet of the KdF, a large state-controlled leisure organization. The letters stood for "*Kraft durch Freude*," which means strength through joy. KdF's mandate was to make cultural and leisure activities—such as concerts, art exhibits, plays, films, books, sporting events, parks, day trips, and holiday cruises—available to the masses (meaning the working class, or blue collar workers now). It was also designed to demonstrate the benevolence of NSDAP ideology to the world as they traveled far and wide. The organization rewarded the diligence and achievements of workers by giving them free tickets, especially those workers who actively supported the Party. By opening the door for the working class to easily and affordably take part in such activities, it was believed that the labor force would become more productive and loyal to the Third Reich.

Opa Marquardt's step-son, Fritz, was employed as an iron worker in one of the Schichau shipyards. Fritz was once rewarded with a cruise on a newly commissioned KdF ship as a bonus for his work. He visited us in Königsberg after sailing along Norway's coastline, and showed us photos of his great adventure.

The KdF made trains available to people who lived in the countryside, so they could get to a city to attend theatre, opera, or orchestra performances, and acquaint them with the work of their great masters of music and literature. Of course, only Nordic-Germanic authors/composers fit the bill for productions. When a well-known classical composer did not quite meet the criterion, Chopin for instance, his ancestry was simply adjusted. The Kdf set up book fairs, which featured books that fit the ideology of the new regime. Most forms of entertainment were controlled by the KdF.

Joseph Goebbels, Germany's propaganda minister, instructed the KdF to sell cheap *Volksempfänger* (people's receiver) radios to every household. They were purposely designed only to receive the broadcasts of the nearest radio stations of the Third Reich. This ensured that propaganda broadcasts would be heard by the general public. Someone gave our family a better type of radio, made by Grundig. I was fascinated with the round "cat-eye" indicator that lit up as you tuned in to a station. When you got the dial to just the right place, the whole eye glowed green. We loved that radio. We listened to music, news, and of course, political speeches by Hitler, and the East Prussian Nazi Party leader, Gauleiter Erich Koch, especially Koch, did he ever love to give speeches.

Another major aspect of the KdF was the attempt to make the automobile a reality for as many Germans as possible. To this end, the Nazis produced the world famous Volkswagen (literally, " people car") and instituted a monthly KdF savings program so that nearly anyone could purchase one. Participating workers purchased a "*VW Sparkarte*" car savings book. Each week, they could purchase stamps—like a postage stamp except with an image of a Volkswagen on it—to stick in their book. They "saved" a minimum of 5 Mark a week until they had contributed 750 Marks to the plan. When they had enough saved up, they got an order number that entitled them to a car as soon as it was made. Though higher-up members of the Nazi party got cars, I don't know of any ordinary people that ever did. One would occasionally see a Volkswagen on the street. My family didn't have money to spare on such things. And unfortunately, those that did participate in the purchase scheme never ended up getting their cars. The Volkswagen factory was turned into a weapons factory as soon as the Second World War started.

It must have been just before the war or early into it that four "Klein U-Boote" submarines docked in the inner harbor, right next to the fish market. I got to go down the gang plank and walk across planks from one sub to the next. I clambered up the rungs on the cunning tower and peered into the dark cavern beneath. Königsberg was a major naval base, so it was common for us to see military vessels. During the war we often saw U-boats docked for repairs. Once, there were nine Type31 U-boats moored side by side in the outer harbor.

The Government often put on special events and parades in full regalia, show off the ships, hardware, weaponry, and regalia of Hitler's rapidly expanding military. On parade day, soldiers marched down the street beside the castle in precise military formation. There were huge flags, banners, marching bands, and much noise and excitement. My Dad and his buddies in Der Stahlhelm were always there in full force. Their whole organization had been absorbed into the Sturm Abteilung (SA), Hitler's own private army of storm troopers, under the leadership of Ernst Röhm. They paraded in the brown shirts, swastika armbands, ski-caps, knee-breeches, and combat boots that were the standard dress of the SA.

Not long after Hitler came to power, dad volunteered for training in a Corps of Army engineers. He had to go to training camps at least twice a year. They specialized in maintaining rail services, restoration of damaged installations, and temporary bridge construction; pretty much anything related to railways. By law, employers had to give their men leave to attend these training sessions. The men were also exempt from general duty in the SA, except for the odd call for participation in parades, torch marches, or mass assemblies. This was fortunate, I suppose, because Dad managed to avoid getting involved in the SA's shady strong-arm tactics. The Brown Shirts attacked or intimidated anyone deemed hostile to the Nazi program: editors, professors, politicians, uncooperative local officials or businessmen. More and more, we sensed the importance of toeing the Party line, and not publically saying or doing anything that was politically incorrect.

It was obvious that Hitler was expanding our military with the aim of taking back the land that Germany felt was rightfully hers. When, in early March of 1936, after the plebiscite, he sent the army in to occupy the neighboring territories of the Saar and Rhineland, the people were ecstatic.

The series of bloodless conquests were called the *Blumenkrieg* (Flower Wars), because jubilant citizens lined the streets cheering and waving, and paved the way of the battalions of German infantry with flowers. Hitler's soldiers were welcomed as liberators. The people in the reclaimed regions, along with the rest of the German people, could not have been happier. Germans were finally being reunited. To us, Hitler was a hero. What's more, we were enthralled to learn that he planned to visit Königsberg soon.

March 18, 1936 was the first time I saw Hitler in person. I was just 10 years old at the time. Königsbergers assembled on mass at the Castle, where Hitler slept overnight in the former king's chambers. We packed into the *Schlosshoff* (Castle Courtyard) and shouted hysterically for him to appear. I was lined up in formation with all the children, *"Das Jungvolk."* With the rest of the crowd, we waved our arms and chanted, *"Wir wollen unsern Führer sehen! Wir wollen unsern Führer sehen! Wir wollen unsern Führer sehen!"* (We want to see our Führer! [Leader]). When Hitler finally appeared on the balcony, the crowd went absolutely wild, I have never again seen such elation. And when the political pundits took the opportunity to hand out pamphlets entitled, *Das danken wir dem Führer!* (We owe it to the Führer), most people agreed.

Things were changing at a dizzying speed. When Hitler came to power, nearly a third of the population was unemployed. Five years later, unemployment had vanished. A shortage of jobs had turned into a shortage of workers. Wages were guaranteed. Inflation had ceased. The birthrate had increased six fold. That was partly due to the public honoring of mothers. At special ceremonies "*das Mutterkreuz*" (Cross for Mothers) was hung around the neck of mothers who had four children or more. That medal came in three categories bronze, silver and gold. You had to have more than eight children to qualify for the highest class, if my memory serves me correctly.

The country had recovered from the Great Depression and showed signs of economic vitality. Hitler had taken back the German rivers, the German railroad, and the German national bank from foreign control. The future looked bright. The Council of the League of Nations unanimously condemned Germany as a treaty breaker, but we didn't care. We were finally freeing ourselves of Versailles.

Later that year, Germany hosted the eleventh Summer Olympic Games in Berlin. It was the first Olympics to be broadcast on TV. Hitler and Goebbels could not have asked for a better propaganda opportunity. They used the Olympics to showcase the "New Germany" and the greatness of the Nazi Regime.

The Nazis came out with a special car in honor of the Olympics, the "Opel Olympia." Its fancy chrome and sleek "gangster" lines made it a true showpiece. They built the world's largest and most spectacular stadium, with a high honor tribune area built for the party elite. They put on the most lavish and impressive Olympic Games ever. Journalists from all over the world were "wowed" by the fantastic facilities and precise efficiency of the whole event.

The German Post Office broadcast over seventy hours of live coverage to special television viewing rooms throughout Berlin. Zeppelins quickly transported newsreel footage to other European cities. A man who lived in our apartment, a travelling salesman, had won a big cabinet with a TV at a tradeshow in Berlin. But unfortunately, the TV signal for the games wasn't transmitted to Königsberg. All he ever got on his TV screen was a fuzzy star pattern. We didn't miss out on all the excitement though. We gathered in the

Sportsplatz am Landgraben, northwest of the city, for our own opening ceremonies.

The Königsberg ceremonies were the most glamorous thing I had ever seen. We stood, abuzz with anticipation waiting for the event to start. Local dignitaries paraded in. The crowd joined the massive orchestra in a stirring rendition of the German National Anthem, *"Deutchland, Deutschland über Alles."* Then, the enormous plaza burst into color like a peacock splaying his showy plumes. Sports teams marched in carrying tall, flowing, multi-hued banners of the Olympics' participating nations. Military bands played musical fanfares. Rows of marchers promenaded in, carrying *Schellenbaum* (Bell Trees) – showy, towering types of instruments that looked like shiny brass trees, decorated with bells, ribbons, and horse tails; some, with xylophones incorporated into their impressive stalks. Those things became part of any marching band.

The entertainment featured a mock torch relay, ribbon dancing, flags, and various gymnastic displays. One athlete wowed us with a ring gymnastics demonstration. Another spun around the colossal stage doing spirals, vaults, and other acrobatics suspended on a *Rhönrad*, a gymnastic apparatus with two parallel connected wheels that are about six feet in diameter. I remember some high wire acts. I held my breath as an acrobat, dressed in white, rapidly spiraled down from the heights, hanging on to a pulley with only his teeth. I'm sure that someone gave a speech, but I don't remember it. The thing I remember the most was how hot it was that day. So hot, that one of the kids holding a banner fainted, and needed to be tended to by paramedics.

Over the next two weeks we eagerly listened to the radio and celebrated every German victory. Germans won the most medals overall in those Olympics, dominating the gymnastics, rowing, and equestrian events. The victories were immortalized by documentary filmmaker Leni Riefenstahl's epic motion picture production, "Olympia." Clips of individual Germans winning medals were shown time and time again as the featured pre-roll in the movie theatres.

The only embarrassing moment of the Olympics occurred when Hitler refused to shake the hand of the African-American gold medal sprinter, because the colored athlete was of an "inferior race." The debacle upset many Germans. Others were not even aware of it, as the incident was probably edited out of the film. I did not hear about it until we were in Canada. But all-in-all, the Olympics were a tremendous success. They certainly elevated our sense of national pride.

During the closing ceremonies, the president of the International Olympic Committee issued the traditional call for the next Games, issuing a "call to the youth of every country to assemble in four years at Tokyo, there to celebrate with us the twelfth Olympic Games."

But there would be no twelfth Olympic Games in Tokyo. In fact, there would be no Olympic Games for more than a decade. Little did we know that instead of competing with each other on athletic fields, the youths of the nations would wind up killing each other on fields of battle in a world war – a war Adolf Hitler was already planning.

6 | NIGHT OF BROKEN GLASS

The German company, *"Luftschiffbau Zeppelin,"* was the world's most successful builder of rigid airships. A symbol of German ingenuity and engineering, the mighty Zeppelins dominated international air transport in the early 1900s. But Versailles' restrictions on German aviation severely reduced the number of airships in Germany's fleet. The Allies seized them, and demanded that most Zeppelin airfields, including the one in Königsberg, be shut down.

When Hitler came to power, he nationalized what remained of the Zeppelin Company and in defiance of Versailles, commissioned a new Zeppelin to be built. Propaganda Minister Joseph Goebbels used two airships, the *Graf Zeppelin* and the newly launched *Hindenburg* in a high profile propaganda campaign. Goebbels instructed the Zeppelins to fly in tandem around Germany for four days prior to the 1936 plebiscite the Nazis had called to ratify the Army's occupation of the Saarland. The Zeppelins sailed low, back and forth over the country, dropping leaflets, blaring music and slogans from large loudspeakers, and broadcasting political speeches from a makeshift radio studio on board.

Also in defiance of Versailles, the Königsberg Zeppelin airfield was reopened for commercial luxury flights. I don't know if this happened before the propaganda campaign, or in conjunction with it, but in any case, I remember the excitement when it was announced that the Hindenburg would land with its first load of passengers at Devau, the regional airport at the northeast edge of the city, and would afterwards fly over the city in several passes.

The closer the big day came, the higher our level of anticipation grew. A visit from the Queen or the President of the United States could not have generated a greater buzz. For weeks, posters about the Zeppelin plastered the city's display columns, and leaflets were handed out at street corners. News headlines pumped up the event in the twice-daily papers, the *Königsberger Tageblatt* and the *Allgemeine Zeitung*. Radio announcers tried to outdo themselves in playing up the event.

I don't remember if we got the entire day off school or were just let out early. But as the appointed time grew near, virtually all the businesses in the city shut down and people gathered in the streets and on plazas to scan the sky for a glimpse of the impressive airship.

My family poured out into the street with the rest of our neighbors and gathered by the gate backing onto the Jewish property. The street was a bit wider there, and the building across the street didn't block out as much of the sky. The roar of the crowd from blocks away gave us advance warning that the Zeppelin was on its way. It wasn't long until the monstrous airship glided into sight. It looked like a giant silver cigar. The crowd erupted in a shout of joy and amazement. A gentle, soft whirring sound came from the propellers. It seemed surreal. It was so unlike the roar of an airplane. We craned our necks in awe, trying to make out people in the large windows of the gondola, as the mammoth slowly slipped overhead. It flew low, not far beyond the tops of the buildings, intersecting the street at a sharp angle and casting a shadow over the crowd as it passed.

It took only a few moments for the airship to pass over our street. But the people were slow to disperse. We sensed that we had witnessed something extraordinary and highly significant. For days after, all we talked about was the Zeppelin.

A year or two later we heard news of the *Hindenburg's* disastrous, Titanic-like demise, when it burst into flames while docking at the mooring mast at Lakehurst Naval Station, USA. It came at the conclusion of a highly publicized transatlantic flight. We were stunned. Before the Nazi takeover, there were no injuries sustained by *Zeppelin* passengers in over more than one million air miles traveled. But with that accident, the era of the *Zeppelin* came crashing to a tragic and fiery end. We could scarcely believe that things could have gone so badly wrong.

In time, this disaster faded from memory. As a young teen, there was so much else to think about and do. Much of my spare time was taken up with my involvement in the Nazi-regulated youth group. Every boy between 10 and 14 years had to enroll in the *Deutsches Jungvolk* (DJ, German Young people/folk), and those from 14 to 18 years old, in the *Hitler Jugend* (HJ, Hitler Youth).

Most boys automatically advanced from the younger to the older group when they turned 14. But those who were identified as having leadership potential remained with the younger boys as leaders. That was the situation in my case. I was never actually a part of a *Hitler Jugend* group. As I got older, I rose through the ranks of the *Deutsches Jungvolk* organization, and was given more and more leadership responsibility.

Girls aged 10 to 14 belonged to the *Jungmädchen* (JM Young Girls), then at age 14 transferred to the *Bund Deutscher Mädchen* (BDM League of German Girls), unless held back to become leaders of the younger girls.

A new law was issued in 1939, forcing any remaining holdouts into the Hitler Youth organizations, with warnings to parents that, unless their children enrolled, they would be forcibly removed from their homes and placed in the custody of state-run orphanages.

The organizations and activities for boys and girls were different. The boys' groups had a heavy emphasis on military training. We participated in *Wehrsport* (military athletics) like marching, bayonet drills, assault course circuits, grenade throwing, trench digging, map reading, gas defense, use of dugouts, how to get under barbed wire, pistol shooting, and throwing spears and knives at dummies. Some cruelty by the older boys toward the younger ones was tolerated and even encouraged, since it was believed this would weed out the unfit and toughen the rest of us up.

The girls' organizations were very popular with most girls, though my sister, Dora, didn't like them much. They focused on music, arts, crafts, theater, community work, clothing design, sewing, and general home economics. Their purpose was to equip girls for their roles as German wives, mothers, and homemakers, and to indoctrinate them so they would pass Nazi ideology on to the next generation.

I was aware of Hitler's *Lebensborn* (Fountain of Life) program in which special places were set up where SS men were encouraged to mate with blue-eyed, blonde Nordic girls, in order to produce "racially pure" German offspring. I actually saw young ladies marching in formation at a *Lebensborn* camp near my Uncle Hans' place, on the Baltic Sea. Like those around me, I didn't think much of it. I simply took it as a way of life. I do not recall the name of that camp, but only that it was near the *Kurort Rauschen*, a popular resort town. The wife of my former business partner had been singled out to go there, but was spared when her mother appealed that her daughter was their only farm help, and that they needed her to keep the farm productive. The girl was white-blond with pale blue eyes—she fit the profile of the ideal Arian woman perfectly.

The DJ and HJ groups were organized into local numbered cells, which met weekly, and in which Nazi doctrines were taught by older leaders. Uniforms were compulsory and differed slightly from one age group to the next. Every group of youth was assigned to a 'Home' (*Das Heim*), as it was called, which was a house or warehouse, often in property that had been confiscated by the government.

My group's *Home* was located on a narrow street in the *Sackheim* area, on the other side of the river, near the Catholic Church. The somewhat dilapidated house had two stories and a huge attic. There were 40 or 50 kids in our Heim. We met there often, to hang out, sing, play various table games, and of course for our weekly meetings. The *Wehrsport* military exercises took place in a park nearby. The marching drills were accompanied by loud singing of political marching songs. For those, we lined up and marched down the street.

A large Deutsches Jungvolk Heim situated in another part of the city

At some point, the meeting times shifted to Sundays. This was likely a deliberate effort on the part of the Nazi organizers to keep youth away from Church. But if anyone noticed this, they wouldn't have said anything. The SA or SS dealt with people who disagreed with the Nazi Regime. It only took a few years under Hitler's rule for everyone to learn to keep their mouths shut and comply with whatever they were told to do—no matter how odd or distasteful the order seemed.

Most of our *Jungvolk* activities were geared towards earning an achievement or proficiency badge. We each had a little booklet, the *Leistungsbuch* (performance booklet) in which we meticulously recorded our achievements and monetary contributions to the club.

There was a long list of compulsory exercises. We had to reach certain standards in the 100 meter sprint, 300 meter run, long jump, shot put, hammer throw, horizontal bar, and swimming. There were a lot of military requirements such as shooting rifles, hand grenade throwing, field exercises map reading, distance judging, and effective use of terrain and camouflage. We had to learn how to pack *Tornister* (backpacks) for our *Gepäckmärsche* (backpack treks). For these marches, the *Tornister* had to be a specified weight, and had to be packed in a prescribed way. A blanket wrapped in canvas square had to be rolled up very tightly and fastened to the outside perimeter of the *Tornister* with leather straps, just like in the military. Of course it was also compulsory to demonstrate that we were well versed in the basics of Hitler's ideas in order to qualify for that badge.

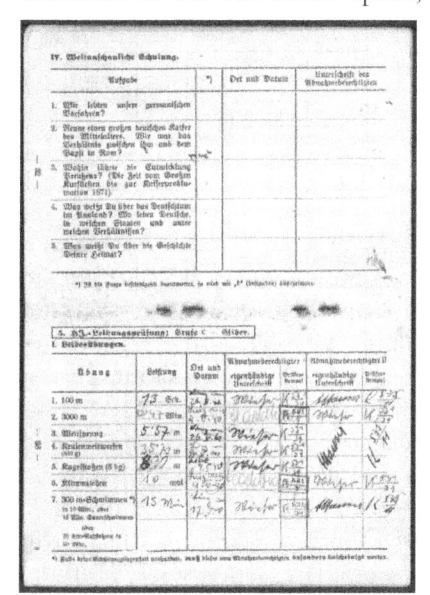

Each achievement in our *Leistungsbuch* had to be verified by the signature of the group leader. But only after the compulsory part of an activity was achieved could recognition for other accomplishments be claimed. For instance, if you could throw a dummy hand grenade 100 feet, but failed the compulsory achievement of throwing it a certain distance 3 times in succession, your hand grenade throw could not be entered and verified in the book. I was good at endurance activities like marching, long distance running, and especially swimming—my summers of swimming in the Pregel River and Baltic Sea had seen to that.

The photo above shows two *Jungscharen* of boys standing in roll call formation at a *Jungvolk* camp. The full group, counting the ones in the background was probably a complete *Jungstamm*. Notice the older boys—higher ranking officers—standing in front of the group. Also evident in the picture, is the requirement that the black pants could not be shorter than a hand's breadth above the knee. During camps, which lasted anywhere from a weekend to six weeks, we stayed in round tents called "*Ostlandzelte*." The flags on the tents bore the ancient Nordic Sig-Rune "S", which was symbolic of victory and the official logo of the *Jungfolk*. The Sig-Rune was the most recognizable and popular Nazi symbol after the *Hakenkreuz* (swastika). The Nazi SS symbol was two side-by-side Sig-Runes. The *Jungfolk* single Sig-Rune was printed on the front of our *Leistungsbuch*, engraved on our award pins, stitched on our badges, imprinted on our publications, and flown on our pennants and flags.

The fourth boy from the right in the photo seems to have "*Das Fahrtenmesser*" on his belt. It was a beautiful dagger with an enameled, diamond-shaped swastika emblem embedded in its black-textured handle, and a silver-colored, stylized bird's head at the butt end of the handle. The blade was engraved with the Jungfolk motto, "*Blut und Ehre*" (blood and honor). The heavy knife was worn on your left side, in a scabbard attached to your belt. A *Pimpf* (a general term for members of the *Jungvolk*) had to pass certain tests before the *Fahrtenmesser* could be worn as part of his uniform.

One of the best memories I have of that time, is of my group going on a long bicycle tour of our province. The highlight, and main purpose of the tour, was to visit the "Tannenberg Denkmal," a stark octagonal memorial to a battle of WW1, in which the revered General Paul von Hindenburg had decisively defeated the Russian Army. Conversation hushed as we walked through the cavernous structure, peering up at its eight towers. It was an eerie place. It felt overpowering somehow—perhaps because of its enormous size, but more likely due to the fact that it was the final earthly resting place of von Hindenburg, who to us was a larger-than-life military hero.

Von Hindenberg, who had turned power over to Hitler after he failed to form a government, had died in 1934. Most of us, as young boys, had witnessed the spectacle of his elaborate funeral procession. His flag-draped coffin, drawn on a gun carriage, was paraded down the Steindamm in Königsberg by magnificently adorned Clydesdale horses. Accompanied by an honor guard, it had moved slowly for days through as many German towns as possible before reaching its final resting place.

As part of the bicycle tour our *Jungvolk* club also toured the *Marienburg*, which was one of the important sites in the early history of the "Black Knights". It was a Gothic style cathedral and fortification combined in one. Our tour guide took care to point out where our German ancestors had triumphed over treachery and deceit. The goal of this tour, like the trip to the *Tannenburg* Memorial, was to give us knowledge and a sense of pride in the history of the German people.

That particular tour was fun, but long and arduous. We camped out in tents, slept in hay lofts, and even under the open sky. We begged for food from farmers and cooked up over an open fire whatever we could scrounge. Often a stay was forced upon us through mechanical problems of some kind. I remember only one injury, though I am sure there were many. A boy lost a piece of his ear lobe while he slept, when a rat bit him. We had a sleepless night in that hay loft, after being aroused by his screams.

Our leaders constantly emphasized the wonderful things that Hitler was doing for Germany. And events seemed to verify those claims. On March 13, 1938, my family crowded around our Grundig radio to listen to Hitler's *Anschluss* (annexation) speech after his successful annexation of Austria. Hitler spoke before a jubilant crowd gathered in Vienna. The crowd cheered. Bands played. Children waved Nazi flags. Austrian broadcasters provided detailed description and gushed with admiring commentary. Like us, virtually all Königsbergers tuned in, and joined in the jubilation.

My club was all abuzz that week, because Hitler was coming to Königsberg to launch his *Anschluss* campaign with a speech at the *Schlageterhalle*. We had to verify routes, hand out assignments, and practice protocol. All of the *Jungvolk* and *Hitlerjugend* in the city were required to line the streets for Hitler's triumphant motorcade.

Friday, March 25, 1938 was the second time I saw Hitler in person. My *Jungvolk* buddies and I lined the cobblestoned Königstrasse at about an arms-distance from one another. I stood at attention on the street with my heels pressed tightly against the curb and my hands clasped behind my back. I stood up tall at the leading edge of the crowd for what seemed like an eternity, until my shoulders and legs ached.

Finally, we saw some action. First, a forerunner rode by on a motorcycle to announce that Hitler was approaching. The sputtering engine of his bike was deafening. When he rode off, and the sound of the motor faded, I could detect the cheers of the crowd from a couple of blocks away. I glanced down the street toward the direction of the coming motorcade and watched it approach. At a distance, I could see a figure, which I knew to be Hitler, stand and salute the crowd. The people went absolutely wild! As the motorcade moved along, Hitler alternated between standing and sitting. Every time he stood and saluted, the cheers of the crowd heightened to a frenzied roar.

As his dark, shiny, Mercedes-Benz convertible limo slowly approached my position, I took note of the huge chrome headlights, the elegant flowing lines of the side aprons, the wide chrome running boards—and the SS agents perched on either side. As his car passed by, Hitler turned our way. And for a brief moment, I looked him full in the face.

The motorcade moved on. The excitement was over. My *Jungvolk* friends and I stood there for a bit longer, and then slowly dispersed along with the rest of the crowd and went home.

I remember feeling somewhat letdown by the whole event. I don't know why. Perhaps it was because of the big build up, the long wait standing at attention, or perhaps because up close, the Führer didn't look quite as grand as he was made to be. But for whatever reason, I felt a mild pang of disappointment after all the hoopla.

Later that year, folks celebrated again when Hitler annexed the Sudetenland—a Czech area along the Polish border, long inhabited by ethnic Germans, known for its crystal and glass blowing cottage industries. The atmosphere in Königsberg was euphoric. It's difficult to describe just how meaningful those annexations were to us. They gave us hope that the Polish Corridor would be repossessed and that our isolated region of East Prussia might one day again be reunited with the Reich.

At the time of the Sudetenland annexation, I was halfway through middle school. The education system in Germany was quite different than the one in North America. Our parents had to choose our career track at about age 10, after we had completed 4 years of elementary school. Most often that choice was dictated by financial considerations. At that point, parents had three choices of secondary education for the student's remaining school years: 8 years *Mittelschule* (Middle School), Teacher's Seminary, or *Gymnasium*.

The *Gymnasium* was a school that prepared students for university admission. It was a highly academic program for students who wanted careers in the sciences, social sciences, or medical sciences. This track was limited to those whose families which had the means to finance it. Teacher's Seminary was for those who wanted to become educators. *Mittleschule* prepared students for practical occupations like engineering, architecture, or construction management and supervision. That was the track I entered. My family was not well-to-do, but the opportunity was made available to me through a subsidy. To this day I do not know where the subsidy came from.

My secondary school was the *Altstädtische Knaben Mittelschule* of Königsberg. It was an old building, four stories high. It held three classes for each grade with about 30 students in each class, for a total of about 900 boys. All the schools at that time were segregated.

Only one street separated the school building from the Königsberg Castle and the *Kaiser Wilhelm Platz* (plaza), which was the busy traffic hub in the middle of the city. So the hum of the heavy crowd mixed with street noise and the screeching of braking streetcar wheels often drowned out the teacher's voice.

The building caused extremes on both ends, cold in winter and hot in summer. It got so unbearable in the summer months that when the temperature reached 25 C° in the shade, classes stopped and we would be sent home. There was a small building nearby, on *Kaiser Wilhelm Platz*, near the castle, which you can't see in the older photo above. It had a large thermometer on the shaded north wall, where a passerby could read the temperature. On warm days, we couldn't go there often enough, to check if the mercury had risen to the level where we could request to be dismissed. Some of us boys tried to help things along a little bit by slipping aluminum

My middle school, the Altstädtische Knaben Mittelschule of Königsberg, is the three story building pictured at the right side of this older photo.

foil behind the bubble of the thermometer to increase the reading. But that ruse usually didn't work for very long, as the plaza was always teeming with people and most of them were interested in the real temperature. They weren't impressed by our shenanigans.

As I went through *Mittelschule*, more and more young men volunteered or were conscripted into the army. The high school English and the geography teachers were drafted. But that didn't really affect our everyday routine. Not initially, anyhow. Other teachers simply took their place.

Our English teacher, Herr Petrat, probably came during the second year of *Mittelschule*. We nicknamed him "Peter." The English he taught us was abysmal! He must have tried to pick up English by reading books. What little vocabulary I remembered from High School was useless when I came to Canada. Nobody could understand the pronunciation I had learned from him.

Herr Petrat also taught our religion class, if you could even call it that. One of the stated aims of the Regime was to restore the true, ancient religion of the pure, northern Arian race. Hitler encouraged Germans to forsake Christianity and return to our Nordic gods. A man named Rosenberg developed what became known as *Deutsch Gottgläubig*, which was essentially a new religious movement involving Nordic gods, which rejected Jewish-based Christianity. Our teacher told us that the Bible was merely a book of fables. Instead, he pointed us to pagan Germanic deities—gods and goddesses of old—whose names were found in ancient Germanic works of literature, various chronicles and runes. Though he passionately sought to convince us, most of us didn't take his rants about ancient pagan worship seriously.

At least Herr Petrat was able to manage our class, which is more than can be said for every replacement teacher. The rector once attempted to replace a male teacher with a female one. She had an unfortunate last name, "Froschman," which in English means "frog man." We were polite enough when the rector introduced her to us. But when she entered the classroom the following morning, the antics started. Everyone in the room burst into a chorus of croaking. Tried as she might, she couldn't stop the frog noises. Things only settled down after the rector showed up and issued a stern warning. But the peace did not last long.

There was an enameled basin of water for hand-washing sitting on a wrought iron stand not far from the teacher's desk. When sunshine hit the surface of the water, it caused a reflection to appear on the ceiling. The boys in the front desk had discovered that they could bounce the floor to make the reflection dance on the ceiling. All the other teachers simply ignored it or made a lighthearted comment about it. But Frau Froschman was determined to keep the boys from bouncing the floor and to keep the class from looking up. The harder she fought for control, the more flustered she became, and the more entertaining the game got. Every time the shadow wiggled on the ceiling, the class burst out in uncontrollable laughter. Poor Frau Froschman didn't even last a day. By mid-afternoon she stormed out of the classroom, never to return.

The quirkiest of all of our *Mittelschule* teachers was Herr Timm. We called him Timmchen, which means "little Tim" (in an endearing way). Timmchen was our language teacher for one term. He also taught biology, gymnastics and swimming, though he himself could not swim.

Herr Timm was the leader of a prominent naturalist club in the city, "the *Kneipp Verein*," which promoted health through natural living and the use of wild plants and herbs for food, or treatment of various ailments with water. He would often take us on field trips, pointing out all kinds of edible plants and fungi. He wore a peculiar hat on those occasions. Boys being boys, we deposited all kinds of things into the depression on top of his hat, whenever he turned his back. The collection of deposited material would come showering down when he bent over. One time, someone put a dew worm on top of his hat. The worm crawled all the way to the edge of the hat's brim and dangled down right in front of his face. Everyone burst out in laughter when he stared at it in disbelief.

But to Timmchen's credit, he taught us just how much in nature is edible and of how great a medicinal benefit many plants could be. I remember helping him prepare dandelion butter. We collected dandelion leaves, chopped them up, mixed them with butter, and spread the mixture on bread.

To this day, when spruce trees sprout in the spring, I snap off some of the tender green shoots and pop them in my mouth like Herr Timm taught me. My Tante Ella in Hermannsfeld used to collect these fresh shoots to make syrup out of them for pancakes.

Calligraphy was Timmchen's specialty. He was extremely particular about how we sharpened large goose quills to be used in calligraphy. He had us make knives for the task, from old razor blades and sticks. First, we placed the blades between folds of paper to prevent cutting our fingers. We broke the razor blades in half. Then we broke them again, at an angle, to a sharp point. We placed the piece of blade in a slotted stick, which had been prepared beforehand, and fastened it to the stick by winding the two split ends of the stick together with heavy thread. Nowadays you can buy knives in different shapes and with replaceable snap off blades, but back then, we had to make our own.

As I said, we used the homemade knives to sharpen quills for calligraphy. But we also used them in art class, to make intricate designs in heavy paper. We'd carefully make little cuts half way through the thickness of the paper, and lift the top layer of paper up ever so slightly, to produce a 3-D effect.

The knives also came in handy for cutting patterns into linoleum, which we used like rubber stamps. We made picture stamps, address stamps, and even stamps of our signatures by carefully whittling away the background of the pattern. The heavy linoleum, which is called battleship linoleum here, had to be glued to a wooden block before working on it. The school had large, variously colored ink pads. We stamped our carved linoleum blocks onto the ink pads and then onto paper. Lino cut is an art form that is used to produce prints even today.

I enjoyed the art classes immensely and excelled in everything creative that could be mastered by manual dexterity. In other words, I was lousy at painting, and other forms of freehand art. But I was great at calligraphy. I even made a few pennies once, when the owner of our little corner grocery store asked me to use calligraphy to make price tags for his display.

A classmate who lived out of town missed the train one day, and came to class late. The student carried a large cardboard box, which he was supposed to have delivered before school. Timmchen told the boy to put the box on top of the classroom cupboard in the corner of the room. There was a small hole in the side of that box and it was not long before one of the boys spotted something poke out of the hole. He nudged his desk mate to watch it. They began to snicker. It wasn't too long before the whole class burst out in laughter when the head of a chicken poked out of the hole, and then pulled its head back in, startled from the loud laughter. Only after several of these episodes did the teacher catch on, and make the boy take the box down from the cabinet and turn it so the hole faced the wall.

Our *Mittelschule* language teacher, Herr Jötkandt, was a stickler for accuracy. We were loaded with homework, making endless lists of different words, lists of synonyms, antonyms, lists of words with the same ending, lists of words with the same beginning . . . he seemed to come up with hundreds of ways for us to make a list. The German language is interesting, in that you can string a series of smaller words together to make bigger words. Compounding the difficulties with some assignments was the fact that German nouns are gender specific. If it wasn't a common noun, we had no idea if it was a "der," "die" or "das", male, female or neutral, which we all had to learn to distinguish. I did not have access to a thesaurus. I don't even know if they were available at that time. But the whole process gave me a love for language. I still love how words can be put together and what image they can conjure up in one's mind.

The language teacher was extremely patient. He never raised his voice. He only looked over the rim of his glasses when needed, and emphatically said two words: "*Leistungsverweigerung, Knabe.*" He sometimes said it as a statement of fact, and sometimes with a long drawn-out raised voice at the end indicating that he intended it as a question. Translated, the phrase means: "Refusal to produce and achieve, young man!" But the English translation doesn't have quite the same connotation—or bite—as the German phrase.

My school was one of the oldest in the city. We had no gymnasium, and therefore very little indoor physical activities. But before he was drafted, our gym teacher, Herr Wellner, took us to another school a few times to use their facilities. He had been a competitor in the 1936 Olympics, and wanted us to become familiar with different gymnastic equipment. He had us try the parallel bars and rings, and gave us demonstrations of his expertise.

I remember trying out the parallel bars. When they were set at the same elevation, they were easy enough to wobble over from end to end, keeping both arms straight. That was all I was willing to try. The stunts on the uneven bars looked far too difficult. I didn't relish the thought of falling and smacking my head on the floor. I did, however, enjoy climbing rope. There were eight or ten ropes hanging from the ceiling along one wall. To win, you had to reach the top and be the first to shimmy back down and touch the ground. In rope climbing competitions, it was easy to get rope burns on your hands or feet.

My favorite activity in the gym required at least two boys. Or better yet a total of four. It was a piece of equipment suspended from the ceiling that functioned like a carrousel. Four ladder-ropes hung down from a Lazy-Susan-type contraption on the ceiling with the lowest rung being about four feet off the floor. The trick was to hold on to the rungs and run in unison as fast as possible and, at someone's command, swing your body up to "fly" around the carousel. As the spinning slowed, you had to pull up your legs, to keep them from dragging on the floor. It was a lot of fun with the right partner or team.

Our math teacher, Herr Bitterkleit, was the rector (principal) of the school. To my knowledge, he wasn't ever drafted. He stayed with us throughout our school years, as did Herr Jötkandt. Herr Bitterkleit was the one who meted out serious punishment, which was usually a caning on your back-end. Lesser infractions received a slap on the hand with a ruler. Teachers could purchase canes at the hardware store, not too far away from school. When a cane became too dry and brittle, it had to be replaced. To add insult to injury, the teacher would send the offender to the store to buy the new cane. This was humiliating, because the store clerk inevitably asked about the nature of your offence.

The canes were about 3/8 inch in diameter and about 3 feet long. When they came down hard, you could hear a whistling sound. It hurt and left large welts. But if you complained at home about a caning, you would likely be given another one. That's just the way it was. When we were in grade 11 or 12, a boy could actually get a caning one day and be called to the Army the next.

Even though the rector was not a very big man, and many of us could have physically overpowered him, I never knew of anyone resisting a caning. It was simply unheard of to resist authority. The teacher's desk always sat on an elevated platform with the front of the desk being at the front edge of the platform. The platform was large enough for the teacher to walk around on. Even when the teacher sat down and called someone up to his desk, the teacher was always "above you".

The best you could do to mitigate the effect of a caning was to wear an extra-heavy pair of undershorts. And that was only possible if you had the good fortune of being asked to report to the rector's office for the caning on the following day. Rumor had it that someone had shown up for a caning with a scribbler tucked into his underwear. Apparently things went worse for him, as he had to strip down and was caned on his naked bum. I don't know if this story was true, but it stopped us from trying to pad our back-ends too much.

If something happened during the rector's class, punishment was immediate and in front of everyone. He taught math—including calculus, logarithm, algebra, geometry and trigonometry. I actually liked him very much. He was a good instructor and I enjoyed his classes immensely. He explained concepts so well that I thought everybody would grasp them. But that was not the case.

I had a friend, Hans Sczabang, who was the creative type. He was gifted in music, but not math. Hans just couldn't understand numbers. I spent many hours at his place helping him with homework, to no avail. He lived quite close to the school, and was an only child. His mom was very concerned about his inability to grasp mathematical concepts, and was appreciative of my efforts to help. I think she spoiled him. I never met his dad. Perhaps he didn't have one, or perhaps his dad had to leave for some reason—like those who had to flee persecution, or who inexplicably "disappeared." In that political environment, it was taboo to ask about such things. I know of one classmate's father who had to go into hiding because he had Jewish ancestors. I even remember this name: "*Buntman*," which, in German, means "colorful man."

School always finished by one or two o'clock, depending on the class schedule. One day, I promised to help Hans with homework right after school. When I arrived at his place, his mom served us some snacks and suggested that we go to watch a movie at the nearby movie house. We didn't have to think twice about her offer. We jumped at the chance.

It was not one of the better movie houses in the city, to say the least. From about ten in the morning until past midnight, the same old movie looped and played continuously for an entire week. After you purchased a ticket, you could walk in at any time during the show. And you could stay all day, if you wanted.

That day, "Catherine the Great" was playing. As we walked in, the image stuttered, and then the screen went blank. A message appeared, requesting patience, as the film had broken and needed to be spliced. Such things were quite common then.

There were lots of seats to choose from. When we settled on ours, we noticed just how many empty seats there were in the theater. Except for a few scattered couples, and a motley group of children occupying two rows near the front, it was practically empty. We observed them as we waited for the film to be patched. Their clothing clearly marked them as Gypsy children. They were noisy and rambunctious. Some noticeably munched on treats. Most of the movie houses did not have concession stands in those days. If you wanted a snack you'd have to bring it with you.

After the movie resumed, a huge black shadow briefly appeared on the screen. Then the shadow appeared again. Something was flying through the air and blocking the light from the projector, but I couldn't tell what it was. A roar of laughter erupted from the group sitting at the front. Then silence. – Another big shadow. More laughter. It happened time and again. And then a huge silhouette of a fish head arced across the screen. It was clear what was happening. The Gypsy kids were eating smoked sprats, and tossing the fish heads into the air. They obviously enjoyed the production of their own show, and didn't seem at all concerned about where the fish heads landed. Catherine the Great and fish heads. . . It was my most memorable movie experience ever!

Germany's military had expanded substantially during the *Blumenkrieg* annexations. More young men were being conscripted for service, and because our city was a major military training base and naval center, as well as a production center for ships and military equipment, the heightened buzz of activity was palpable. But apart from that, life in Königberg seemed to go on as usual. That is, until the night everything changed.

*Above: The Jewish Orphanage. Below: The Jewish Synagogue.
The backs of these buildings were located just across the street from my home.*

That night, I awoke to the sound of panicked shouts, and a big commotion in the street. Flickering reflections of flames danced on my bedroom wall. The Jewish Synagogue was on fire! Only the street and a few warehouses separated us.

Dad shut the window to keep the bits of glowing ember from flying in and starting a fire in our living room. I peered out at the spectacle. Fierce flames shot high into the sky. The once graceful dome was being ravaged. Yet the Star of David remained clearly visible—two black intersected triangles in the midst of bright raging flames. Firefighters dowsed the string of warehouses while the Synagogue burned. I could see that the firemen were concentrating their efforts on the small woodworking shop at the back of one warehouse, directly adjacent to the Jewish property, and weren't even trying to save the Synagogue. Plumes of smoke billowed into the air. The acrid smell of smoke stung my nostrils.

A large group of neighbors had congregated beneath our suite, in the recessed doorway of our apartment building. I could hear the tension and concern in their muffled voices. Then gunshots rang out, and mom pulled me back from the window.

In the morning, I heard that SS men had tried to shoot down the Star of David that had been so clearly silhouetted in the midst of the flames. But as far as I can remember, that star remained on top of the burned out skeleton of the dome for quite a while, perhaps even until bombs in 1944 destroyed what was left of the building.

Dad went down to find out what was going on. When he came back with the explanation, mom started to cry, *"Das is das Ende von Deutchland! Das is das Ende von Deutchland!"* (This is the end of Germany) she sobbed over and over again. I couldn't understand the whole thing, and was ordered to go back to bed. I lay awake for a long while, wondering what had happened, and what it all meant.

Later, I found out that it was part of a coordinated attack on Jews carried out throughout Germany by SA Storm troopers and angry civilians, orchestrated under the pretense of retribution for a Jew's assassination of a German diplomat in Paris. The attack was called *"Die Kristallnacht* (literally "Crystal Night"), alluding to the enormous number of shop windows broken that night. The attacks left the streets covered with broken glass from the windows of Jewish-owned stores and buildings.

Many Jews were killed in the attacks, and many more arrested and incarcerated in concentration camps. Jewish homes, hospitals, and schools were ransacked, as the attackers demolished buildings with sledgehammers, and set fire to many of them. Tombstones were uprooted and graves violated. Fires were lit, and prayer books, scrolls, artwork and philosophy texts were thrown in the flames. Hundreds of synagogues in Germany were either burned down or smashed until unrecognizable, and thousands of Jewish businesses damaged or destroyed.

I had to step over fire hoses on my way to school that morning. The fire seemed to be out, but I could see a small group of Jewish children being "evacuated" from the orphanage. They huddled together against a wall and tried to protect themselves against the spray of a fire hose, as a fireman seemed to use the flow of water to herd them together. I walked by, not daring to appear concerned. I was less than 150 feet away. I had a horrible sick feeling in the pit of my stomach. I don't know if any of the orphans were kids I had played soccer with in my younger years. I was simply too stunned and afraid to look.

Up to now I had never known just how many Jewish businesses or offices of professionals I had walked past on my way to school every day. But there was no mistaking now, and I didn't care to count. Windows were smashed, stores were looted or the content thrown out. The Star of David and the ugly, accusatory label, "*Jude*," (Jew) was scrawled or painted on numerous walls and doors, often making the original signs undecipherable.

A dark pallor seemed to have settled over the city. Even the normally bustling Fish Market was not the same. Very few people were out and about. The fisher-women, who were notorious for loudly hawking their wares, sat in silence. The hardware store, where I had often accompanied other boys to buy fishhooks, was in shambles. It was the store where teachers sent us to get new canes. I believe the name of the store was Drewenski & Krebs.

It was normally a 20 to 25 minute walk to school when the bridge wasn't open. But this day was anything but normal. With my heart pounding and my head churning I arrived at the school late. If I remember correctly, it was the English teacher, Herr Petrat, who went from class to class that morning to explain and justify the events.

A few days later, after the pall over the city had lifted a little, curiosity overpowered caution and I decided to have a look into the inside of the Synagogue. I knew it was forbidden territory, but the place held such an intrigue to me that I couldn't resist. It was now or never.

The front door of the Synagogue had been boarded up after the fire. Climbing the gate that we boys from the neighborhood had often climbed was not an option. Someone might spot me. It was too dangerous. But I knew how to get to the side door of the Synagogue by sneaking through the property of the little cabinet shop across the street. There, I would be able to get in undetected.

Now, more than seventy years later, I can still recall the fear and tension that gripped my heart when I saw the side door hanging wide open lopsided on its hinges. I paused for a moment, looked around to ensure no one was looking, and then took a big gulp and went in. I had to struggle over some debris to enter what seemed to be a large coat check. Black cloaks hung from the hooks. They were covered in dust and ashes.

A large archway to the left led into the sanctuary. There were some very dark areas around the perimeter where I could not discern anything, and I did not venture there. The fire did not cause as much damage as I had anticipated. Several rows of heavy pews seemed to be untouched except for being covered in a layer of ashes. But the air was thick with the smell of destruction—extinguished fire, smoke, dust, and debris.

That smell became all too familiar in the war years, only added to by the unmistakable smell of death. Standing there in the Synagogue, I first experienced what would eventually become an unforgettable sensation. I'm not sure how to describe it. It's a combination of disbelief, fear, disgust, helplessness, and stunned astonishment at the carnage and destruction humans are capable of. It's the feeling that made those times so unforgettable, and even now, news coverage of some horrific event on TV seems to tangibly bring back that sensation.

There was a massive darkish marble table dominating the space in front of the pews. I wiped a smudge of ashes off the surface. I couldn't clearly see the color of the marble, but it seemed to be reddish-brown with light veins. I also seem to remember scrolls, either on the table or on the shelf underneath although some historians say that the scrolls were put on a heap and set on fire. From what I remember, the scrolls had round, silvery knobs on their ends. I moved through the Synagogue quickly, for fear of being found out.

I have the most vivid memory of the office. Light streamed through those windows, which were still intact. It was obvious that the room had been ransacked. Cabinet and desk drawers were ajar or tossed on the floor, their contents strewn knee high. Dirty footprints and other debris covered the once white paper. The biggest piles seemed to be behind the desk. On the right side, on top of a desk or shelf, was an addressograph—a machine used to print addresses onto envelopes with little metal plates, which bore the names and addresses of the Synagogue's constituents. Some plates were still in their containers. But hundreds and hundreds of them were dumped next to the desk. I was tempted to take one of the plates as a souvenir, but feared it would not be worth the risk. It was dangerous for me to be there. There's no telling what might have happened had I been caught by an SA or SS officer. So I didn't tell anyone what I had done. I kept that entire venture to myself for many years.

Shortly after *Kristallnacht*, Jews had to wear an appliqued badge with a "J" prominently displayed on their clothing. First, the badge was just worn on the front. Later, the word "Jude," in stylized Hebrew letters, was sewn on a yellow Star of David, which was also required to be worn in a larger format on their backs. Orders were given that Jews had to step into the gutter when other people were on the sidewalk. We saw fewer and fewer of them on the street, and it was rumored that they had been moved into a ghetto to be amongst their own kind.

They weren't the only ones "branded." Polish workers had to wear a diamond shaped badge with a purple "P." French workers wore a blue "F." Slavic workers wore a white-on-blue "OST." All foreigners had to wear labels identifying them as outsiders. This was due to the Nazi quest for racial purity and preservation, which was a mainstay of eugenic philosophy at the time.

Eugenics was a social movement in the early 1900s that sought to improve the genetic features of human populations through selective breeding and sterilization. It was based on the idea that it's possible to distinguish between superior and inferior elements of society. Eugenics was practiced around the world and was promoted by many governments and influential individuals and institutions. The ideology was popular with Hitler, but also with American academics such as Margaret Sanger, the founder of Planned Parenthood, and American organizations like the Carnegie Institute and Rockefeller Foundation. Eugenicists advocated for the removal of genetic "defectives" such as the insane, "feeble-minded" and criminals, and supported the selective breeding of "high-grade" individuals. It seems inconceivable today that the entire Western world had adopted that concept. But that's where Hitler got his ideas. He was to a considerable degree simply voicing the conventional wisdom of his time, and he had the means and power to actually apply the ideology.

In the summer of 1939, my dad had to report for service with the Corps of Army engineers he had trained with for several years. His unit was situated on a strip of railway not too far from the main station. The long train was painted in camouflage colors. At least one of its locomotives was kept under steam at all times, to keep all systems functioning, and to be ready to move on a moment's notice.

Every weekend, the Corps had regular visiting hours. When we went to see him, there was always quite a crowd in front of the living accommodation and sleeper cars. But civilians were not allowed to go inside. A strange mood seemed to prevail, and the visits did not last long. The last time we went to visit, the train was gone and Dad with it—No one knew where.

7 | FIRST GUNNER

The war started on September 1, 1939 with extra editions of the newspaper and a radio address by Adolf Hitler. After the oppressive uncertainty of the previous weeks, we almost felt relieved. People greeted each other in the streets again. A positive mood buoyed up our spirits. Tension seemed to dissipate. We were glad that Hitler was responding to the Polish aggression against Germans in Danzig. His stated aim was to reclaim "The Corridor"—land which rightfully belonged to Germany and to protect Germans in Poland from more attacks.

Years of suffering and separation as a result of the heavy hand of Versailles were finally coming to an end. We were excited and hopeful that East Prussia would soon be re-united with the Reich.

Two or three days after Hitler's declaration, I heard anti-aircraft fire in the distance. I ran outside into the street just in time to see a small ball of fire and black puffs of smoke appear around a small object in the sky. A small Polish airplane had been shot down. It was the only time during the first few years of the war that combat came anywhere near Königsberg.

I was familiar with the sound of antiaircraft guns, and with the characteristic puffs that the exploding shell left behind. There was an anti-aircraft training facility near a town called *Brüsterort*, close to my Uncle's place on the Baltic Sea. There, trainees practiced by shooting at a target, which was pulled at a distance behind small planes. The target looked like a large windsock without the taper. The plane looped around for its next run close to where we often sat on the beach. Sometimes the windsock looked tattered, either from the wind or from being hit. Whenever we heard the "boom . . . boom" of anti-aircraft guns, we'd look up and scan the sky, to see if the trainee had hit his mark. They used heavier long-barreled 88 mm anti-aircraft guns, not the rapid-fire light ones. The ammunition exploded at a set distance. The puffs of smoke looked like dots from a type writer.

It took less than a month for Hitler to conquer, divide, and annex Poland with his *Blizkrieg*. Germans generally supported the initiative. Travel by train to Germany had been a puzzling uncertainty, with Poles stopping trains at a whim, or arrogantly rubbing salt in our wounds by halting traffic on the only highway connection that supposedly guaranteed unimpeded travel between East Prussia and the Reich. We were thrilled that the trains would now make it through. People could travel by any route and would no longer be restricted to one highway.

Königsberg celebrated the reclamation by putting on one of the biggest, most exuberant victory parades imaginable. A beaming parade marshal, wearing a hat topped with a massive feather plume, led the procession down the main street past the Königsberg Castle, setting a high-spirited tempo with his high prancing steps and swinging baton. Bands played. Regiments of soldiers marched in formation flanked by officers dressed in fancy parade uniforms like the ones I had seen at Uncle Paul's tailor shop. Military vehicles followed. A mass of onlookers waved *Hakenkreuz Fahnen* (Nazi flags). They cheered and shouted. Some wept for joy.

Dad came home after the Polish Blitzkrieg, bearing some prized spoils of war: cans of Australian corned beef. The meat came in rounded rectangular metal cans you had to unzip with a slotted key. The meat was nicknamed, "*Toter Indianer*" (Dead Indian) due to its unmistakable reddish color. Mom cooked it up in pea soup the first time we ate it. It was absolutely delicious! To this day, I think of that happy occasion every time I see a can of corned beef—which even today comes in those distinctly shaped cans with a windup zipper.

After just a couple of weeks however, Dad got called back into action. We didn't know exactly where his unit was going, but suspected that it was being sent to France. We knew that trouble was brewing there. France and Britain had pacts with Poland, and had issued a joint ultimatum requiring German troops to evacuate Polish territory. They had declared war on Germany three days into the *Polenfeldzug* (war with Poland). At the time, I thought that Germany would just have to defend our territory against the French along the Maginot line, which was a series of heavy fortifications, gun posts, and other structures that France had built along the French-German border. I had seen reports in the weekly news about the corresponding, impenetrable defence system that Germany had built, called the *Siegfriedlinie*. The Siegfried Line was a defence system stretching more than 630 km (390 mi) with more than 18,000 bunkers, tunnels, tank traps, barbed wire, and heavy fortifications. It ensured that we would be safe from any attack. I never expected Hitler to launch an offensive against France. And I certainly didn't imagine that I would ever be drafted to the army and be sent into combat.

Germany invaded France in the spring of 1940. We got a letter from Dad some time later, verifying that he had indeed been sent to France to support the troops. He informed us that he'd been shot and wounded in battle . . .

but not to worry—he was convalescing, and would be re-assigned to a military training school in Berlin, to help instruct officers in equestrian skills. He would not be sent back into active military support duty. Mom was relieved, to say the least.

Over the next several months, Hitler's *Wehrmacht* overwhelmed Belgium, Holland, and France. It was hard to keep up with all that was going on; the war progressed at a dizzying speed. But most news was good news. The Blitzkrieg period was ten months of almost total triumph for Germany. We thought that the hostilities might resolve after the decisive victory and armistice with France, but instead, the whole continent seemed to erupt in conflict.

There was war everywhere. Virtually every country lined up and chose sides. Britain, France, and Poland had a pact. Germany and the Soviets had a pact. Germany, Italy, and Japan had a pact. Pacts were made. Pacts were broken. The Soviets fought the Fins. The Italians fought the Greeks. The Hungarians fought the Yugoslavians. The Japanese fought the Thais. The Thais fought the French. The Brits fought the Iraqi. All the residual political tensions caused by Versailles and all the power struggles over boundaries, all the conflicting philosophies and political ideologies of competing governments finally burned down the fuse and blew up the powder keg that was the Eurasian continent.

Shortly after the French armistice, the *Luftwaffe* (German Air Force) engaged in an attack on British airfields. The Royal Air Force (RAF) retaliated with an aerial bombing campaign against Berlin. Hitler was incensed that Britain would target civilians, and immediately ordered the *Luftwaffe* to deter from its original plan of decimating the RAF and bomb British cities instead. Apparently, it was a critical error. The Battle of Britain became Hitler's first major setback. What's more, it was the first time that German civilians experienced the atrocities of war on German soil. We were particularly concerned about Dad, who was stationed in Berlin. A military training school would most certainly be high on the list of bombing targets.

I listened to a radio broadcast of a speech Hitler gave in late 1940 or early 1941. His oration was even more theatrical, passionate, and forceful than usual. He reminded us that France and England had declared war on Germany with the intention of ripping the Rhineland away, and splitting our country up once again. He criticized the barbarism of Britain in attacking Germany's civilians. He lamented that France and Britain were intent on keeping us subservient, that they fiercely opposed German unification, and refused to allow us to peacefully reclaim what was rightfully ours. He lashed out at the United States, which was poised on the verge of interfering in Europe's affairs. He appealed to the pride, will, and determination of the German people.

Hitler worked himself and the crowd into frenzy. At the highpoint of his speech he screamed out the question: "*Wollt ihr den totalen Krieg?*" (Do you want an all-out war?) The crowd matched his mood of righteous indignation and fury against the world by screaming back in the affirmative: "*Ya – wir wollen den totalen Krieg!*" ("Yes, we want an all-out war!"). I was shocked at Hitler's intensity, and equally shocked at the hysteria of the crowd. Did they know what they were asking for?

Other than the Polish plane being shot down, war hadn't yet come to Königsberg. At least not in the gruesome reality of air raids, bombs, tanks, fire fights, destruction, and death. But nevertheless, our city was definitely affected by the ongoing conflict. Mild food rationing started early on. Obviously, since we were a sea port, fish were always plentiful. But other food products weren't. We were issued food stamps, and could only buy restricted portions of certain items. Even the famous pastry shop "*Petschliess*," which was at the end of the same block as my *Mittelschule*, started to demand ration stamps.

I was crazy about all the delicacies that were sold there. *Petschliess* was world-renowned for its marzipan, which was made of ground almonds, powdered sugar and rose water. It came in different shapes and had various sugary decorations. But I usually settled for the cheaper *Rumschnittchen*—left over baked goods that were soaked in rum and topped with vanilla sugar icing. It's amazing how things change. I hardly ever eat sweets now.

Besides the food rationing, another obvious sign of war was the constant influx of battle ships and subs. It became commonplace for us to see naval vessels and personnel in the harbor. Some areas had been re-zoned for restricted military access. In late 1941, and a few times over the subsequent years, Soviet bombers targeted some key military sites in Königsberg. But by far the most obvious sign of war was the depletion of young men from the general population, as more and more were drafted and sent off to serve.

As the younger teachers at my high school were drafted, the remaining older ones were given more and more teaching responsibilities. Many subjects were dropped altogether. We had only about six weeks of French and Latin when the teacher of those subjects was drafted. Eventually, because of the dwindling number of teachers and senior students, my *Alstädtische Knaben Mittleschule* was combined with another school, the *Kneiphöfische Gymnasium*, even though that school was exclusively for University preparation. We abandoned our building and started going to the *Gymnasium* facility, which was on the former University campus, just behind the Immanuel Kant Library. I think that happened sometime during grade 11, likely during the fall of 1941. Our school building required a lot of coal for heating and the rationing made it impossible to keep the temperature at a comfortable level.

The following photo was taken in my homeroom on the final day at my old school, before we moved over to the *Gymnasium*. I am standing at the back, beside the cabinet where the cane was stored. The tall teacher standing in the forefront is Herr Bitterkleit, the rector who meted out punishment. The teacher beside him, wearing glasses, is Herr Jötkandt. He was the one who made us write the many lists of words. The boy on the extreme right is "Buntman," whose Jewish father went into hiding because of his Jewish ancestry. The next photo is of our combined class in front of the gym of the *Kneiphöfische Gymnasium*, sometime in 1942—I am in the back row at the far left.

Gruss aus Königsberg i. Pr.

Königliches Wilhelm-Gymnasium

The war was showing no signs of letting up. By summer, Germany was fighting on two fronts: on the Western Front against France, England, Canada and the United States; and on the Eastern Front against the Russians. Hitler had just launched another big offensive towards Stalingrad. So it came as no surprise that during our summer vacation that year, most of us boys were "mustered" in preparation for our upcoming drafts.

"Mustering," involved groups of 16 and 17 year olds being summoned to one of the army facilities for a battery of physical and aptitude tests. We were assigned a number, and our names and vital statistics were entered into a "*Soldbuch*"—a small record booklet that we kept for the duration of our time in the military. Based on the mustering results, we were earmarked for future service in the tank corps, marine, U-boat, air force, or infantry. We could express our preference for the branch of the army we wanted to serve in, but we wouldn't necessarily get assigned to what we requested.

There was a funny story going around as to how one could ensure getting an equestrian assignment. Prior to mustering, you could use grass to wipe your bottom after a bowel movement. Then, when the military officials examined that part of your anatomy, the proof that you were a "country bumpkin" would stare them in the face!

We were eligible to be drafted to the military around our 18th birthdays. Near the end of the war, with more and more casualties, boys as young as 15 years were sent to battle. There was often pressure exerted on us to enlist for service prior to our official draft date. Furthermore, some of us were conscripted into the *Kriegshilfdienst* (War Support Service). Others had to serve in the *Arbeitsdienst* (Work Service) prior to being drafted into the military. So in my final year, more and more classmates had to leave school. In some cases, they couldn't even say goodbye to friends and teachers. They were just gone. It was inescapably true and undeniably real. "*Der Totale Krieg*!"

The mood in the city shifted dramatically that winter. Up until then we had heard the odd report of bombings in Germany, but generally, it sounded as though the Axis was faring relatively well. However by early 1943, with the defeat and surrender at Stalingrad, and dramatic German losses on all fronts, the deteriorating situation could no longer be concealed from the population at large. When appeals came for women to knit socks for the soldiers, it became apparent to us just how ill equipped our army was for the realities of fighting on the brutally cold Russian front.

Women started to be employed to work 10-12 hours a day in factories. Young women in the *Bund Deutscher Mädchen* (League of German Girls) were called upon to operate searchlights and anti-aircraft guns (*Flieger Abwehr Kanonen*). My sister, Dora, was trained to operate a *Messgerät*, an optical instrument that determined distance of aircraft for the anti-aircraft guns.

Rumors started circulating about the suspicious demise of several respected high-ranking military officials and war heroes. People coined a term to describe their demise. They said, "*Er wurde gestorben,*" which means, "He was made to die." Though the Nazi's tried to cover it up, we knew that the officials had likely been given the choice of a dishonorable execution or an "honorable" suicide by poison. Many took the poison. Like Rommel (The Desert Fox), who received an elaborate state funeral with all the pomp possible during a time of war after he had been forced to commit suicide.

We found out that Allied carpet-bombing on several German cities, particularly Berlin and Hamburg, had killed hundreds of thousands of civilians. Slowly, it began to dawn on us that we could potentially lose the war, and see our country decimated in the process.

My schooling ended in January 1943 when I was conscripted into the *Kriegshilfdienst*. By then, only 10 or 12 students remained. Normally, we would have continued classes until June, but due to the diminished class size, they fast-tracked us, and we graduated early. Some of the guys that were conscripted into the *Kriegshilfdienst* had to go back a few months later for a final exam, but because I had good marks, I didn't have to.

The *Kriegshilfdienst* (War Support Service) was different than other types of obligatory youth work service. Traditionally, when students graduated from the Hitler youth groups and finished their education, they were obliged to serve the country in the State Labor Service, the *Reichsarbeitsdienst* (RAD), for one year of compulsory "*Arbeitsdienst*" (Work Service) for males, and "*Pflichtjahr*" (Duty Year) for females. This service year could be postponed until after graduation by those attending University. Initially, the RAD provided cheap labor to do essential civic work such as building roads, draining marshes, and various agricultural construction projects. During the war, however, it provided important combat support, functions like repairing damaged roads, constructing and repairing airstrips, constructing coastal fortifications, and laying minefields. You were obliged to work for the RAD if you had finished your education, but were not yet of draft age.

Because I had progressed through the ranks of the *Jungfolk*, I was conscripted to *Kriegshilfdienst* duty as a streetcar conductor in lieu of the other compulsory Work Service. As directed, I reported for duty with the *Königsberger Straßenbahn* (streetcar) in January of 1943. I was issued a uniform, black boots, a leather money belt with a metal coin dispenser, a paper punch, and a whistle. After a quick one-day orientation, I started my first shift.

Each streetcar was managed by two workers: the driver and the conductor. The driver's only responsibility was to drive the car according to schedule, which could be somewhat of a challenge, given the fact that the roads were shared with all other possible conveyances, such as hand drawn carts, horse drawn wagons and coaches, trucks, automobiles, and bicycles. It wasn't uncommon for the roads to get congested and chaotic—especially along the docks, and in the heart of the city, around *Kaiser Wilhelm Platz*. There were two routes where the streets had steep grades. There, the driver had to operate a lever to disperse sand onto the tracks from a reservoir. This provided better traction for braking coming downhill, and for acceleration going uphill. The photo shows the beginning of the climb from the *Kaiser Wilhelm Platz* to the *Gesekus Platz*.

Most streetcars had multiple carriages, depending on the busyness of the route. Each carriage had sliding doors and large platforms on either end, onto which passengers could step up from the street. There was a center aisle running end to end, and seats on each side.

It was my job to jump from carriage to carriage to collect fares and issue transfer tickets. I had to mark each transfer with the punch that was attached to my money belt with a chain. The punch mark was unique to each conductor. By examining it, the inspectors could identify which conductor had punched the ticket. The ticket also indicated the date, time of issue, line number, and direction of travel. Transfers could only take place at designated transfer points. I had to check the tickets of people transferring onto my streetcar, to ensure their transfer was valid. I also had to keep passengers informed on transfer points, routes, and related issues. Needless to say, I got to know my way around the city quite well, and became familiar with the location of most businesses and buildings.

A conductor's biggest challenge was to accommodate as many of the waiting passengers as possible at each stop. We often had to squeeze through a standing-room-only crowd to do our job. The streetcars got especially crowded if we were the first or second streetcar on either side of an opened bridge. When a draw bridge was opened to allow a ship to pass, all traffic would grind to a halt, and people would continue to pile into the streetcar.

The streetcars ran continuously from 5 o'clock in the morning until 1 o'clock at night—and actually longer if you take into account the time they took to pick up and drop off street car personnel. Each shift was about ten hours long. I had to alternate between early and late shifts, with only one day off every ten days. One of the happy "fringe benefits" of the job was free entrance to movie houses when in uniform. I took full advantage of that, though I slept through many a film because I was so exhausted from work.

Somehow, I became disillusioned with the Nazis during the time I worked the streetcars. They had promoted me to the rank of *Jungstammführer*, which was a regional officer that had authority over several *Heims*. *Jungstammführers* planned meetings, oversaw awards, facilitated communication, and made sure that everything in the organization ran smoothly. I knew all the politically correct rhetoric, but deep down I knew that things were not right. The ideology just didn't ring true. I was getting tired of the manipulation, fear and intimidation. I was getting tired of being pushed around.

I managed to avoid attending any more meetings by citing the excuse that I was just too busy contributing to the "war effort" (*Kriegshilfe*). That seemed to satisfy them. I would only pop in at *Jungfolk* headquarters once in a while, when they needed help with the mimeograph. (Oddly enough, it was the same model of mimeograph machine that I later operated here in Canada, at Calvary Baptist Church, to print the church bulletin.)

Several weeks after I started work as a streetcar conductor, a card was in our mailbox when I got home. It bore the Nazi swastika, and was addressed to "the Volunteer, Ulrich Thomas." It instructed me to appear at a specified time for an entrance examination to Hitler's SS force, and threatened severe punishment for non-compliance. I was dumbfounded. I hadn't volunteered for the *Shutzstaffel (SS)*—Hitler's Protection Squadron, who swore absolute loyalty to the Führer. I had no interest in serving in that elite, but despised group. I suspected the card was a clever ruse to get me to volunteer before my official draft date, since the Nazis didn't have the legal right to conscript me earlier.

I informed my mother that I planned to ignore the directive. I had no intent of showing up as instructed. She was frightened. I don't know what scared her more—the prospect of what might happen to me if I didn't report for SS service, or the prospect of what might happen to me if I did. She didn't have to worry for long. The card for my inevitable draft to the army arrived about a month later, with my enlistment date set for late June or early July 1943—just a few weeks before my 18th birthday. I was slated to become a gunner on a '*Leichtes Infantrie Geschütz*'.

The Prussian Army had a long history, rooted deep in tradition and pride. In times of peace, it was comprised of solders who had chosen the military as a career. But now it was part of the German *Wehrmacht*, and populated by soldiers who had been conscripted into the army against their wills.

When the appointed time came, I said good bye to Mom and Dora. I took the train to *Braunsberg*, a garrison town about 80 km southwest of Königsberg,, to enter basic training in the 21st infantry Division of the *Wehrmacht*. .I took only a few specified personal items along. Army life started that very afternoon.

In the basement of the garrison, we had to strip off all our clothes, place them in fabric bags labeled with our names, and fasten the long draw-string closures. We turned these bags in for safekeeping at the garrison.

I never saw those clothes again.

I went to a counter with the other conscripts to pick up our dog tags. They were thin, oval disks made of aluminum, fastened to a leather lace to wear around our necks. The oval had a series of slits, like a perforation, running horizontally across the tag. It was stamped with identical information above and below the perforation line: our soldier ID number (*Personenkennziffer*), and our blood type. The tag was designed to be broken in two pieces if the soldier wearing it was killed. The upper half would remain with the body. The lower half would be collected by the medics and sent to headquarters, so the family could be informed. I studied the tag. I hoped my mother would never be the recipient of news like that. She had already lost my younger brother and sister to diphtheria. I feared that another loss would be more grief than she could bear.

We congregated in a long line and moved from wicket to wicket to receive the items for our drill uniforms. As we filed past, piece after piece was thrown on top of our outstretched arms without any regard for size or fit: *Feldbluse* (Field combat tunic), *Arbeitshemd* (service shirt), internal suspenders, *Koppelhaken* (belt Hooks), *Keilhosen* (tapered trousers), *Hosentraeger* (trouser suspenders), *Feldmütze* (Field Service Cap), Socken (socks), and *Schnürschuhe* (Low Combat Boots). The few guys that dared to say something about the items being too big or too small soon learned to keep their mouths shut.

Back in our assigned rooms, we frantically exchanged sizes so we could rush to the exercise ground in time for inspection. I have large feet, and a small head, so I ended up scuttling out with my heels protruding and stepping on the backs of my too-small boots. An overly large cap flopped down low over my forehead and blocked my vision. It would have been comical had it not been for the bellowing reprimand from the drill sergeant, who berated one after another of us for being a disgrace to the German Army. He shouted at us to run and come back on the double, in proper attire, after we exchanged sizes at the storehouse.

I was relieved to get a pair of combat boots to fit my size 13 feet. The *Schnürschuhe* were a lace-up paratrooper-type combat boot made of brown pebbled leather. They weren't the only boots we got. We were also issued a loose, calf-high boot for marching, called a "Jack-boot," or "*Knobelbecher.*"

Knobelbecher means "dice cup." This boot was made out of smooth, black leather. When broken in, it would develop a characteristic dimple above the ankle, which looked like a leather dice cup. That's how it got its name. Both boot types had hobnailed leather soles. Metal bars, shaped like horseshoes, rimmed the back of each heel. It was our responsibility to maintain the correct number of nails in the sole of the boots and to replace the heel-irons before the metal wore through.

We wore no socks in the *Knobelbecher*. Instead, we learned how to wrap soft flannel "*Fußlappen*" (foot wraps) around our feet to prevent pressure points. For long marches, we sprinkled foot powder on the flannel pieces before wrapping them around our feet. Then, during rest stops, we'd replace the wraps with fresh ones. *Fußlappen* were so much better than socks! Socks almost always produced blisters. But *Fußlappen* kept your feet comfortable and dry. At least they did for those of us who mastered the wrapping technique. Some guys just couldn't seem to get it right.

The loose-fitting shank of the *Knobelbecher* was a feature that proved extremely useful. During combat, we'd stuff as many *M-24 Stielhandgranate* (stick grenades), handle-side down into the side of our boots as we could. These grenades were called "potato mashers" by the Allies due to their long wooden handles. The handle acted as a lever and significantly improved the throwing distance. The *Stielhandgranate* were too bulky to tuck under our belts. And we couldn't hang them on our belts like we did with the *Eihandgrante* (egg grenades). Stuffed in our boot shanks, the long grenades were out of the way, leaving our hands free to use other weapons. Yet they were nearby and easy to grab when we needed them.

Besides the uniform, I also received the standard issue of basic field gear for the German army: A Mauser K98 rifle would be my weapon. My steel "coal scuttle" helmet (*Stahlhelm*) had a rim that flared down at the sides and back and at a right angle across the forehead like a short visor, to shield my eyes from the sun. The sturdy belt (*Koppel*) and combat harness (*Tragriemen*) provided space to fasten my ammunition pouch (*Patronentasche*), folding trench spade (*Klappspaten*), gas mask canister (*Tragebüchse für Gasmaske*), gas cape (*Gasplane*)—a thin, light protective sheet to protect against sprayed blister agents such as mustard gas, my scabbard (Scheide), bayonet (Seitengewehr), as well as my field canteen (*Feldflasche*), mess kit,(Kochgeschirr) and bread bag (*Brotbeuel*) to carry emergency combat rations. My belt was fastened with a large aluminum buckle (Koppelschloss) engraved in fine detail with a Reich's Eagle clutching a swastika, and the historic inscription of the German Army, "*Gott Mit Uns*," which means "God With Us."

We were issued two standard "booster" foods to provide us with extra energy on long marches or when going into battle. The first was a heavy, dry, square biscuit, which we tucked into a special pocket of our tunics. The second was a flat, round red tin of *Scho-Ko-Kola*, a high-energy chocolate that was scored into wedges so it could be easily broken. We carried the *Scho-Ko-Kola* in our bread bag, along with our emergency field "Half Iron Rations" (*Halb-Eiserne Portionen*). The Half Iron Ration consisted of a small tin of meat and a dried *Zwieback* cracker, which we would eat when the tactical situation prohibited the field kitchen from providing a meal for more than 24 hours. We could only eat these items on order, and only as much as our commander allowed.

All our non-essential combat gear fastened onto a separate assault frame (*Sturmgepäck*). We were issued a blanket (*Mannschaftsdecke*) and a shelter quarter (*Zeltbahn*). The *Zeltbahn* was a multi-functional piece of waterproof camouflage cloth. It could be fastened to other shelter quarters to build a tent, used as ground cover, turned into a flotation device, used as limber to move a wounded soldier, or worn as a protective rain cape. Often it became a burial shroud.

In addition to combat gear, everyone was issued personal items such as a toothbrush holder, soap container, shaving kit, sewing kit, shoe polishing kit, extra hobnails, a small pad of paper and pen for writing letters, a windproof refillable petrol cigarette lighter, storage container (*Tornister*), and an army mess kit (*Kochgeschirr*). The mess kit contained all our eating utensils: knife, fork, spoon, eating tin, drinking cup. The mess kit was attached to the *Brotbeutel*, which was attached to the belt or combat harness. Each soldier was also issued a colorful butter container. Mine was orange. We stored all non-essential items in our *Tornisters* and left them behind when in combat.

We needed mess kits because when away from barracks, we would be served meals from a field kitchen (*Gulaschkanone*). In the morning, we'd be issued our bread ration for the day. *Kriegsbrot* (War Bread) or *Kommissbrot* (Army Bread), as it was known to us, was a dark, dense, multi-grain type of bread. When we actually did get to the field, we sometimes got scrambled eggs to eat with our bread. But mostly, it was eaten with cheese (*Käse*), jelly or preserves (*marmalade*) and perhaps hard sausage (*Dauerwurst*) for breakfast.

The hot coals in our horse-drawn *Gulaschkanone* were kept going all day. The main cooking containers sat in an oil bath, so our food was never burned. Stew or thick soup, called *Eintopf* (One Pot), which was served at noon, was normally the largest meal of the day. Seldom did we eat anything but *Eintopf*. The few times we got separate dishes of potatoes, meat, gravy and veggies, we felt as though we had attended a feast. The evening meal looked much like that of the morning, using the remainder of the bread issue, with perhaps the addition of soup (*Wehrmachts-Suppekonserve*). Somehow we always got coffee, not Tim Horton's or Starbuck's, but a brown brew made from roasted barley, acorns and horse chestnuts. But during training, we didn't have to worry about all that. We took all our meals in the mess hall.

This was what a standard field kitchen looked like

After we were issued all our equipment, the next order of business was to meticulously record every item we got in the *Soldbuch* we had received when we were mustered. The *Soldbuch* contained each soldier's details including a photo, name, rank, promotions, pay grade, clothing, equipment, next of kin, awards, medical information, and a history of unit assignments. We were to wear it in the breast pocket of our uniform on the left side. We were told that this booklet had to be produced on demand by any superior officer at any time, even on the battle field. And just to be double sure we kept track of what belonged to whom, they made us memorize the serial numbers of our weapons.

The following day, military training began in earnest. We had already learned many of the marching drill commands in *Deutches Jungfolk* and *Hitler Jugend*: *"Attention. Fall in. Fall out. Right face. About face. Forward march."* And because of our compulsory involvement in those organizations, most of us were in excellent physical shape. Now, we had to add combat training, field training, and weaponry into the mix. We learned how to properly position our rifle: *"Present, ARMS. Order, ARMS. Right shoulder, ARMS. Left shoulder, ARMS. Port, ARMS."*

The traditional German army salute consisted of an open hand, with the index finger touching the forehead, the same as for most armies in the world. Most of the officers in my battalion were long-time military professionals who had been trained to salute in the traditional manner. They didn't like the *"Heil Hitler"* salute because it took away from army tradition. They insisted that we use the old army salute when we were wearing our helmets.

This photo is from a unit in my battalion. It seems to have been taken at the time a command had been given regarding the position of the rifle. Often in the process of executing one of these orders, the container for our gas masks got out of position, which is so clearly portrayed in the picture.

Nothing was routine during our military training—not mealtime, sleep, hygiene, housekeeping or mess hall duty. Every exercise was geared to exact one and only one thing from us: total unquestioning obedience. We were trained to quickly and unflinchingly follow even the weirdest commands. We learned how to march and parade, how to handle and clean rifles, how to throw hand grenades, and how to operate machine guns. My group, who were all born in 1925, were perhaps the last soldiers to be trained under the old "Prussian Army discipline and training." Every command and every requirement was stringently regulated and enforced. Discipline was rigorous.

Normally, artillery soldiers went through 6 weeks of basic infantry training and a further 3 months of artillery training (as opposed to 4 months of infantry training for infantry troops). But the situation in the war meant that things were far from normal. Basic training was rushed due to the severe need for soldiers on the front. Those of us who were earmarked for artillery service went through the basic training, and then a mini crash-course artillery orientation, for which we were divided into two groups: *Fahrers* (Horse handlers) and *Kanoniers* (gunners).

Two weeks after reporting for service we were allowed to have visitors. My sister, Dora, came to see me. A couple of weeks later, we were marched to the station to board a freight train; destination unknown. We had been in training for less than a month.

The rest of the artillery trainees and I had orders to load our things into a box car. The car was fragrant with the smell of fresh straw. We piled all our gear on one side and left a large open space for ourselves on the other. I am not absolutely sure if the canons, horses, and handlers were with us on the train, or if we met up with them at our destination.

It was a beautiful sunny summer day, so we decided to keep the doors of the box car wide open. As the train pulled out, we could tell we were headed east. But we didn't know where we were going, nor did we know what we might encounter when we got there. I picked up a piece of straw to chew on. Then, I settled down on the edge of the open car next to the other guys. No one said much. Buried in our own thoughts, we dangled our legs out over the side and watched as the countryside passed by.

The train finally pulled onto a side track somewhere in Estonia, near Pleskau. I was glad it wasn't Russia. Apparently, our unit had been assigned to occupation duty rather than frontline combat. That was a relief. But for some reason, we had to unload the train in a hurry and rapidly march to an isolated brick building. We soon found out that it was due to the threat of being ambushed by guerrillas.

The first briefing for us newcomers stressed the fact that the building had no functioning toilets. We had to use an outside latrine. However, this posed a slight problem. At night, soldiers had been killed in the latrines by guerrillas under the cover of darkness. The Estonian guerrillas were trying to disrupt rail-lines and demoralize the German troops. They attacked whenever the opportunity presented itself, either in small groups or solo. We were warned not to go relieve ourselves without reporting to the guard station first. Every trip to the latrine at night required three soldiers: one to carry the toilet paper, one to carry a flashlight, and one to carry an automatic weapon to protect the others.

After our orientation, we met the new recruits who had arrived on earlier trains. There were probably about 150 of us all together. We were introduced to our superiors, who would also go into combat with us. Then we commenced what was known as "field training." Field training was combat training that involved live ammunition. Training was different here than it was at *Braunsberg*. Instead of fear and intimidation, the officers fostered comradeship and respect. We felt more like a team. It was drilled into us that in live combat, we would be dependent on one another for survival.

I was trained on the 75 mm *Leichtes Infanteriegeschütz* (Light Field Artillery) infantry support canon. It was a Howitzer-type gun that used large shells, which were about 18 inches long, 3 inches in diameter, and were pointed like bullets. The gun could be aimed in direct or indirect fire, and could theoretically fire 15 to 20 rounds per minute to a distance of about 4,000 yards. It was typically set up just behind a rifle company. The artillery crew was protected by an armored shield and advanced the gun by hand (and harness) for approach and final position.

A 75 mm Light Field Artillery Team

The gun in the photo seems to be positioned in the upper range for indirect fire, as the slit for the gun sight is not open. The thing dangling below the slit is the cover for the stubby muzzle. There's an eye on the axel of the wheel, to which we'd attach our pulling harnesses. These harnesses are visible in the photo on the Number 1, Number 3 and Number 4 gunners. Another eye was located at the back, beside the hand of Gunner Number 3, on the far right of the photo.

It took a crew of 6 soldiers to operate the 75 mm gun. The Number 1 Gunner wore a single triangle patch on the left arm of his uniform. It indicated that he had been trained in the use of the *Richtkreis*. Since I wore the triangle patch, it was my responsibility to direct the aim of the gun by looking through the sight and cranking the wheel to raise or lower the elevation, thereby fine-tuning the horizontal aim that had been set by the Number 3 gunner. In the photo, the Number 1 Gunner is the one without a helmet. The Number 1 gunners often took their helmets off, as the rims got in the way of looking through the sights.

The *Richtkreis* (gun sight) was a simplified theodolite instrument. It could be removed to mount on a tripod. In the photo, you can see a red and white striped pole stored on the spur of the artillery. There is a second one on the other side. They could emit a small slit of light for use during the night. If I was aiming the gun for an indirect shot, I had to pull the poles out and plant them in the ground in front of us at a prescribed distance. This established a baseline so that I could make the right adjustments to the direction of the barrel. When shooting indirectly, I couldn't see my target, but had to rely on a spotter to tell me how many degrees of adjustment I needed to make.

The Number 1 gunner directed the gun. Number 2 gunner operated the firing lever on my command, except during rapid firing, when everything was done as fast as possible and I had to adjust the aim whenever possible. Number 3 handled the ammunition, made a rough adjustment of the gun's position, and took care to secure it. Numbers 4, 5 and 6 were responsible to handle the ammunition, unload it from the *Protze* and prepare it for the different requirements or targets. They had their hands full when things got rough. They had to open the ammunition containers, prepare the charges going into the *Kartusche,* set the detonator on the grenade, and feed the ammunition to the Number 3 gunner. The *Kartusche* contained the propellant for the ammunition, and was ejected after firing.

The driver of the *Protze* would move it out of harm's way if possible, and come back with more ammunition. The weapon was pulled by the *Protze* when we had to move greater distances. The gun could also be broken down and split into six loads (a maximum of 165 pounds each) for transport in mountainous areas.

Our *Protzenfahrer's* (Horse Handler/Driver) name was Hans Soltek. He was a simple country guy, from the southeastern region of East Prussia, near the border. He was somewhat on the slow side, and couldn't read or write. But he was fantastic with horses! He loved them and fussed over them like they were his children. The last memory I have of Hans was from when we got hit with a barrage from a *Stalinorgel* (a multiple rocket launcher) while going through a bush as we changed position. He was kneeling beside his beloved horses and sobbing uncontrollably because two of them had been hit. He had to quickly cut them out of their harnesses so we could move on. This was probably in the early summer of 1944.

I don't have a clear picture of the faces of the other guys on my group and I can't remember their names. I won't say much more about the 75 mm field canon. If you search for "*Leichtes Infanriegeschütz*" on the internet, you can find some sites that show actual combat footage.

Days in Estonia passed with a combination of field training and occupation duties. Frequently we had to comb the nearby wilderness for guerrillas. We shot several of them down out of trees, where they hid in an attempt to ambush us. A few of the older guys, most of them Sergeants, went into town from time to time to befriend locals and hook up with some girls. We called it the "*Kattofelfreundschaft*" (Potato Friendship). The odd one was killed by guerillas and didn't make it back. Whether they were set up by the Estonian women, or were killed when they came across guerillas haphazardly, I can't say.

Our Company had been informed that it was on "stand-by." We had to be ready on short notice to re-enforce the troops in the battle that raged around Narwa, near the southern tip of Finland. Specifically, we were to replace the 227th Infantry Division (the Stern Division). The Soviets had launched an initiative to push the German Army back from the strategic Narwa Isthmus, so they could eliminate our forces in Estonia, and push through Latvia into East Prussia and Central Europe.

We never had much of a sense for how the war was going. We had no idea that the mighty Scharnhorst had sunk in December 1943, or that the Allies had begun a massive bombing campaign of Germany. We got mail, but it was censored. Bad news simply didn't get through.

While we waited for our marching orders, we were dispersed into the Estonian country side in small groups, to hunt down more guerrillas. Our group stayed at a small farm, where I tasted the best bacon I have ever eaten. I also experienced a typical sauna for that area: a sod hut with a built-in brick stove, which was fired from the outside. The inside of the stove was doused with water, which was extracted from wood barrels that stood near the door. The seats were arranged at different levels. It was so hot and steamy up on the highest seat that it took your breath away. To induce more sweating, you could beat your body with green bunches of birch branches, and then go outside and douse yourself with cold water, or roll in the snow.

Speaking of snow, we were issued skies for patrolling. But I was an ardent tree-hugger. I couldn't have gotten around on skis if my life depended on it. So I was quite happy when orders suddenly came to move further south. Some of the larger group remained with the 21st Division. My infantry crew was assigned to join the newly reorganized Heer 214th Division. "Heer," which phonetically sounds like the English word, "hair," is the German word for "army." The guys nicknamed the 214th division the "Herring" (as in pickled fish) division. That's because during the years leading up to the reorganization, two-thirds of the division had been stationed in Norway and Denmark, where army life was characterized by luxury and ease. Those "preserved" soldiers were ill prepared for the rigors of fighting on the Eastern Front.

Our unit's tactical sign was a cross on top of a globe situated over two waves. I'm about certain what it stood for. In any case, in April 1944, under the command of Generalleutnant Harry von Kirchbach and General Field Marshal Walter Model, the "Herring" Division was moved to the 4th Panzer Army XXXXII Corps of the Army Group North Ukraine, at Kovel, to fight against the Red Army's 1st Ukrainian Front. I was about to find out what front line combat was really like.

8 | THE HERRING DIVISION

Kovel was the city which was the north-western hub of the Ukrainian rail system, with six rail lines radiating outward from its center. It was of great strategic military importance because of its various westward leading road and rail connections. The Russians had surrounded the German-occupied city, and our unit was being sent in to help push them back.

The military train dropped us off south of Kovel, in the Pripyat Marshes; infamous as the location of the modern-day Chernobyl disaster. The Pripyat Marshes are a forested, swampy area with numerous bogs, lakes, waterways, and canals. The terrain was difficult. It was impossible to use field artillery there—not only due to the brush and trees, but mostly because the heavy equipment would have gotten stuck in the mud, as our boots often did. The ground was so soft and the water table so high, that every incoming explosion created a crater that quickly filled up and became a small pool. It would have been futile to try to dig in and establish underground shelters or bunkers, so we set up a log house as our base. Since we weren't able to use field canons, we gunners were ordered to join the infantry soldiers in combat.

It took a long and concerted effort to make any progress. Every forward movement was met with heavy resistance from the Russians. The fighting was fierce. It was my first time in active combat, and the only time my unit was exposed to explosive rifle and machinegun ammunition. That type of ammo was outlawed by the Geneva Convention, but the Russians ignored those stipulations and used it whenever it suited them.

The incendiary bullets were designed to detonate. Instead of cleanly piercing flesh, they exploded upon contact and ripped their victims apart. The casualties were high and the wounds horrendous. The deafening gunfire . . . the screams . . . the wounds . . . the blood—the images are too horrible and unspeakable to even mention.

It was in that first battle, I think, that I turned my emotions off. *Shoot. Take cover. Reload. Survive.* That was all I could do. I couldn't allow myself to feel anything. No horror. No pain. No compassion. No mercy. I was just 18 years old, and whether I liked it or not, I was a soldier. I had to follow orders. Do or die. Kill or be killed.

Over the next several weeks, with the Luftwaffe Focke-Wolf bombing and strafing the enemy lines, we were able to slowly advance and push the Russians back about 10 kilometers east of Kovel. The heavy casualties continued. The medics laid the corpses along the side of the road to be collected and buried. There were so many of them. They were lined up side by side like sardines in the Königsberg fish market. The bottom half of their aluminum ID tags had been snapped off, so telegrams could be sent back home to inform waiting mothers.

We were still in the Pripyat Marsh region, but the brush wasn't as thick and the ground wasn't as swampy as on the other side of Kovel, so we were finally able to set up tents and establish a camp. The officers seized the opportunity to do some training. They assembled us to demonstrate how to use a *Panzerfaust 30* (tank fist)—a one-shot, disposable, pre-loaded anti-tank rocket that could be operated by a single soldier. To use it, we had to take off the safety, aim, and, with a little squeeze, fire the projectile.

We sat around in a circle on the ground, listening to the instructions. Obviously the guy demonstrating the launcher didn't know how to use it properly, and didn't heed the warning written in large red letters on the upper rear end of the tube, *Achtung! Feuerstrahl!* (Warning! Backblast!) When he accidently discharged the weapon, the projectile killed one soldier sitting in front, and the exhaust severely burned several others behind. One of the guys had all the skin burned off his face. It was not a great morale booster, to say the least.

Better terrain allowed us to establish a more favorable frontline. We set up on a small bluff whose elevation provided better sightlines and a slight tactical advantage over the enemy. Here, we began to get a sense for just how formidable their forces really were. The Russian infantry attacked in multiple waves. We mowed down the first couple of waves with little effort. But like a swarm of insects, the waves of Russians just kept coming and coming. I noticed that the subsequent lines didn't even have weapons. As they ran toward us, they picked up guns from their wounded and fallen. Some made it through to our line with upstretched arms and were taken prisoner. Though they were poorly equipped, it was obvious they greatly outnumbered us. It was all we could do to hold them back.

After weeks of heavy combat, we were bone weary. Our lines seemed to be holding, but just barely. The officers could tell that we needed a break, so they ordered a rest period from the front lines and provided some booze for revelry. The down time lasted less than a day. Early the next morning, someone burst into our camp shouting: *"Die Russen kommen, zurück, zurück!"* (The Russians are coming, retreat, retreat!) The Italian forces south of us had pulled back and Russian forces had broken through. We were roused from drunken slumber, having celebrated the reprieve a little bit too much and too long. Instinctively I scooped up my gear and made it out of the tent. On leaden feet and muttering: *"Die Russen kommen"* again and again, I took a few steps in one direction, just to go back again, not able to think clearly. Then I saw our driver come up with the gun hitched to the *Protze*.

He did not stop for any of us to clamber up to our usual seats but motioned us to fall in behind. I grabbed a hold at the top rim of the gun's shield and stumbled along. When I saw some guys donning their helmets, I began looking for mine until someone pointed to the helmet on the muzzle of the gun. I was told that I had placed it there in the evening, saying that some idiot had failed to cover the muzzle. We sobered up fast. There was no time to dwell on the stupid things done 'under the influence'.

I was horrified that my carelessness might have resulted in capture. The Russians were known for their brutality. Being taken as a Russian prisoner of war and subjected to their inhumane treatment was out of the question. It was a fate worse than death. As I ran, I strapped on my gear and eyed the grenade hanging on my belt. I would never raise my hands in surrender to the Russians. I'd use the grenade to blow myself up first. Refusing capture was the only decision that I controlled. I vowed I'd never let my guard down like that again. That night was the only time in the war—and the only time in my life—I was ever drunk. Even as I write this, the feeling of bewilderment and disorientation comes back, as if it was yesterday.

I don't remember how long it took before we regrouped and settled into a more routine situation, if there is such a thing on the battlefields. But there would be no more advancing. We were now under orders to systematically retreat.

In the process of our stage-by-stage retreat, we lost some horses in a rocket barrage. Another time, a trigger happy or very nervous German soldier threw a hand grenade that exploded behind us, wounding a buddy of mine. He had lots of shrapnel in his back and was bleeding profusely. I couldn't leave him there for the advancing Russians, so I slung him over my shoulders and raced through a burning village to the nearest first aid post. The entire village was an inferno. It was set aflame as we retreated—probably in emulation of Stalin's scorched earth policy, and to slow down the Russian advance.

When we reached the Panzer position, we dug in. As usual, our commanders ordered us to keep our eyes open for spies that were coming back with military intelligence. But apparently, the spies didn't pick up enough information to accurately predict the enemy's plan. According to historians, Hitler expected the Russians to direct the *Schwerpunkt* (heavy point) of their attack north of Kovel. In anticipation, he had sent reinforcements from our area up north. It was an unfortunate miscalculation. The Soviets planned to attack south of Kovel, at the juncture between the Heeresgruppe Mitte and our division.

Soviet records indicate that by early July, the Soviet 1st Ukrainian Front had amassed over 1.2 million men, 2,200 tanks and 2,806 aircraft. By contrast, the opposing German formations comprised 600,000 men, 900 tanks and 700 aircraft. Thus, according to Soviet reconnaissance, their forces greatly exceeded ours. A concerted offensive effort would almost certainly succeed.

The offensive began at 3:45 am on July 13 with a tremendous artillery bombardment. The infamous Katyusha led the chorus. We called them *Stalinorgel*—Stalin's Organs—because the racks of rockets resembled the pipes of a massive church organ and made loud howls as they were released. The sound was ominous and spine chilling. Compared to other artillery, these multiple rocket launchers delivered devastating quantities of explosives to a target area in a short amount of time. They weren't extremely accurate—but they didn't need to be. The sheer volume of missiles and the barrage of flying shrapnel and debris ensured widespread destruction.

The Russian *Kaffeemühle* (coffee grinder) light aircraft joined in the attack, adding the ratchety sound of their 100 horsepower engines and a rainfall of shells to the howling refrain. The attack went on for hours and hours, filling the night sky with arcs of light, ear splitting explosions, screams, and terrible carnage.

I was glad I was with my gunning team, manning the light field artillery, and not in the front line, surrounded by the dead and the maimed. As day broke, the incessant howls gave way to more traditional combat sounds . . . the rumble of tanks, the whistle of anti-tank missiles, the rat-tat-tat of machine gun fire, and rifle shots of the advancing assault infantry. Wave after wave after wave of infantry attacked. No matter how many we killed, more came.

It was some of the heaviest fighting of the war. Sleep was out of the question. One day stretched into the next. Survivors later stated that they had never seen such concentrations of men, tanks, artillery, and aircraft. Though much of it was a blur, some vivid snapshots remain in my mind. I remember a Russian soldier trying to exit the turret of a tank that had been blown up – falling down to the ground as the explosion engulfed him. I remember the panic of trying to free our equipment after being stuck in the mud. The vivid images of men being blown to pieces are ones I have tried to forget.

Three or four days after the Russians hit us with their *Schwerpunkt*, we were overrun by Russian tanks and our division collapsed and fell into disarray. Instead of an orderly, systematic retreat, pandemonium ensued.

Several of us were separated from our unit and jogged together in the direction of the retreating Panzers, trying to catch up. The military term for dispersed soldiers was *Versprengter*, which literally means sprung loose. When we crested a hill, a German officer came running towards us, waving his pistol, shouting at us to stop our retreat. A soldier behind me snidely retorted, "*Du hast wohl Halsschmerzen!*" and shot him dead.

Literally the phrase is translated, *"You surely have an aching neck (throat)!"* It was a well-known derogatory saying that inferred someone was doing something incredibly stupid merely for the sake of recognition; in hope of being awarded a *Ritterkreutz* medal to hang around his neck.

I had just witnessed the murder of an officer. And it barely fazed me. *Kettenhunde* (Chain Dogs) had the authority to shoot a soldier on the spot if they suspected him of leaving the front lines. But the officer wasn't wearing the characteristic eagle, swastika, and left arm band of the Military Police on his uniform and helmet. Besides, we had no intention of defecting and leaving the front line—there was simply no front line to return to. To turn back would have meant certain death or capture.

I don't know when or how I caught up with my unit, but I remember being stopped by a group of *Kettenhunde* who were, in fact, organizing a group of stragglers to send back into combat. Thankfully, I spotted one of our motorized 150 mm guns nearby, beside a row of trees. The military police had stopped them too. I hurried over to clamber on the truck just as the driver gunned the engine to take off. It was akin to suicide to be forced into those groups of last resistance.

Somehow we found what was left of our Company and re-organized just outside of a small village. That evening, someone went to a farm house and came back with a pot of soured milk—a common summertime drink. It made me think back to the time when the nurses in Königsberg force-fed me milk to help me beat diphtheria. That's what led to my milk aversion. My army buddies gulped down the sour milk while I cringed. We were huddled against a clump of bushes. Only a few stars glimmered in the sky. There were trees overhead. As I glanced up, I noticed small red berries hanging beneath the leaves. *Were those cherries? Yes, they were!* I popped several in my mouth and savored their fresh sweetness. It was a taste of goodness and normalcy, defying the death and insanity that pressed in and threatened to overcome us. It's funny the things a person remembers. More than sixty years have passed, and I still remember those cherries.

When daylight broke, we took up position near an area controlled by an enemy anti-tank gun. The rapid, high velocity weapon was stationed up in the bell tower of a church. The Russians shot at everything in sight. We were ordered to get our gun ready, pull out from the bush, and take the Russian gun out. The trouble was we had to pull our gun into position, adjust the calibration, and fire in clear view of the Russians—who already had their gun aimed in our direction. It was ludicrous to think we could get off a shot before they did. Such was the insanity and arrogance of poorly trained young officers. It was a stupid order, but we had to obey. We pulled out from behind the bushes . . . and as anticipated, a shell exploded overhead before we even had our gun ready to fire.

I felt a thud on my leg. The gunner behind me dove for cover, badly wounded. My team and I managed to pull back into the bushes before I collapsed. A piece of shrapnel had hit me below the left knee and my boot was rapidly filling with blood. My buddies quickly loaded me on a one-horse buggy stationed nearby. It carted me away on the very road controlled by the gun we had been ordered to take out. The driver dodged his way through artillery fire to a busy and chaotic field hospital, where I received a tetanus shot, had a tag with the letter "T" hung around my neck, and was immediately loaded into a departing Red Cross hospital train.

I was one of the lucky ones. Historians recount that eighty percent of German soldiers didn't make it out of the Battle of Kovel. Most were killed in the fight. The remaining wounded were finished off by the Russians. The able-bodied were captured and sent to Russian concentration camps—few returned. Only about twelve thousand men escaped—most through the town of Biliyi Kamin, on the northern bank of the Bug River. It was the only door the German army managed to hold open for units and stragglers to escape to the south.

By the evening of July 21, Biliyi Kamin was in flames and Soviet infantry were advancing like a swarm of bees. The air was full of the thunder of advancing Russian tanks. It's said that there were so many things bombed out and burning that the smoke—coupled with the dust thrown up by exploding Soviet bombs and shells—blotted out the sun.

The Red Cross train clattered its way west across Poland and Germany. In those specialized hospital trains, passenger railway cars were emptied out and fitted with cots stacked three-high and end-to-end lengthwise down each side. This maximized the number of wounded that could be transported. I was only vaguely aware of what was going on. But I must have been in a middle cot, because I could look out the window at the countryside as it zipped by. It crossed my mind that I had never travelled this way before, and that this would be my first visit to the Reich. I wished I were lucid enough to stay alert and pay more attention to the scenery, but I was exhausted from months on the battlefield. I slipped in and out of consciousness and slept most of the time, relieved to leave the battlefield.

The train stopped at numerous stations along the way and made several unscheduled stops due to air attacks, strafing and bombings. Some of the more severely wounded were unloaded early on—presumably in order to get them to civilian hospitals to give them the best chance of survival. Soldiers who had received adequate medical attention and who were ambulatory, could get off at any station to return home and recover on convalescent leave. Those of us who needed additional medical attention remained on the train.

At one train station, I was taken aback by a strange sight. On the platform outside of my window, soldiers of the German Army were saluting with outstretched arms! Apparently, Hitler had ordered the abolition of the old military salute, to be replaced by the *Heil Hitler* salute as a sign of total allegiance. I later learned that he did so because some Army officers had tried to assassinate him. The attempt, dubbed "Operation Valkyrie," failed miserably.

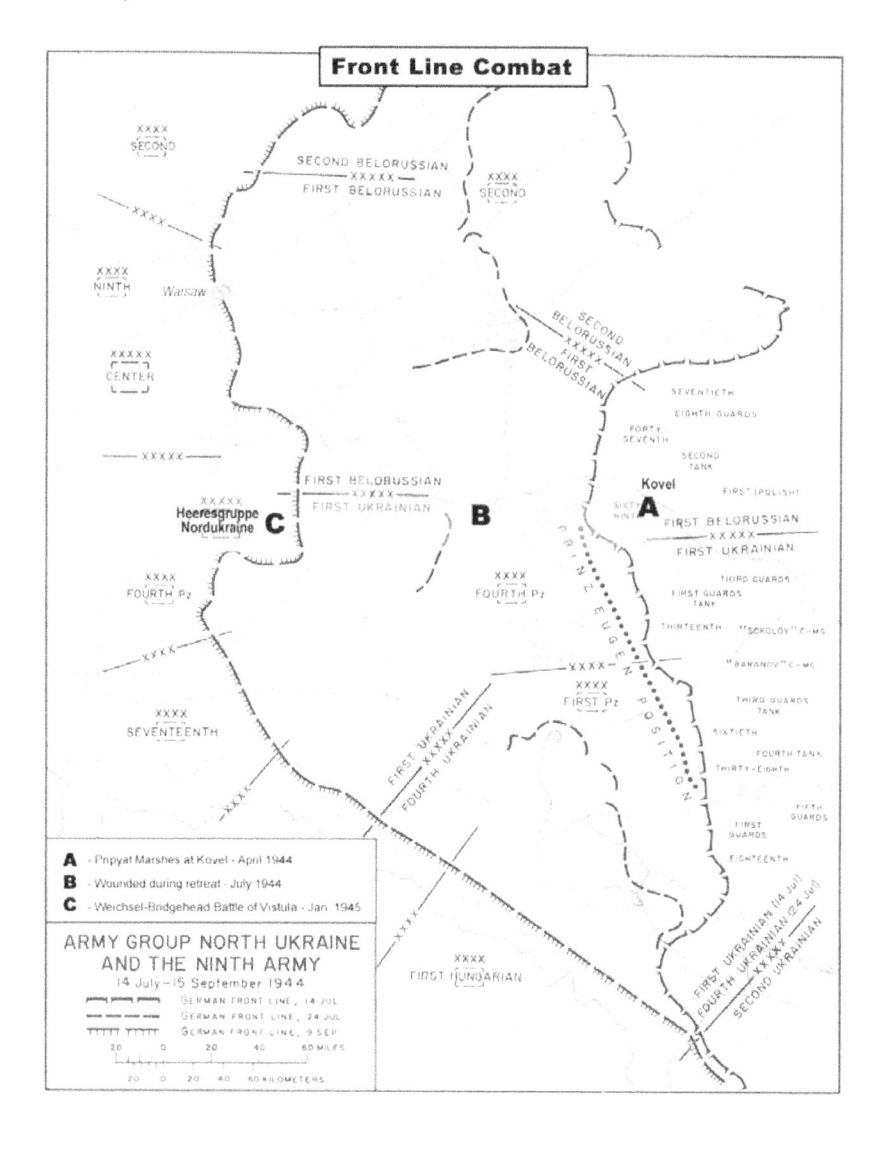

I don't recall how long it took to cross Germany and reach Bremen, the final stop. The trip took far longer than it normally would have, due to all the stops and interruptions along the way. I only knew where I had landed when I was placed on the ramp of the train station and could read the sign.

Like Königsberg, Bremen was a port city, and an important commercial, industrial, historic, and cultural center. From news reports early on in the war, I was aware that Britain's Air Force had repeatedly bombed the city, and had even "carpet bombed" it with a thousand airplanes during the Allied *Thousand Bomber Campaign*.

I wasn't in very good shape when they carted me and the remaining patients off the train to *Saint Joseph Stifts Hospital* and its adjoining concrete bomb shelter. Dark, caked blood stained my uniform. I was unkempt after weeks of combat. I'm certain I didn't smell very nice. Though there were nurses on the train, they were kept busy looking after the more severely wounded and preparing for unloading the next batch of wounded at the next station. Having had no treatment, other than the tetanus shot I got at the field hospital several days earlier, my wound hadn't been cleaned and was probably beginning to fester.

The doctors got to me as soon as they could, given the overwhelming number of patients waiting for treatment. They surgically removed the shrapnel embedded in the bone, and immobilized my leg in a thick white cast. They cut a square window in the heavy plaster, from which a drainage tube protruded, dripping yellowish-crimson discharge from the wound. After the operation, I continued to fade in and out of consciousness for several days.

When I was finally able to take note of my surroundings, I became aware of the frequent blasts of the air raid sirens. Hardly a day went by without them sounding off. Sometimes the incessant howls were followed by the single, long, *all clear* signal. But more often than not, the siren was joined by the drone of airplane engines, the whistle and explosions of falling bombs, and the crash of crumbling buildings—sometimes distant and sometimes nearby—until silence fell and the *all clear* sounded again. Some nights the air raid sirens went off several times and blared for hours. Being wounded, we couldn't evacuate to a bomb shelter for safety. We waited each air raid out, wondering whether the hospital would be hit next.

At one time I shared the room with a lower ranking officer in the SS. I was shocked by his accounts of how he "dealt with" Russian and Polish civilians, and how he had tortured prisoners in his keeping. What had circulated amongst us soldiers as unbelievable rumors about such conduct by Hitler's elite became undeniable reality!

It was in early September, after a bombardment with an explosion in the yard of the hospital that shook the building so much that the beds moved around, that I learned of the destruction of my home town. Apparently, the British had repeatedly carpet-bombed Königsberg at the end of August, dropping a thousand tons of high explosive fire bombs and incendiaries on its historic center. My heart froze. *Had Mom been injured? Had she even survived? What about Dora and Dad? Where were they? Were they alive?* My mind raced through all the potential scenarios. If I could have, I would have set out immediately to find them. But I was still immobilized, so I just lay there, feeling helpless and hopeless . . . *It would take a miracle for all of us to come out of this war alive!*

Several weeks later, an influx of wounded soldiers from the *Battle of Arnheim* in Holland crowded the ward. They provided a glimmer of good news, which by that time in the war was extremely scarce. Apparently, they had fought back advancing British forces and secured a decisive victory. As more and more wounded arrived, creating a demand for every possible hospital bed, I got a bit more good news. The doctor cut me out of the cast and pronounced that I was well enough to go home on convalescent leave. *I could go home!* My leg looked pitiful. The skin was pasty and inflamed, and the muscle was wasted away after weeks in a cast. The ugly deep red hole beneath my knee hadn't completely filled in yet. There must have been some nerve damage from the shrapnel too, because the inside of my calf lacked sensation. But even though the leg was useless for walking, I could make my way around on crutches well enough. I had been away from Königsberg for just over a year. It felt much longer. I was anxious to make my way back to learn of my family's fate.

I don't remember anything about the trip or the exact timing of it, though it must have been about the beginning of October. But I do vividly remember my arrival at Kaiser Wilhelm Plaza in the heart of the city. The memory still stirs up overwhelming feelings of horror and loss. I had seen a lot of destruction on the battlefield, in Bremen, and along the way, but this was worse, far worse.

I stood there for a long while, stunned with utter shock and disbelief. Everything was burned out and in ruins. The air was filled with the foul stench of explosives, dirt, dust, oil, fire, and death. I felt numb, devastated, hopeless, overwhelmed.

The once majestic cathedral was reduced to a scorched shell. The crumbled tower of the Castle formed a jagged black silhouette against the sky. No trees or vegetation remained. My school, the University, the shipping quarter, the Fish Market . . . all had been utterly destroyed. It was simply gone. Everywhere, beautiful historic buildings had been turned into tragic piles of charred rubble. There were no fisher women plying their wares. No men with long grappling hooks propelling barges from bollard to bollard. Even bollards had burned down to the waterline. No button man collecting and selling rags. No lovers feeding swans at the Schloss pond. No boys racing down the steps by the Holzbrüke to sneak a quick dip in the Pregel. No first graders skipping home with colorful *Ranzen* on their backs.

Königsberg, as I knew it, was dead. Its heart had stopped beating. The place was utterly ruined and desolate.

I tried to push down the huge lump of panic that was growing in my chest and rising into my throat. How could anyone have survived such a brutal attack?

I hobbled over to the Altstädtische Langasse Street to go in the direction of our apartment. It was hopeless. The road was impassable. It was filled with craters and mountains of debris. The bridges of Königsberg no longer functioned. The districts of Altstadt, Löbenict, and Kneiphof were decimated. The warehouses were gone. Uncle Paul's house was gone.

Jagged Ruins of the Königsberg Castle

A lone passerby just shook his head sadly when I asked about the Lomse. I sat down on a large pile of rubble that until a few short weeks ago had formed the walls of my high school, trying to collect my thoughts and to grasp the fact that I was now homeless. The life I knew had irrevocably disappeared. Everything was gone. Bombed. Incinerated. Obliterated. I was too stunned to cry. It was simply too much to take in.

Numb and desperate, I began to hobble around, inquiring about my mother. I don't remember how or when I found out where her employer lived. Apparently, he had an apartment in Maraunenhoff, on the edge of the city.

The outlying areas were not as badly damaged as the core. The roads had been cleared, the streetcars were running, and there were a few more signs of life. Maraunenhoff, in the northeast part of the city, hadn't sustained any damage at all. But even so, a deep, inconsolable grief hung dark and grey in the air. Mom's boss and his family had a spacious second-floor flat in that neighborhood, with a wrought-iron-railed balcony overlooking the street. I maneuvered my crutches up the steps and hesitantly knocked. A woman answered. It took a long moment for it to sink in that it was my mother. She was alive!

The reunion was bittersweet. Both of us were in shock at everything that had transpired since I left. I learned that Dora, who was now 17 years old, was assigned to an anti-aircraft unit stationed outside of Königsberg. Thankfully, she had survived the Allied attacks. Dad was stationed in a military supply compound in town. It had not been hit. Only a few of the industrial areas and harbor installations had been bombed. Residential areas were the hardest hit during the campaign. It appeared that the Allied forces wanted to wipe out the German population, but preserve the industries for the advancing Russians. Nearly half of Königsberg's housing was destroyed. The warehouse district, where mom's employer's business was located, was also decimated. Due to this, and the constant air raids and impending Russian invasion, he and his family had decided to flee. He told Mom that she could live in their flat for as long as she wished.

In a trembling voice, Mom described her long night of terror. Our neighborhood had been blown to bits and engulfed in flames when the firebombs started to fall. The RAF dropped a mixture of bombs and massive oil bombs to start fires, and high explosives to feed and ventilate the flames. There was nowhere to hide from the inferno. Mom bolted from our apartment down the street, dodging her way through the crumbling buildings, exploding incendiaries, fires, and deafening chaos, to dive into the river. Many friends and neighbors were crushed and incinerated attempting to do the same thing. Even those who managed to make it into the water of the Pregel weren't safe. Hundreds who had escaped the initial onslaught burned alive in the water when a thick layer of oil, released by sunken and damaged ships, ignited. The firestorm was so severe that metal bridges melted and buckled into the river. Wave after wave of British bombers continued to rain destruction down on the heart of Königsberg until it was crushed and scorched, and no beauty or life remained in her. The city burned for days. Incredibly, unbelievably, Mom survived sitting in water for several days, submerged up to her chin.

I couldn't bring myself to tell her what I had gone through on the Eastern Front. I was still alive. My family was still alive. That was all that mattered.

Mom got word to Dad that I had come back to convalesce. He managed to get leave for a day to come see us. We didn't talk much. I think we were all in shock. It was impossible to put the horrors of the war and our feelings of bewilderment and uncertainty into words. What was there to talk about? It's not as if we wanted to relive or share our nightmarish experiences. Miraculously, we were all still alive, but the war wasn't over. More horrors were certain to come. I would have to return to the front. Königsberg would be overrun by the Russians. Mom would have to flee. Dora's antiaircraft station and Dad's military supply compound were prime targets for air raids. Our chances of survival were extremely slim. In light of the general situation, we agreed to make Dad's birthplace our place of refuge. Somehow, Dad got the information to Dora. If any of us survived the war, we would meet up at my Uncle's home in Hermansfeld.

As I regained strength and became more agile on crutches, I ventured out a few times to catch a film at a movie house. I also rode the streetcars, to check out all my old routes. Some streets were impassable. The streetcars were halted by craters, piles of rubble, or damaged lines. Other routes had been discontinued for lack of passengers. Many of the residential areas were no longer habitable. It was eerie traversing the broken city. I didn't meet anyone I knew. No old neighbors. No old schoolmates. No old *Jüngfolk* members. No old teachers. No one. The few people riding the street cars were grim and sullen. The hustle and bustle of Königsberg had been silenced. Only a quarter of the population remained.

After about six weeks, my convalescent leave came to an end. By then, I didn't need crutches and managed with the help of a cane. I had orders to meet up with other recuperated soldiers in Siegen, a city about 120 kilometers northeast of Frankfurt/Main, to be shipped back to our units. Resigned to my fate of returning to the Eastern Front, I said good bye to Mother, and hopped on the train.

Travel in Germany was getting quite chaotic, to say the least. I don't remember how many times the trip was interrupted by bomb raids or strafing by fighter planes. Whenever enemy planes attacked, the train screeched to a halt and we all jumped out of the cars to crawl underneath for shelter. We stayed there, plugging our ears to the sound of the droning engines and explosions, hoping we wouldn't be hit. Train connections and routes constantly changed due to unpredictable schedules, damaged trains and tracks. What's more, every delay or change in route had to be documented and verified by the military police at the next stop. It took me a long time just to make it to Berlin, where the bombings had turned most of the buildings along the route into hollow shells or mounds of rock.

When I took the underground train through Berlin, I was astonished to see throngs of people living in the tunnels. They sat on suitcases, stretched out under blankets, tended crying children, and huddled in corners trying to keep warm and remain safe from the frequent air raids. Their faces registered shock, bewilderment, and deep sadness. No doubt most of their homes had been destroyed. I thought of Königsberg, and wondered if the goal of the Allies was to keep bombing civilians until every German was homeless.

The next leg of the trip was even worse. Attacks were more frequent, schedules only tentative, and progress extremely slow. It was obvious that the army was also falling into a state of chaos. Somehow I had to report to Hanau, but at the train station post, was directed to Siegen. When I finally reported to the barracks in Siegen, I was ordered to go help out at an observation post on the outskirts of town. There, I spent a few nights scouring the sky for enemy parachutes. It was not the threat of an invasion, which prompted the round the clock watches; not paratroopers, but enemy airmen who had to jump from damaged planes, we were on watch for. We were to take them into protective custody, shield them from the wrath of civilians. Apparently some enemy aviators had made it to the ground to be assaulted, even killed by angry civilians, hostile over the loss of their homes or loved ones.

Someone came to give me orders to report to Giessen, a city southeast of Siegen. I dutifully reported to the military police at the train station in Giessen to get the requisite stamp of verification in my *Laufzettel,(checklist)*. I was given the address of the barracks, and pointed in the general direction. I had quite the time finding it. Here, too, bombs had taken out a lot of houses and not many people were on the streets to ask for direction. When I finally reached the barracks, I was immediately ordered to double back as the unit was no longer there. It had been moved to Frankfurt/Main. So I obtained the necessary documentation, and returned to the train station to check for a possible connection.

I didn't mind the mix up and delays. I must admit that I wasn't in a hurry to get back to active duty. There was food available at Red Cross stations or military kitchens near every train station. And there was far less chance of getting killed here than on the Eastern Front. But I couldn't dawdle too much getting to my assigned destination. The *Kettenhunde* were everywhere—and they didn't hesitate to shoot or hang any soldier suspected of desertion. They often hung the body of suspected deserters from makeshift gallows with the sign "traitor" or "coward" hung around their necks. The public display was a stark reminder of what happened to anyone who refused to support Hitler's senseless war.

There was some semblance of order when I arrived at the barracks at Frankfurt/Main, where I joined the soldiers waiting for their orders. We spent most of our days sleeping. Nights, we hunkered down in a basement shelter waiting for the inevitable bomb raids. Falling bombs shook the earth while plaster and dust from the ceiling rained on our heads. After the air raid sirens sounded the all clear, we ran into the city to search for and rescue civilians.

We clawed through the rubble of collapsed buildings with our bare hands, carrying the wounded and dead to be where they could be taken to a hospital or morgue from. It was horrible having to deal with the battered and broken bodies of women and children.

A small group of us were outfitted for combat and sent to a freight yard to board a transport train. I never thought I'd be grateful to be sent back to the front. But anything was better than helplessly sitting in the shelter every night waiting for the room to collapse, remembering the previous night's horrors, and wondering if the next bloodied corpse pulled from rubble might be mine. I think all the guys were relieved. After what we had seen, we felt we would rather die fighting than trapped under fallen buildings.

As always, the freight car had a layer of straw for bedding on one half of the floor, and room for our gear on the other half. As the train headed back east, it often stopped and backed up onto a switch to hitch up with more freight cars and engines. Sometimes we waited on a side track for several hours or a day for another train to arrive and take us to the next stop. We were the only car ferried around and felt like unwanted goods. Just who determined our movement seemed a mystery.

We arrived at a small station and spent Christmas day waiting on a switch in the tracks. A few of us seized the opportunity to hop off the train to check out a couple of nearby farmhouses in hopes of getting some food. I don't remember if we had any luck. That Christmas and the next are to this day the bleakest and most devoid of hope in my entire life. Without fail, every Christmas since, the picture of that drab train station with the Red Cross service comes to mind, almost to a point that I can taste the brew we called coffee in those days. After a few more switches and several air attacks, the train got fairly close to the front lines, and we were dropped off to hike the rest of the way. We arrived at the Weichsel bridgehead on New Year's Eve 1944.

I walked around the camp searching for familiar faces. Of all the guys that went into battle with me at Kovel, I recognized only one. I was shaken. A lone, lower ranking officer appeared to be the only man in my unit that had made it from Kovel to the Weichsel without being injured, killed or captured! The rest were new recruits . . . sixteen and seventeen olds. They were just kids! I was incredulous. At the ripe old age of nineteen, I was one of the "*Alte Hasen*" or "Old Hares" of the 214th Infantry. (Slang for military veterans who'd survived front-line combat.)

I spent the opening days of 1945 getting oriented and then was sent out to scout enemy activity at our advanced observation point with a communication specialist. They were called *Funkers*. Prior to my injury the Wehrmacht had used field telephones. In those days, the *Funkers* were responsible for stringing and maintaining the telephone lines, spools of which were strung across the ground and spliced to extend their reach or when damaged. That happened quite frequently, and *Funkers* often lost their lives trying to maintain communication. I'm sure they were relieved when the "*Bertha Geräte*" came into use. It was a portable communication unit which could be carried on the *Funker's* back. But they were not for voice communication in general, as the transmissions could be picked up by the enemy. They were slow and cumbersome to use since we had to code and decode all communications. By the time I got back to the front after convalescent leave, the technology had advanced to the point that wired field

We Will Be Free

telephones were no longer in use. *The Funkers* used radio communication instead.

We were dug in on the west side of the river Weichsel with a clear view of the river and the activities on the other side. That's where the Russian front was situated, barely within range of our guns. Our repeated appeals for heavy artillery support went unheeded. We had received some strange orders from our high command. We were to fire at Allied air planes with our guns—a near impossible task, given the limitations of our equipment. Though an observer plane would circle above us once in a while, we knew better than to fire at them.

We could see the steady build-up of weaponry and tanks on the other side of the river. The fresh churned-up soil where tanks had gone into position formed a jagged black scar across the white of the winter landscape. We watched with dread as more and more infantry amassed. It was obvious the Russians were preparing for a massive assault. It was also obvious that we were severely outnumbered.

Historians report that we only had 569,000 men against their 1.5 million, 700 tanks against their 3,300, and 1,300 aircraft against their 10,000. Though we were severely outnumbered and outgunned, we had orders to stand our ground. All we could do is wait for the inevitable.

In the early morning hours of January 13, 1945, all hell broke loose.

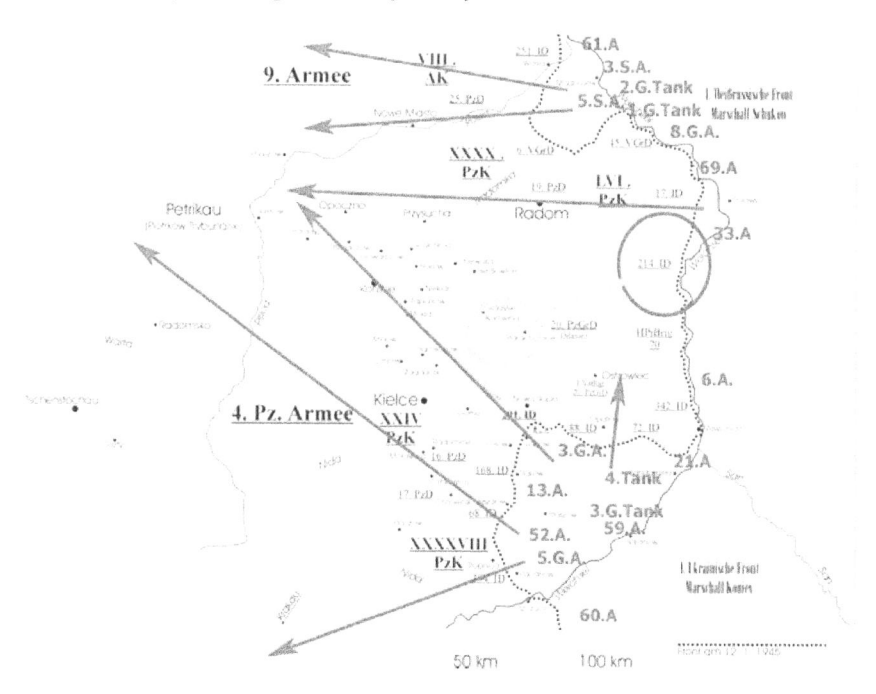

The Herring Division

The attack started with an intense barrage of artillery and rockets. The shrieking, deafening explosions went on for hours. Then, the Russians rolled their tanks across hastily built bridges. Though our battered troops fought desperately, we were able to put up little resistance. They overran us and the front collapsed all around me. In less than a day, the Russian offensive completely broke through our front, decimated the 4th Panzer army, and obliterated the 214th Infantry Division, which they'd surrounded in a trapped pocket ("*Kessel*") near *Starachowice*. Only a small fraction of the troops were able to retreat to Silesia. The large circle on the map shows our position at the Weichsel bridgehead. The smaller circle indicates the positon to which we were ordered to retreat. The arrows indicate how we were surrounded and overrun by Russian forces.

As the Russians overran us, I was separated from the rest of my division and caught behind enemy lines. I became a *"Versprenger"*—a loner who was separated from his unit in combat. I have not met anyone from the entire Division since.

Somehow, I would have to get back to the German front alone. I hid until I could move under the cover of darkness. A few times over the next few days, I attached myself to other groups of retreating soldiers or joined one of the endless treks of fleeing civilians. While walking with one such group, I became aware of the familiar sound of tanks rumbling up the road behind us. Thankfully I wasn't at the back of the group and had time to react. With my heart pounding in my ears, I ran for the forest. Moments later, the tanks overran the civilians and mowed down anyone and anything that failed to get out of the way—driving right over top of them. I lay down and tried to camouflage myself with brush and snow amongst the trees, and waited it out while the Russians passed by. I decided to travel mostly by night from then on.

Having witnessed a few instances when lone German soldiers had fallen into the hands of Poles or Russians, I desperately wanted to avoid any such encounters. I vowed again that I would use suicide to avoid capture and torture. I kept the grenades handy and slept with my rifle cradled in my arms. For extra measure, I picked up a handgun from a body beside the road and tucked it into my belt. I wasn't supposed to have any unauthorized weapons, but I didn't care. Better to risk a tongue-lashing from a German officer or '*Kettenhund*' than being captured by the enemy.

I can't remember the exact sequence of events during my lone trek back to the German front. My memories are more like isolated snap shots amidst the blur of those weeks. One night, I spotted some German Army vehicles at a farm complex. As I crept closer, I heard boisterous German voices coming from the farm house. I knocked, and found a small group of soldiers making merry, oblivious to the Russian advance. I asked them if I could settle in the house for the night—for some warmth, shelter, and rest—but they wouldn't let me in. Irritated at their lack of hospitality, I made my way to a nearby barn. Little did I know that their rude behavior would later save my life.

The barn was filled with pigs. I chased a sow out of the first pen and forced her out into the aisle. I blocked off the way with a bale of straw, piled up some loose straw for a bed, and settled in for the night. During the night I was startled awake when the door to the barn flung open. Silhouetted by the flames of the burning farmhouse behind, I saw the unmistakable outline of a Russian soldier. I glanced up and saw that there was a small window above the pig trough beside my bed. I jumped through the window, crashing the glass and taking the frame out with me. I ran across the snow covered field with bullets whizzing past. The soldier must have checked for more people in the barn, or was hampered by the sow, because I had gained some distance before the shooting started.

The noise of artillery was just a distant rumble one night, when I came to an isolated farm off the beaten track. Freezing cold, I decided to cautiously enter. An old Polish couple sat at the kitchen table. They were startled and undoubtedly frightened to have this unexpected visitor in their home. They spoke no German, but offered me a bowl of soup, which I gratefully wolfed down. I could sense their unease when they hastily took me to the barn to bed down for the night. It was the first warm food I had had since the day before the Russian offence, and was the only one for a long time to come.

Having written down this account, I lay awake last night, trying to remember what I actually did eat along the way. I really can't say for sure, but there was so much discarded stuff that fleeing civilians left behind along the road—like luggage, backpacks, and carts—that scraps of food were generally available. The only difficulty was finding something that could be eaten frozen, as it was January, and the thermometer relentlessly remained below zero.

In my determination to go West, I had no need for a map or compass. The distant rumble of artillery and the carts and goods discarded along the road were my directional guides. I stayed near the westward road that ran north of Kalisch, wanting to avoid the possibility of encountering the enemy in the city. But on one occasion my rumbling belly and the possibility of a warm meal weakened my resolve. I carefully approached the edge of Kalisch. The streets seemed deserted, but there were obvious signs of battle. Buildings were damaged. A destroyed tank sat by the side of the road. I crept into the first house on my right. It was a mess on the inside—probably destroyed by enemy soldiers searching for Germans. All I could find for food was a crock pot containing a heavy crust of molasses. In haste I scraped some of the heavy brown sweetness into my mouth and bolted back out the door and away from the city, back toward the road. Foraging for food in a city occupied by Russians was just too risky.

The Herring Division

Early one evening I came upon a cluster of German tanks in a forest clearing. I found out that they had orders to stay in position until nightfall and then retreat to establish a bridgehead. The tank group were part of the elite SS tank battalion and had a couple of the newest *Königstiger* (King Tiger II) tanks. Those tanks had superior fire power and higher speed than any other on the battle field. Another loner joined us in the clearing. The commander of one *Königstiger* was extremely friendly and chatted with us, and offered us a ride. He shared some food and cigarettes, and gave us a few instructions about how to ride on a tank. We were happy to have the opportunity to ride and not walk, and to make some good headway west. When darkness fell, the commander started up his engine. The other loner and I jumped on, and the battalion headed into the night.

A couple of hours into our journey we were accosted by Russian tanks and engaged in fierce battle. The hatch to the turret was closed. There was nothing I could do but hang on for dear life. The turret turned every which way and the tank shook when the gun was fired. The engine exhausts glowed red from constantly running at high speed. The glowing exhausts were a means of distinguishing friend from foe, because each model of tanks has different location or arrangement for the mufflers.

Flares, flashes of cannons, and explosions lit up the scene and were accompanied by the deafening sound of turrets grinding, tank canons firing, metal hitting metal, and machine gun fire. In the end, the Russian tanks were no match for the *Königstigers*. I saw several of their tanks explode. Nevertheless, I have no idea how I managed to cling to the tank and avoid getting thrown off or hit by enemy fire. At the time, I was unaware of the miraculous protection I had experienced. In retrospect, it's virtually unthinkable that I could have survived a battle riding on the outside of a tank. The other soldier wasn't as fortunate. I don't know what happened to him. As for me, I jumped off the tank at the first opportunity as dawn approached, not even thanking the commander for his kindness.

The most extraordinary experience of the entire war came a few days later. I had cautiously avoided a little village and taken shelter in a large culvert. During the course of the day a heavy snowstorm settled in, reducing visibility to a point where I felt safe to move on. The road seemed to be well travelled but without the normal refuse and debris of hasty retreat. As I approached an intersection on my right I could see smoke rising from barely visible houses. At the intersection I saw someone walking down the road towards me, though it was hard to see in the heavy snow. The person stopped and so did I. After another few hesitant steps toward one another it became clear to me that he was a Russian soldier and to him that I was a German. He reached for his weapon as I scrambled desperately to get mine off of my back. But then, suddenly, he turned on his heels and walked away. I was stunned. Why didn't he shoot me? Why did he turn his back on me, knowing I could shoot him? It had been a one on one encounter with an enemy, almost face to face, though I could not see his face clearly. Will I meet him in heaven? Will we share our stories there? I should have seen the hand of God in it then but did not.

After several weeks of travelling west I was halted on the road by the familiar order: "*Halt! Paßwort!*'(password)" I knew that I had finally made it. It was January the 27th. I had made it to the first village on the German border. In the two weeks since the battle at the Vistula I had covered more than 300 kilometers as the crow flies, and that by foot, except for the ride on the Tiger II.

After initial questioning, I was sent to the nearby command post in the village. I looked around for the familiar signs of conflict, but the village seemed to be quiet. The streets were clean. There were no carts or possessions littering the sides, which indicated that the people here hadn't felt the need for a hasty retreat. A soldier on guard duty at a warehouse pointed me to the command post—the house down the street with a tank parked in front. When I reported there, I was questioned again, and told I could settle down for the night in the farmhouse directly across the street.

The unit had orders to remain in position, I was told. They were to be joined shortly by a larger contingent of troops and more tanks. A few more loners were sent to join me in the farmhouse. Late in the afternoon two buddies with a horse and small cart arrived. They had wanted to travel on but were ordered to leave the cart in the yard and tie up the horse in the barn. There were five of us in the farmhouse altogether.

I could hardly believe it. I was back on German soil. I was going to sleep in a bed . . . a bed!!! The thought seemed almost too good to be true! One of the guys in our group had found a food depot along the way and had persuaded the guard to let him have several Christmas fruit cakes, the only food stored there. I was grateful that he shared it with me. The five of us had an absolute feast! With a full belly and relieved that I could finally rest and let down my guard, I stripped off my boots and gear, put my belt and weapons on the table, and settled down for a good night's sleep.

Little did I know that I would wake up to experience the darkest most horrifying day of my entire life.

The Herring Division

9 | EVERYTHING PASSES

Startled awake by a commotion in the pre-dawn light, I found myself staring into the barrel of a sub-machine gun. It was aimed squarely at my head by a stony-faced soldier dressed in mustard-brown. Another mustard-brown-clad soldier riddled some bullets through the wardrobe door, gunning down the Christmas cake guy, who I barely caught a glimpse of as he jumped in there to hide. It took me a moment to fully come to my senses. Mustard-brown uniforms! RUSSIANS!! What? How? Where did they come from?

Pain gripped my heart, wound upwards, and sent shockwaves to my brain. My eyes darted over to look for the gun and grenades I had discarded on the table the night before. The Russian's eyes narrowed and followed my gaze. The corner of his mouth turned up in a slight curve, daring me to try. I knew it was futile. So I slowly raised my hands in defeat. Yelling orders in Russian, and gesturing so we'd understand, the *tovaishtsh* (comrades) herded the three of us out into the yard.

Three of us. The Christmas cake guy was dead. One of the horse-and-cart guys was missing. Apparently he got up in the middle of the night to tend to the horses and didn't return. Where was the German Panzer that had been parked in front of the command post across the street? Tanks make a tremendous noise when they move. How is it that we didn't hear it move out? And where were all the other soldiers? Why didn't the commander send someone to wake us? How could they leave us behind?

The Russians shouted and gestured at us to strip down. We stood barefoot, shivering buck-naked in the frigid dawn as they searched us for the telltale SS tattoo; small black ink letters specifying the SS member's blood type. The mark was generally located on the underside of the left arm, near the armpit. Satisfied that none of us were members of Hitler's elite force, they threw our outer uniforms back at us, pockets emptied. No underwear. No shirts. No coat. No *Feldmütze*. No socks. No boots, just the field-gray combat tunic and pants.

A few more German loners were dragged into the yard and subjected to the same routine. I couldn't calm my racing heart. About a dozen of us stood assembled there, with ashen faces and raised hands, lost in our thoughts, fearful of what was to come.

Dawn broke, and with it, the sound of fighting nearby. The Russian soldiers were antsy to get going. They marched us off in the direction I had entered the village, out into the forest. The ground was frozen, but there wasn't much snow in the forest. The scattered twigs poked into our bare feet. The pain intensified and then dulled as our extremities froze and grew clumsy and numb with lack of sensation. But I scarcely noticed my bare feet. I suppose that the fear of the unknown over-rode all other sensation.

After much gesturing and shouting, I gathered that the Russians wanted us to sing. I don't know why, but for some reason I had a knack for understanding Russian. I understood enough to satisfy them, and quickly learned to interpret for others too. At the time, I thought it was because I had been exposed to the prattle of the Königsberger fisherwomen, but now I see it as a special gift from God. The ability to understand the language meant that I had more value to the Russians than the average POW. In the time to come, it helped spare my life.

If they wanted us to sing, sing we would. We sang traditional German folk songs and wandering tunes. There was an adaptation of one popular song that we sang repeatedly. The original words were: *"Es geht alles vorüber es geht alles vorbei, nach jedem Dezember kommt vieder ein Mai."* "Everything passes. It all comes to an end. For every December, May follows again."

On the Eastern front, we sang our own version of the folk song. *"Es geht alles vorüber, es geht alles vorbei, drei Jahre in Russland und dann sind wir frei."* . . .

"Everything passes, all things will flee, three years in Russia and we will be free."

Fighting on the front we anticipated that the war wouldn't last more than three years, and that we'd be free to go home at its end. But being captured by the Russians was a fate worse than death. As Prisoners of War, would we ever be free again? We sang the words boisterously, with feigned confidence, trying to sustain hope. How could anyone survive their infamously inhumane treatment?

As I trudged along singing, I replayed the sequence of events like a badly scratched record over and over in my mind. The village had looked secure. Why did I let down my guard? Why didn't I sleep with my gun? Why didn't I secure the door or arrange for the guys to take shifts on watch? Why didn't I wake up when the army moved out? Why did they abandon us? Yes, I was in rough shape after my ordeal of two weeks on the run. But why hadn't I been more vigilant? Why did I take off my gear that night? Why did I miss the opportunity to kill myself rather than be taken alive? I had blown it. My worst nightmare had come true. What little control I had before was now totally gone. The grim, appalling reality began to sink in: I had been abandoned by my own people, was at the mercy of the enemy, a prisoner of war.

Every year on January 28th I re-live the turmoil of emotions I experienced that day, still marveling at how God brought me through it all. Though hope felt as leaden as my numb feet, I just kept singing: "Everything passes, all things will flee, three years in Russia and I will be free."

When we reached a clearing in the forest, our first guards were replaced by others. Two of our new guards were so drunk that they could barely stand up. They made us sit in a circle in the center of the clearing. One of the drunken guards came into the middle. We noticed he had a hand gun dangling from his wrist with a leather strap. Mocking us, he started to dance—or perhaps it would be more accurate to say that he attempted to dance. He swayed, staggered and stumbled in every direction, singing loudly in Russian, as he swung the gun at our heads. One of the sober guards tried to subdue him. Incensed, the intoxicated soldier discharged his gun into the air several times. We dared not move. His Russian comrades did nothing more to intervene. He was totally out of control.

He and the drunken soldier on the perimeter continued to sing and torment us until a Russian officer showed up. The soldier on the outside of the circle seemed to sober up instantly. He quit the incoherent singing and stood at attention. The 'dancer' in the middle got worse, if that was possible, and did not respond to the officer's orders to stop. All at once, the officer pulled out his pistol and shot him dead. Then he marched us off and left the drunken soldier's body in the middle of the forest, right where he had fallen.

We prisoners glanced at each other in disbelief. The accounts were true. Russians were brutal. And if they had such little regard for each other, there was no telling how they would treat us.

We were marched past a few Russian soldiers on an elevated road. They were shooting at people in the field, who were running to dodge the bullets. We were told that these targets were SS and '*Hiwis*' ("*Hilfswillige*"—*Volunteer Helpers*), which had been identified as such, and were to be killed—but I'm not certain that was true. It may have just been ordinary civilians they were using for target practice.

An explanation is in order about the '*Hiwis*'. They were foreign workers, who had come from the Ukraine or Poland to work in Germany. These workers were regarded as traitors by Poles and Russians, merely because they had worked in Germany. The hatred of the SS was not unfounded, however, and the effort to find them was relentless. I don't know how many times I had to bare my upper arm to prove that I did not belong to that group.

We marched and marched, pausing only to sleep for a few hours each night. We constantly heard sounds of intense fighting in the distance. I am not able to say how many days passed. I felt despondent, and my physical condition had started to deteriorate. More prisoners were brought to join our group, which by this time had increased to somewhere between 80 and 100, and continued to increase thereafter.

One evening, something extremely unusual happened. We were being kept in an outdoor chain-link fenced area for the night, adjacent to some sort of building, when the guards suddenly threw an older man into the enclosure. That wasn't the unusual part. We were always being joined by more POWs. But this guy was a civilian. Not only that, he carried a heavy backpack. A backpack! No one was allowed to carry a backpack! Needless to say, we were all overcome with curiosity as to what it contained. The man motioned for us to gather around and sit down. He then unfastened the straps to reveal its contents. It was filled with New Testament Bibles! Obviously, this was a pastor who had somehow convinced the guards to allow him to distribute the paperback volumes to us prisoners of war.

For the next few minutes, we listened to him preach. He told us that God loved us, and that through Jesus we could have forgiveness of sins. He urged us to make peace with God, and to rely on Him to help us through these dark times. When he was done, he asked those who wanted to receive a Bible to raise our hands. About 30 of us did.

Some guys undoubtedly felt stirred as they listened—as I had that time as a boy, when aviator pilot Hans Bertram came to our church. They planned to read the gift. But I had different plans for it. Everyone smoked in those days. Tobacco had been a regular ration on the Eastern front, and we got it from time to time from our Russian captors. But it was extremely difficult to get our hands on cigarette rolling paper. The paper in these New Testaments was extremely thin, and perfect for the job.

My conscience gave me a twinge the first time I opened it to rip out a page. So I decided to harvest the paper from back to front. That way, I would burn up the references, Proverbs, Psalms, and Epistles first. Chances were that I wouldn't get enough tobacco in captivity to ever get to the gospels, and smoke the words of Jesus.

I have no idea why the Russian guards allowed that pastor in, nor why they allowed us to keep the Bibles. It's one of several unusual and unexplainable things that happened to me during the war. In retrospect, I realize it was God's way of trying to get through to me. And I should have paid closer attention, because things were about to get worse. A lot worse. As the Pastor had surmised, we were headed for extremely dark times.

The decent guards were replaced by ones that lived up to the terrible Russian reputation. It wasn't long before I had no need for cigarette paper. We were barely given any food and water, let alone luxuries like tobacco.

Our suffering intensified when Polish militia replaced the Russians. Day after day they paraded us down the road like trophies, as ceaseless columns of Russian tanks and Army vehicles passed by. The incoming soldiers mocked us and pelted us with rocks and debris. At times we were marched east, but mostly west, into Germany, in the same direction as the troops and tanks. I imagine that the purpose of this was to boost the morale of the Russian troops and to taunt and demoralize the remaining German citizens.

This is a group of German POWs captured by Russians in 1944. Notice that many of them were barefoot or had feet wrapped in rags.

We were not fed at all by the militia, nor were we given anything to drink. To get food, we had to jump out of the column and grab something edible from the wayside. There were all sorts of discarded goods from refugees who had passed that way—carts, clothing, household goods, dead animals. But we risked our lives whenever we stepped out of line. Our captors shot anyone they caught leaving the group. I risked my life once when I darted out to retrieve a severed pig's head. I gnawed on the raw, frozen meat, trying to suck down as much bloody tissue as possible.

Thankfully, we were often forced into the ditch to allow Russian troops to pass. During these frequent stops we quenched our thirst by drinking from little puddles, or popped chunks of ice into our mouths. We ate whatever edible scraps we could find, no matter how rotten, and scavenged discarded clothes to stuff in our tunics for warmth. Those of us without footwear used rags to bind up our feet. Not everyone had their boots confiscated. But I went without footwear for the entire duration of my internment. I was grateful when once during my time in camp, I found a couple small pieces of wood to use as soles under the bindings.

There were no trains running in the vicinity. The only way to transport prisoners was to march them. So week after week we marched. Many succumbed to sickness and malnutrition. It was not uncommon for emaciated prisoners to simply fall down dead, or die during the night. Every morning we left bodies behind.

I was malnourished, ill, and my feet were getting worse. I had severe frostbite and gangrene was setting in. There was no way I could have survived any more marching. I simply couldn't go on. I was singled out to stay with a small group of prisoners in similar condition. We were housed in a stable, and watched over by two Russian female guards, though we probably didn't need guards—no one was in any condition to run away. The farm was likely a recognized first aid station for prisoners. At one point, a German civilian was brought in. Shot in the stomach, he was bleeding profusely and in terrible agony. It didn't appear that there were any doctors or surgeons around. He didn't last long.

I was a mess. I did not have the strength to get up, and I couldn't control my bodily functions. Like others around me, I lay in my excrement on a thin bed of straw. I must have picked up some underwear along the way, because I had to discard them, due to the maggots swarming in the filth.

The guards brought us food once a day, but most of us couldn't eat. Those who tried were unable to keep anything down. The stench of filth and sickness must have been overpowering, but I was too feeble to notice. In the midst of delirium, however, I did notice the kindness of one of the female guards.

Soldiers of the German Wehrmacht considered it shameful that Russians sent women into combat. We called female soldiers *"Flintenweiber."* A *Flinte* is a hunting gun, and *"Weiber"* means woman, but with negative, patronizing undertones. It was a derogatory term . . . one that this particular guard didn't deserve. She cradled my swollen feet and gently lanced the many large, tough black ulcers. Bloody puss drenched the surrounding straw. Were it not for this kindness, I would have most certainly been overcome by the infection and died.

I have no recollection of how or when I was moved, but I next found myself in a "hospital" for prisoners. It was set up in a former German school, and guarded by Polish militia. The "beds" in our room were constructed by able-bodied German prisoners, who were kept in a different part of the building. The beds consisted of three long, layered decks of plywood. There were perhaps twenty patients laid out side-by-side like sausages on each layer. The decks were sloped with the head side higher than the foot side. A plank at the foot of each deck ensured that patients wouldn't slide off.

The triple-decker contraption was built to house people like me, who had suffered frostbite or had other wounds in different stages of infection. The slope allowed the fluid from our wounds to drain down to the foot of the bed, drip down to the next level, and ultimately down to the floor. It was a relief to be assigned a spot on the top level.

We received no medical attention at all. No medications or cleansing or dressings for wounds. Basically, if your body managed to fight off the infection on its own you survived. If it didn't, you died. It's astonishing that anyone managed to stage a recovery in those cramped, unsanitary conditions.

No one talked much. What little conversation we had tended to drift toward fantasies about food. We could occasionally hear the rumbling of artillery fire in the distance. Inevitably, someone would offer his opinion that the artillery fire sounded closer than it had before. He was certain it was a sign of our imminent rescue. With hollow eyes we stared at the doors for hours and days on end, hoping to see them flung open by liberators. But our German *Kameraden* never came. The sound of artillery grew silent. No one told us that Adolf Hitler was dead. Nor that on May 8, 1945, Germany unconditionally surrendered. There would be no liberation. No freedom. The Russians had secured control. And although the war with Germany was over, they had plans for what they would do to exact revenge.

As far as I can tell, it was shortly thereafter that a handful of fellow patients and I were deemed well enough to be discharged from the makeshift medical facility. Polish militia were assigned to march us to our next assigned internment facility. En route, we passed through the Polish city of Częstochowa. It was famed for the iconic painting of the Black Madonna of Częstochowa, Queen of Poland. As we walked, we spotted the telltale spire of the Jasna Gora monastery in the distance. Legend ascribed miraculous healings and surprising answers to prayer to the virgin. Thus, the monastery had been a pilgrimage destination for Roman Catholic Poles for centuries and still is today.

At that point, we definitely could have used a miracle. We had no idea that our trek would end about a hundred kilometers south of Częstochowa, at the world's most infamous concentration and extermination camp. I recall one night spent sleeping in a school storage room, and another stretched out on top of student desks at a different school along the way. On that occasion, perhaps it was even the day we passed through the home of the Black Madonna, two or three of us talked late into the night. We discussed the predicament we were in, and bitterly concluded that if there truly was a God, He would not allow such suffering.

I vividly remember passing by the ominous knobby barbed-wire electric fence of the concentration camp, which I later learned from an inmate was named "Birkenau"—the largest and most lethal of the *Auschwitz* camps. At the gate, the Polish militia handed us over to the Russians. The Soviet soldiers escorted us into the camp. Row upon row of barracks stretched out before us. We started down a wide road, and then they pushed us into a barbed wire compound at the second barrack to the left. As best I can tell by looking at maps, my barrack was near the north end of the complex, close to the perimeter and across from the partially completed "Mexico" camp extension.

Prisoners milled around the yard. I could tell which guys had recently been captured. They were thin, but their bodies weren't yet emaciated. Then there were the guys who had been prisoners for a while. Their uniforms were tattered. Muscles atrophied. Teeth missing. Eyes vacant. Skin taut, magnifying every bone beneath. The heat was oppressive. No one smiled. No one spoke. No one acknowledged us newcomers.

At nightfall we were herded into the shadowy humid barrack. The long walls were lined with dull blood-red brick compartments. The floor was also covered in bricks. I was assigned a space that amounted to the surface dimension of a large coffin. Getting comfortable on the stone surface was impossible. I was given no straw, no mattress, no blanket—nothing to lessen the pressure of my bony hips and shoulders against the damp bricks. I could feel their clammy claws reach through my skin to squeeze each throbbing bone. The roosts were moist because the entire inside of the barrack was hosed down each day and scrubbed with coarse brooms. Perhaps it was a feeble attempt at cleanliness, I don't know. But I suspect that at least part of the reason was to increase our suffering.

To relieve ourselves we used the honey barrel near the doorway. It was a large metal drum, cut in half, with two opposing holes burned through the sides. A pole was fed through the holes whenever the container was full, so two prisoners could carry and dump its contents at the designated spot. The holes also served as an overflow. When the barrel was full—as it most often was—the urine could run out onto the ground, while the heavier excrement sunk to the bottom. We were given no toilet paper or rags with which to clean our feces, and no water to wash our hands. Looking at photos of Birkenau, I see that there were barracks with a succession of dozens of toilet holes cut into a long slab of concrete. I don't recall ever being allowed to use those facilities. But perhaps that's where the foul sludge was dumped.

We were fed once a day. A heavy cast-iron pot of soup was brought into the yard. Two prisoners carried the pot on a pole, taking great care not to spill a drop. We lined up as soon as we saw them coming. Everyone had some sort of *kummchen*—that is, a small bowl or food container. It was one of the few personal possessions we were allowed. Some guys had the good fortune to keep their mess canteens, minus the knives, of course. My *kummchen* was an old tin can with a makeshift wire handle. When not in use, I carried it around my waist on the piece of rope or strip of fabric I used as a belt. It was just as well I didn't have a belt. By that time I was so thin it would have surely run out of holes.

Our ration for the day was one ladle full of thin soup. I always told myself not to wolf it down. It was all the food I'd get until the following day, so I wanted to eat it slowly, though it was nearly impossible to do so but eating it too fast would result in severe stomach cramps. The meager broth never satisfied my hunger, but only served as a cruel reminder of how famished I actually was.

Some prisoners were conscripted to do odd jobs like hose down the barrack, empty the "honey" barrel, or bring in the soup kettle. But the majority of us did nothing but mill around aimlessly outside. We were only allowed in the barracks at night. Temperatures in that area often reach 35 degrees Celsius (95º F) in July and that summer was no exception. The occasional fight broke out when prisoners jostled for standing room beside the barracks, which provided the only available shade. It's farfetched to call it a fight, the stronger one yanking the weaker one away from the shade. Ever under the watchful eyes of guards on the watchtower, we tried to follow the order: "Do not cluster in groups"! We had all adopted the classic prisoner mentality. Keep your mouth shut. Keep your eyes cast down. Comply. Do nothing to arouse attention.

Sitting with our backs against the barrack, we passed the time by finding and killing the lice that hid in the seams of our clothing. It wasn't easy. First you had to catch one of the sesame-sized tormentors. Squishing them with your fingers didn't work; their outer shells were too hard. So we had to get one on top of a thumbnail and press down with the other thumbnail to crack its shell and grind it flat.

One week stretched into the next. Then suddenly one day we were ordered to line up. What was happening? No one knew. The guards marched us through the length of the camp down the road past the long string of barracks on either side. They took us out through a barbed wire gate, and marshalled us along a platform beside some railway tracks. A train stretched down the expanse of track. We were being transported somewhere. Were we being taken to another camp? Or perhaps back to Germany? Or, heaven forbid . . . to Russia, our most probable destination.

We had been lined up in the usual 'five per row' formation for the easiest way to tally. The guards crammed us into the boxcar and shut the door. Everything went dark. There must have been a hundred of us in that boxcar. We were so cramped for space it was impossible for all to sit down. The only light was the daylight that shone through the narrow crack at either side of the sliding doors. When the train moved, those cracks provided some ventilation. But POW transports were not high on the priority list, and the train often stood still for days on end, the sun's scorching rays creating suffocating conditions in our cramped quarters.

Our "toilet" was a metal chute connected to a hole in the wall, which was a little larger than a fist. It was difficult to jostle through the bodies to get there. Some of us had diarrhea, and could never make it in time. Don't try to imagine the condition around that toilet chute and the condition in that boxcar in general. There was no sitting room, no water, no paper, no bedding, and no way to avoid the stench, filth, and agony.

Once a day, the dead would be removed from the boxcar and a bucket of soup pushed in. Once they gave us pea soup—which was nearly impossible to digest in our condition, and greatly added to our misery instead.

To this day the Poles deny that Auschwitz was used as a collection and shipping facility for transporting Germans to Russia. The best I have been able to find to substantiate my experience is a copy of a letter to UNESCO, which gives a detailed list of transports, and states that the camp was used up until 1948 for this purpose. The majority of people transported were German prisoners of war, but some were German-sympathizers; civilians from former German friendly nations. The letter estimates that over 90,000 people were shipped from Birkenau to Russia during that time.

Russian officials recently unsealed classified documents verifying the practice, and more information is constantly coming to light on the internet. The Auschwitz-Birkenau memorial and museum website was updated in 2013 to admit that "the Soviet military authorities established transit camps at the sites of the Auschwitz main camp and Birkenau for German POWs and for Polish citizens of Upper Silesia, Bielsko, Biała, and the vicinity who had signed the *Volksliste* [declaration of German ethnicity] during the occupation. The State Bureau for Public Security (Państwowy Urząd Bezpieczeństwa Publicznego – PUBP) participated in administering the camps for Poles. The transit camp in the main camp probably existed until the fall of 1945, and the one in Birkenau until the following spring." (www.en.auschwitz.org).

It's interesting that the Auschwitz museum site reports that the facility was only used to collect and deport Germans until the spring of 1946, whereas UNESCO says the Russians used it for this purpose for more than three years after the war, up until 1948 . . . But if there's anything I've discovered, it's that the "official historical storyline" of the war and the Allied treatment of Germans doesn't ring true to my experience, nor to the experience of other Axis soldiers and civilians.

If the UNESCO letter accurately lists the different transports, and judging from the listed destinations, I surmise that I would have been among the 2,850 people (2,700 POW and 150 civilians) that were shipped to Russia on

We Will Be Free

July 11, 1945, final destination Stalinogorsk (Novomoskovsk). Our transport must have been about 35 boxcars long, given that one was the kitchen, at least one was a "morgue" for stacking dead bodies, one boxcar for supplies, at least one or two for the guards, and 28 rail cars crammed with about a hundred prisoners standing in each.

I can't say how many days or weeks I was on the train. Historians say such trips often lasted 14 days. Given the inhumane conditions, it's a wonder any of us made it there alive. When we were finally ordered to disembark, most of us were so weak we could barely walk. Two or three boxcars of prisoners, feeble and covered with excrement, were unloaded at my stop. As the guards marched us toward the camp we saw a woman laden with two pails of water dangling from her carrying yoke. Water! The guards couldn't stop us from swarming her and fighting for a drop. The frenzied fight unleashed an equally frenzied barrage from the guards, who kicked us and hit us with the butts of their rifles to restore order. We cried in pain from their brutal blows, but even more so over the water that was cruelly denied and spilled to the ground.

I've tried to piece together the storyline of my life as a POW in Russia as best I can, but due to the malnourished and poor physical state I was already in by the time I got there, there are many things that I didn't notice and simply can't recall . . . although to this day, forgotten memories still pop up from time to time. As best as I can tell, I worked in four or five different labor camps—spending time in three or four of them before being hospitalized for several months. I was interned in one more camp after my hospitalization.

The camps were in the Donbas (Donets) Basin, a major industrial region of eastern Ukraine and southeast Russia north of the Sea of Azov and west of the Donbas River. The area contains one of the densest concentrations of industrial factories in the entire world.

The name of the nearest city was Voroshilovgrad (Luhansk), which administered the Voroshilovgrad Oblast (province). I also remember hearing about Shachty, which was the site of a big smelter operation in Russia, not far south of us. Several places had the word "*shacht*" in their names, which in Russian means "shaft." This was due to the many coal mines in the region. In looking at a map of camps for POWs in the Donbas basin, I presume that I was in Voroshilovgrad camp-complex #144 or #474, each of which consisted of numerous sub-camps.

Conditions in the camps varied, but all were deplorable. The barracks were overcrowded and filthy. The type of work and schedules also varied, but we were required to put in up to 14 hours of hard labor each day, seven days a week, year round. The guards were ruthless and didn't hesitate to beat or execute POWs—sometimes for no apparent reason. The amount of food we received also varied, as food rations designated for the camps were often diverted by Russian officers to be bartered or sold on the black market. The UN sets the minimum food requirements for heavy labor at 3100 to 3900 calories per day. The thin, meatless gruel and hard bread we received provided only a fraction of that amount—I'm sure that we often got only a few hundred calories a day; especially when food was punitively withheld for failing to meet our work quota. POWs routinely died of malnutrition. Disease was rife. Average life expectancy was one to two years. But due to the steady stream of Germans herded like cattle off the arriving trains, the deaths were inconsequential. The Russians simply replaced the prisoners they had worked to death with new ones.

After the water incident, we were marched down a dusty road to the first camp. The area was obviously rural. There were no other buildings in sight. Apparently, the camp had been built by Germans and used as an army base during their occupation. It was a familiar setup with several barracks around a large yard, surrounded with a barbed-wire-topped perimeter fence to keep people out but used in our case, to keep us in. There was a large gate near the mess hall. This first camp was unlike any of the others— due to its German construction, but more so because all the guards and the Commandant were German NKFD.

NKFD stood for *Nationale Komitte Freies Deutschland* (National Committee for a Free Germany). The NKFD was a German anti-Nazi organization that operated in the Soviet Union during the war. Members were communist Germans who fled Nazi Germany when Hitler came to power, as well as German defectors, who had been indoctrinated, trained and molded into trusted servants of the Russian State. They proudly wore white bands over their uniforms on their right arms, with NKFD printed in bold black letters on the white background. Instead of guns they were equipped with "walking sticks" capped with solid metal knobs, which they used liberally, but not for walking. We secretly called them "*Knüppelhunde.*" "*Knüppel*" is the German word for a Nightstick or long Billy-club. The last syllable, "*hunde,*" means dog . . . in other words, "beating-hounds." It was an apt nickname. The NKFD were even more abusive and brutal than the Russian guards—which I hardly thought possible. I suspect they felt they needed to prove their communist loyalties, distance themselves from German prisoners, and demonstrate that they had what it took to serve their adopted Mother Russia. After the war, many from that organization assumed high positions in the DDR, Communist East Germany.

During our first assembly, the Commandant introduced himself in flawless German. He was dressed in a khaki colored French uniform with the traditional ship-like hat and tri-colored pin of the French army perched on his head. His name was "Vogel"— an unmistakably German name. Yet he claimed to have come from Alsace, France. Apparently, when Germany tried to conscript him, he deserted. His lip curled into a sneer. Looking at us with obvious disdain, he gave us a glimpse of how he and the rest of our captors felt about soldiers of the Wehrmacht, and what type of treatment we could expect from them: *"Wenn einer von Euch Schweinen krepiert ist für mich ein Feiertag!"* . . . "Every day one of you filthy pigs perishes is a day of celebration for me!" He and the commandants of the other camps must have spent a lot of time celebrating.

The Commandant organized us into work brigades and introduced us to the rudiments of the quota system, which regulated every aspect of life in a communist society. Our guards and Russian supervisors were also subject to quotas. He explained the system: If we exceeded the work required of us, we would get extra rations. If we met the quota, but didn't exceed it, we would only get the basic ration of food. Those who failed to meet the required work quota would have the basic ration of food reduced accordingly. As I said before, a 'normal' day's ration was only a bowl of gruel and a piece of small, hard bread. In other words, those who were too sick and feeble to fulfill the quota would be starved to death even more rapidly than the POWs who were still able to be productive.

We started a regimented daily life with plenty of assemblies in the yard. Standing at attention, and watched over by guards, we wearily feigned to listen as the Commandant launched into yet another long discourse. His frequent tirades appeared to be an attempt to degrade, humiliate and shame us. Standing in the yard, it was impossible not to notice the American-built trucks that rumbled past a few times a day. The back was crammed full of Russians—mostly women—standing together on the truck-bed on their way to or from work. On cue, they broke into boisterous song as the truck came near the camp, but after the truck had rolled by, the singing stopped as abruptly as it had begun. The singing was to demonstrate to us, no doubt, how happy they were to work in communist Russia. After all, according to the familiar slave labor camp motto, *"Work in the Soviet Union is a Matter of Honor and Glory."*

I only remember one work assignment at that camp, which took place on two consecutive days. We were ordered to line up by brigades, and to come equipped with our spoons. The utensils that most of us used for eating could hardly have been called "spoons." Most of them were crudely shaped out of discarded scraps of wood, or pieces of tin-can or metal we had picked up from a ditch somewhere along the way. In any case, we assembled in the yard at attention, "spoons" in hand. With NKFD guards flanking both sides of the column, we were marched out of camp down the road. They wanted us to sing of course. A POW near the back of the line started to sing the old familiar folk tune, and it wasn't long before we all joined in: *"Everything passes, all things will flee, three years in Russia and we will be free."*

I don't know whether the NKFD were happy about our song choice, but there wasn't much they could do about this subtle collective symbol of defiance.

We were marched to a distant field. At its edge, we were ordered to face the field and stand shoulder-to-shoulder in a single line. Our assignment was to plant the large field with turnip seeds—which seemed ridiculous to me, since it was nearly the end of summer, and there was no hope that turnips would germinate and mature in time to be harvested before winter came. Nevertheless, we were instructed to use our spoons to dig holes an inch deep and three inches apart, drop three turnip seeds in each hole, and then cover them with dirt. We were supposed to stay in line and only move forward on cue to plant the seeds in the next row. No one was supposed to stand up unless he needed more seeds.

The seeds were given out a hand-full at a time. We were so starved that not many of them got into the ground. Crouched over, shielding our transgression from view, we were able to stuff the seeds in our mouths while only pretending to plant them. The next day we carried on planting rows from where we left off. As you can imagine, our "spoons" weren't in the best of shape after using them to dig in the dirt all day—especially the wooden ones. But nevertheless, they were all we had, and we had no choice but to continue using them to eat our meager daily gruel.

I remember the small residue of ground up soybean at the bottom of my '*Kummchen*' after receiving my ladle of soup. We could not digest that stuff and were happy when it settled at the bottom. We would drink the liquid on top and leave most of the solids, and eat only a bit of the gritty stuff at a time. It was harder to digest than pea soup.

From the first day in captivity one event became almost routine. It followed no script, was an ever present threat, and was always unscheduled, undignified, unsupervised, and unescapable. It was the search for contraband.

The definition was simple. Contraband was anything that could cause bodily harm, or could be used to facilitate or aid in a prisoner's escape. We soon learned that it often had another meaning—it was anything we had that the searchers decided they wanted. We were at their mercy. Most of the time two individuals conducted the search. One of them would check the naked prisoner, while the other one would go through the belongings. No bodily cavity was spared in that search. Even the smallest scrap of paper with handwriting was sure to be taken.

Some POWs had such an intense craving for salt that they would steal from the job or barter meager rations to obtain salt, often with the help of guards who got it for them on the black market. The only form of salt available was rock salt with all the impurities. Sometimes it was a good thing that the POWs lost the salt in the search because our bodies could not handle much salt and the person consuming it would get very ill and die.

One thing that was highly sought after by most POWs and never confiscated, no matter how many pieces nor how large a piece was found, was charred bits of wood or raw charcoal. We would chew on the pieces at the first indication of diarrhea. Sometimes drinking large quantities of water would help stave off the trots. But it was very risky to use the water remedy, it could have the opposite effect and kill you.

One other constant from the start to the end of my captivity, was being mocked by all the Russian soldiers in their guttural voices with a four-word phrase. We heard the phrase uncountable times . . . over and over again. The words are deeply embedded in my mind. The first two words were spoken like a gleeful undeniable fact:"Gütler kaput!" The Russian language has no "H" sound—Gütler was their word for Hitler. "*Kaput*" essentially means broken or defeated. I can't bring myself to mention the final two words or their meaning. They are lewd and horrible. Essentially they were a leering promise of what the victors were going to do to German females.

Stalin encouraged his army to take vengeance by sexually helping themselves. His promise was turned into a catch-phrase with which the Russian soldiers tormented German prisoners of war. The phrase was sexually sinister and evil, and often accompanied with leering and lewd gestures. They mocked us relentlessly with it. It was extremely emasculating to realize that they meant to carry through with these heinous crimes, that many already had, and that there was nothing we could do to protect our sisters, mothers, wives, and daughters. Knowing what Stalin had endorsed them to do to our women intensified our emotional agony. To this day, the phrase is stuck in my head and from time-to-time replays like an evil, nightmarish taunt.

The first camp must have been an initiation and distribution point for other camps in the area because it wasn't long before my brigade was moved to top up the dwindling numbers in another facility nearby.

The next camp had a large gravel yard with a dense, high wire fence on the perimeter. It was one of several in the area that supplied the work force for a large industrial complex. Every morning we were marched to our assigned site.

POWs from surrounding camps kept that huge industrial complex in operation. From the mining of coal to the filling of the smelter, from burning of sawmill scraps to emptying of the slag basin to the production of concrete blocks after the slag was ground in rolling mills, an ever renewed supply of prisoners worked on the "Restitution." Heavy physical labor was done by new arrivals.

Prisoners with trade skills, such as sheet metal workers, coopers, blacksmith and mechanics were the most sought after trades around the camps. Tailors were frequently called to repair uniforms for soldiers or even sew a custom fit uniform for some high ranking officer These were more fortunate than the rest of us. They enjoyed some privileges. I had just turned 20, and didn't have a trade, was suspect when listed as a student.

Somehow I became part of a brigade, who was assigned to unload crates of china and glassware which had arrived from Germany in boxcars on a railway siding. The crates were marked in German: "*Vorsicht Glass*" (Glass-Handle with Care) on all sides. The tracks, where the cars sat, were on an embankment, about eight feet high. We decided to build some kind of a ramp. With our guard's permission and their collaboration we scrounged for suitable material and had just started to put things in place, when an overseer arrived.

He was furious that we hadn't yet unloaded any crates. Blustering, he ordered us to clear aside our half-constructed ramp. He would demonstrate that we didn't need a ramp to get the job done. He climbed into the car, put his shoulder to the first crate, and with the help of a lever pushed it to the edge of the car and out the door. Down tumbled the crate, smashing the contents in the process. Incensed, he shouted at us that he didn't care how we did it, but we'd better just hurry up and get the job done . . . or it would mean cut rations!

After we removed what little of the ramp was built, we had a very successful day by following his example. Not only that day, the next day also, we produced way over our quota. Another brigade was to unpack the crates and store the content in the corner of a warehouse. They became over achievers as well, using scoop shovels to move the shattered porcelain. We were rewarded with a couple extra bites of food, which we gratefully wolfed down. But victories like this were few and far between. Having our rations cut back was just as frequent of an occurrence.

Russian soldiers were our guards and just as persistent slave drivers as our NKFD guards had been. We were under constant physical surveillance. The Commandant was particularly ruthless. His punishment toward anyone who dared to step out of line was swift and brutal. One day the guards chased down some prisoners, who had escaped, and dragged one unfortunate fellow back. The Commandant decided to make an example of him.

There was a space under a stair with a wrought iron gate. We called it 'Das Loch'. It was in plain view next to the assembly area. The captured escapee was shoved into 'Das Loch', a space designed for severe punishment, where a person was forced to stay in a cramped position not able to stand, nor sit down. After a few hours, he was in agony. Every time we assembled in the yard, which was at least twice a day, we were forced to see his suffering. They kept him in there until he died. Theft from the kitchen or workplace was punished with varying length of confinement in that hole.

One evening, in the fall of 1945, dozens of soldiers suddenly appeared around the perimeter of the camp, shouting loudly in Russian and shooting their rifles wildly into the air. Not knowing the reason for the pandemonium, some prisoners panicked. One ran and tried to climb the fence. The guards immediately gunned him down.

Later that night we learned the reason for the commotion. Japan had surrendered. The war was over. We weren't certain what that meant for us. We held out a thin glimmer of hope that we might be released, but we also feared what the Russians might do to us now that they were the victors and in charge.

One thing that happened right away was that they began a relentless quest to identify "war criminals." They called us in to be interrogated at any time during the day or night under the pretense that our documents had been lost, and that they needed to reconstruct the history of our military service. The questions they asked through the translator were always the same: Where did you grow up? What did you do there? When were you drafted? Which unit did you serve with? Who was your immediate superior? Where did you serve? Where were you captured? An administrator recorded answers on a form. They tried to trip us up and find inconsistencies in our replies. A couple days or weeks after being questioned they called us in to go through the process all over again, claiming that the forms had been lost. If you didn't answer in exactly the way you had the first time, then they said that you had lied, and categorized you as a war criminal.

I suspect that they had quotas for how many war criminals they had to identify. They used any shred of evidence, no matter how scant or inconsequential. Often they twisted our words or fabricated evidence. Certain military units were on their black list—anyone serving with such a unit was automatically branded as a war criminal. All former members of the SS and anyone with ties to the SS were condemned. Teachers and scholars were branded as war criminals because they supposedly contributed to propagating Nazi doctrine. And if you were branded as a war criminal, you had no hope of ever leaving Russia alive. War criminals were sentenced from 25 to 100 years of heavy forced labor.

I was grateful that my initial military unit had been disbanded and reorganized. Had they known that one of our unit's assignments at that time had been the hunting down of dissidents in Estonia, I would have likely been categorized as a war criminal and sentenced to many years of forced labor.

It may have been information that I offered during one such interrogation that led to my assignment to paint propaganda banners. The Russians wanted me to prove that I had indeed had calligraphy lessons in high school. They gave me the supplies to paint large canvas banners extolling the victorious Red Army. By that time I had a good working knowledge of Russian. I remember the slogans well. One was "Hail to Our Heroic Army!" Another was "Hail to our Red Army."

I rolled the strip of fabric out on the floor and began to paint the slogans in large letters. My work must have satisfied them, for they conscripted me to paint banners on several successive days. Banners were strung out everywhere—across streets, on buildings, on bridges and on fences. Everywhere we looked, we were reminded that our captors were the victorious war heroes, and that we were nothing but despicable criminals. It may also have served as a propaganda tool for the general population.

After the war, food was scarce everywhere in Europe, perhaps more so in Russia. Prisoners were not the only ones on rations. Civilians were on rations also. This created a situation where food and other scarce items became valuable trade commodities on the burgeoning black market. Our Russian guards took full advantage of this, and of their favorable position. Bribery and corruption were commonplace. Much of the food that was allocated to feed POWs never got to us. Furthermore, guards and officers often used food to bribe prisoners to help them cheat the Communist system.

I don't know who masterminded the ingenious scheme. One prisoner from my brigade was selected to participate in a scam at the nearby industrial plant, involving a truck driver, Russian guards, and a select group of able bodied POWs. After arriving at our work site one morning, the guards and chosen prisoners jumped into the back of a truck that was headed to the plant to deliver supplies. They hunkered down and concealed themselves under tarps. After the driver dropped off the supplies, the guards and prisoners loaded and stole a large electric motor from the plant. The motor had been readied for pickup by conspirators who worked there. The motor was hauled out of the plant and directly to the black market to be sold. At the black market, no questions were ever asked as to where the goods came from. The conspirators sold the motor and split the proceeds. The Russians each got a few Rubles (A Ruble is about a dollar) and the prisoners got some food and cigarettes as payment.

The irony of the situation was that the motor was needed to operate a piece of essential equipment. The plant couldn't operate without it, so the plant was forced to buy back their own property from the black market. I suspect that the same truck driver who was part of the scheme to steal the motor was hired to transport it back to the plant. Trucks and drivers were not that plentiful in the area. So he benefitted richly from that scheme. We often heard about such schemes, bribes, and corruption, but kept our mouths shut and looked the other way.

My brigade was ordered to shovel gritty slag. Slag was formed when hot liquid residue from the blast furnace was poured into basins of water. The red glowing residue came in special rail cars, which looked like a giant pear supported on two sides. A cranking mechanism tilted the pear-like drum to empty the content into a huge water filled basin in the ground. Loud, boiling sounds accompanied the billowing steam when the liquefied stuff hit the water. The stuff crystallized and became the slag we had to shovel after the water residue was drained.

I was given a shovel and told to scoop the heavy grit from the basin onto *nasilki*. A *nasilki* was a contraption that looked like a stretcher, except it had a flat wooden platform on top of rough wooden poles. Two POW "porters" carried each *nasilki*. Hundreds of prisoners, bearing *nasilkis*, moved like ants in an ever-circling chain to transfer the slag from the basins to the concrete block factory stockpile. Day after day the routine was the same. The shovelers constantly shoveled, the porters marched their heavy loads down a well-trodden path, strode up the slag pile, tilted their *nasilki* to dump their burden, and trudged down the pile and back to where they had come from, for their next load. Not even the shouting of the guards changed much. "*Davaii, davaii, bistra! Nasilki davaii!*" ("Move, move, faster!" "Stretcher, move!") were the constant shouts.

As I said earlier, the slag was one of the major ingredients used to make concrete blocks. The blocks looked similar to the standard grey hollow concrete blocks used for construction today in North America. The POWs involved in the concrete block production process moved the slag from the stockpile in the corner of the yard on *nasilkis* to a crude mill, where it was mixed with cement and water. Other prisoners then moved the thick heavy mixture in the same fashion, as described above, over to the press. The press had a mold that used a mechanism of weighted rollers to apply pressure to the mixture and extrude one concrete block at a time. The whole process was extremely labor intensive and inefficient.

Shoveling slag onto the *nasilki* was physically demanding labor. My body was weakening. Each night I fell onto my bunk, not knowing if I would find the strength to rise again the next morning. On top of the physical demand came the never ending attacks by our ever-present tormenters: lice. If the work didn't kill you, the lice just might. The plague of lice in that camp was so bad, that we jokingly said that we had to be careful not to be carried past the guard house by the critters. Though we tried to make light of our tiny tormentors, in actual fact having lice was no joke. Lice sucked your blood, and drove you crazy with the intolerable itch. The bloody scabs, as a result of all the scratching, were an entry point for the lice to get under your skin. What's worse, they carried and transferred disease. We heard stories about entire prison populations that succumbed to typhus fever epidemics we called it '*Fleckfieber*" spot fever), which were spread by lice, and was almost always fatal. My skin was covered with itchy red bumps, bloody sores, and scabs—some of which didn't heal for many years. One sore on my left leg opened regularity each winter during the first years in Canada. I still have scars from lice.

The commandant and guards in another camp were just as cruel as the previous ones. But the stench and filth were worse. The pall of death was thicker. There were more lice, more bedbugs, but the most significant hardship was that it wasn't only food that was scarce, so was the water. We only got about a liter a day. And that amount had to suffice for drinking, washing, and any attempts at keeping ourselves or our eating utensils clean. I learned how to "wash" by letting a mouthful of water trickle into my hands to wash up. I also learned to keep a small pebble in my mouth to keep my saliva flowing and my tongue from drying up and blistering.

Several brigades from my new camp had to do various jobs to keep a large sawmill operation running. Here too, results were tracked with the quota system. An overseer came by every day to record results. The logs arrived in rail cars, which sat on the track a few hundred yards from where we had unloaded the china. One group of POWs was assigned to uncouple and push the rail cars to the designated site for unloading. The next group was given the task of unloading the logs from the rail car. They crouched under the car and attempted to simultaneously pound out the crude wooden rungs that held the logs in place. Theoretically, the rungs were supposed to come out at the same time, allowing the logs to roll off the car and down the embankment in a more or less orderly way. But things rarely went according to plan. Most often, one of the rungs would get stuck, and the logs would fall off the car and down the embankment in a jumbled tangle. It was a dangerous situation as workers could easily get caught or hit by careening timbers. When the tangle became too great, the car had to sit on the tracks until the logs could be unjammed from under the wheels. When this happened, the brigade pushing the rail cars had to move the next rail car to another spot for unloading.

The wide road at the bottom of the embankment indicated that motorized machinery had once been used to unload and move the logs. But either the shortage of equipment or the availability of free POW labor changed all that. After the work brigade untangled and lined up the logs side by side on the road, another brigade moved the logs from the road to the conveyer-track. A final brigade was assigned to roll the logs along the conveyer-track toward the saw mill. The conveyer-track consisted of two parallel lines of timber—about 8 feet apart— raised up on stubby piles that protruded about 2 feet above the ground. It was like a wide, elevated, railway, with logs for rails instead of iron. The process of transporting the logs to the saw mill required a huge labor force, for no machinery was used. The heavy timbers were all moved manually. First, I was assigned to work with a brigade that untangled the fallen logs. Later, I was on a brigade that moved logs down the conveyer-track to the saw mill.

As I said earlier, each evening an official came to tally how many logs we had moved that day. He marked our final log, and then counted the number of logs between it and the log he had marked the previous evening. The production of the entire sawmill was calculated from that count. Our work supervisor was also rewarded and punished according to the quota system. He knew that without cheating, it was unlikely that we would meet our quota. So, first thing each morning, he made us move the marked log ahead on the conveyor-track to help with the tally for that day. Moving the marked log forward over the other logs required a herculean effort. But everybody was happy when the quota was reached or even exceeded. We would get full ration or a bit extra food that night.

Weakened from the excruciating physical labor, the lack of food and water, and the deplorable, unsanitary conditions, prisoners didn't last long. I don't remember when and how I became ill—much of that time is just a dark hole in my mind. I do know that somehow I ended up in the hospital, where I remained for about three quarters of a year. While there, I survived three bouts of pneumonia and two cases of pleurisy. For a long time I have been wrestling to recall and piece together the details and sequence of events of my many months in the hospital. But I've come to the conclusion that I will not be able to give a coherent account. The best I can do, is to lay out my memories like snapshots in no particular order.

POW Hospital-5929 was in the town of Pakamony (Now called Pervalsk), in the southwestern part of the Voroshilovgrad Oblast, about 40 kilometers from Voroshilovgrad (Luhansk). Any prisoners in the region who were too ill to work were taken there. For most, it was just a matter of time before they ended up in the morgue and then in an unmarked grave on a field not far from the building.

The hospital building had been a school before the war, its large classrooms converted to patient rooms. I vaguely remember being moved from a dark room on the ground floor to a bright room with large windows on the second floor. The long hallway on the second floor had doors to at least six or eight classrooms. I was taken into the room across from the Bärenweibchen's (bear's wife) desk. That was the nickname of a stout, matronly Russian woman who was in charge of dishing out our daily food rations: one ladle of thin soup and a piece of heavy bread, about the quantity of half a biscotti biscuit or a quarter slice of Texas toast (About 1 ½" long x 1"wide x ¾" high). Anyone who was able to walk had to pick up their food from her station in the hallway and take rations back to those who were unable to walk.

It was around Christmas 1945, near the beginning of my stay, when every prisoner in the hospital received one boiled potato as a gift from the Red Cross. We had to sign a receipt, acknowledging that we had received the gift of food. The receipt didn't specify that the gift was a half rotten and barely edible potato. But even that was so special that I see the scene clearly before my eyes to this day.

A string of 4 twin-sized beds—wooden planks on a metal frame with no mattresses—stood against the wall to the side of the doorway, shoved together, end to end. Each twin-sized platform was occupied by 2 patients. Eight beds were shoved together in pairs and lined up end to end in a row down the middle of the room. At least 4 or 5 patients occupied each pair, so a total of 16 to 20 patients lay side by side and head to foot in the middle row. Another 6 beds were lined up against the far wall, with the heads of those beds toward the window.

Those beds were perpendicular to the middle row. Again, 2 patients occupied each twin-sized bed. So on average, there were 36 to 40 patients crammed into a room at any given time. Given the number of rooms and patients on my floor, I figured there were several hundred POWs in that hospital. I have since learned that from 1944 to 1947 it had an average occupancy of about 800.

There was an open space at the front of the room, where the teacher's desk would have stood. This area was reserved as a treatment area. Privacy was non-existent. If a guy was getting treated, all the other patients in the room could see. And it was impossible to ignore his groans and screams.

Dr. B, (I am not sure of the rest of his name and can't get any information about him) was in charge of the hospital, had served as a doctor in the German army. It was said that he had survived Stalingrad. Besides German, he spoke fluent Russian and Hungarian. He obviously had greater expertise than any other medical personnel in the area, because part of his responsibility involved training a group of Russian medical residents. Plus, he was often called out to surrounding homes to attend to Russian civilians. Dr. Tomas was one of his residents. She was a small Russian woman, who tried her best to learn German. She was the doctor who looked after me and the other POWs on my floor.

Initially, I was placed on one of the doubled-up beds at the front and center of the room, with an unobstructed view of the treatment area. I had 3 or 4 other patients as bed-fellows. Often, I was the only patient out of my group who survived the night. I don't know why, but it seemed that most guys seemed to pass away quietly in the dark. Each morning, the dead bodies would be removed and new sufferers would take their place. I remember one man by the door in the other row who suffered immensely but struggled a few days to stay alive. The reason for this particular guy to stand out in my mind is the fact that most men didn't resist death as hard or as long as he did.

Though it was called a hospital, the facility at Pakamony was ill-supplied and ill-equipped. Medicine and basic sanitation were virtually non-existent. There were only two "medicines" available to the doctors to use for treatment: chlorophyll tablets and camphor oil. There were no other drugs—no antibiotics, no pain killers, and no anesthetics.

Chlorophyll tablets are made of plant greens. Most prisoners were given one chlorophyll pill when they were first admitted to the hospital. Given regularly over a period of time, the herbal supplement may have helped detoxify the liver, or could have possibly worked as an anti-inflammatory agent for conditions such as pancreatitis. But one pill wasn't going to make a difference for patients as sick and malnourished as we were. I think it was given more for its placebo effect than for curing anything.

Camphor oil injections were administered more frequently. Camphor is an essential oil that comes from distilling the bark and wood of the camphor tree. It has a strong eucalyptus-like smell that most people today associate with Vicks Vapor Rub. Though it's effective as a liniment, camphor is actually toxic. Taken internally it can cause severe side effects, convulsions, and even death. At the time however, doctors didn't know that. They thought that injecting camphor might stimulate our hearts and help our bodies fight off infection.

Dr. B. injected camphor oil into our shoulders with a needle the size of a turkey injector. It was at least 1/8" in diameter. He said that it had to be thick because of the consistency of the oil. He also made it clear, that the best he could hope to achieve with the few treatment options at his disposal, was to stimulate our circulatory systems and hope that our bodies would begin to heal themselves. Another technique he used to stimulate our circulation was to draw blood from our arms and inject it into our buttocks. That didn't hurt nearly as much as the camphor injections.

Cupping was also a common treatment. It's an ancient Chinese form of alternative medicine that uses small vase-like cups to create local suction on the skin. This is believed to increase blood flow and promote healing. The doctor had us straddle a wooden chair with our backs arched toward him. He created a vacuum in a cupping glass by holding it upside down over an alcohol burner, thus removing the air from the glass. When placed on the back, it sucked on so tightly that a patient's skin and underlying flesh bulged into it. After twenty minutes or so, the doctor removed the cups and the patient returned to his bed, covered in large red welts.

The location of my bed meant that I was a front-row spectator to all treatments. I remember one occasion when one of the POWs had an abscessed tooth. A dentist was called in from the community. He was a huge man who spoke only Russian. He made the patient sit down on the chair in the tub, put his huge hand on the patient's head, and indicated that he wanted the patient to open wide. Then he reached into his pocket for a pair of common pliers to yank the tooth out. Boy did the POW ever holler! He spit mouthful after mouthful of blood into the tub, and rested on the chair for a while before he staggered back to his bed.

It was unusual to see a tooth get infected so much that it needed to be extracted. Mostly, our teeth just loosened and fell out on their own. Guys were always loosing teeth. Like baby teeth, they wiggled and got loose, and then fell out on their own—or you pulled them out without trouble. I lost about 16 or 18 teeth over the course of my captivity. On the upper left hand side of my mouth I have no teeth remaining behind my eyetooth.

There was a large shallow tub in the treatment area at the front of the room. The tub was unlike anything I had seen before. It was constructed of a mosaic of flattened cans. The graphics on the cans indicated that they came from the United States. Originally, they were large and rectangular- shaped, and contained some kind of processed meat. They were similar in size and shape to our modern-day one gallon canisters of olive oil. The meat cans had been cut open, flattened, and joined together in a mosaic to form a tub about six feet in diameter and about six inches high. The POWs, who constructed the tub must have used dozens and dozens of cans, and yet somehow managed to make all seams watertight.

The tub was used for POWs who were going into acute kidney (renal) failure. Renal insufficiency was a common malady. It's a condition in which the kidneys fail to adequately filter waste products from the blood. As the toxins build up in a guy's system, he starts to retain fluid, causing swelling in his feet. He might also experience chest pain, shortness of breath, nausea, and confusion. His belly swells up and distends like an overinflated beach ball. At this point, medical personnel place him naked on the wooden chair in the middle of the tub. He only survives if his body can handle the shock of sudden "draining". To drain the fluid, they poke up to ten needles into his belly with syringes. The needles stay in place and he begins to spout water like an elaborate fountain. His skin collapses like a deflated balloon as the water sprays out. Often, patients went into cardiac arrest or seizures and died during the procedure. I witnessed these scenes more times than I care to remember, and have seldom talked about it.

I was glad when they moved me from my front and center vantage point to a bed under the window. I can't say exactly when that happened. I was hanging on to life by a thread, and was constantly drifting in and out of consciousness. I never went into kidney failure, so I never had to be drained, but I experienced every other treatment available—even the one the doctors reserved as a last-ditch resort.

The last-resort treatment for guys on their deathbed involved a rapid infusion of fluid under their skin. The solution contained saline, and probably also contained a bit of sugar. It was a way to rapidly rehydrate the body and provide a rush of glucose energy to the system. A similar (but gentler) procedure, called hyperdermoclysis (HDC), is used in hospice and palliative care centers to this day.

Every school room back then had a wooden map stand with a telescoping extension on three iron legs. Maps were hung from a hook on the top to teach geography. But the hospital had repurposed the map stand to function like an IV pole for this procedure. A large glass bottle, like the old half gallon milk jugs, filled with saline and plugged with a rubber stopper hung upside down from the hook. The rubber stopper attached to a length of red rubber tubing with a large needle fastened to its end. It may have been the same type of needle used for camphor injections. I'm not sure.

The doctors inserted the needle under the skin of a patient's leg, just above the knee. With gravity assisting, they forced a liter or more of solution down the catheter tubing and into the patient's leg. A nurse massaged and kneaded the enlarging pocket of fluid to coax it to accommodate at least a liter of saline.

The patient was left with a massive fluid-filled bubble, the size of half a volleyball, on his thigh. Needless to say, this was also an extremely painful procedure. For many POWs, it was the last treatment they got before they died.

Somehow, I survived the HDC-type procedure. I had pulled through two bouts of pneumonia and a bout of pleurisy. But another bout of pneumonia led to an even worse pleurisy episode. Pleurisy occurs when the membrane that lines the inside of your chest cavity and surrounds your lungs becomes infected. The inflammation makes breathing extremely difficult. Every breath in and out is accompanied by searing pain. As pus and fluid builds up in your pleural cavity, it becomes increasingly difficult to breathe. In order to relieve the stress on my system, and to try to prevent cardiac failure, the doctors ordered that the nurses regularly extract the pus.

The nurses made me straddle the chair in the middle of the tub in the same posture as for the cupping treatment—with my back exposed and curved. Then they plunged a long-tipped aspiration needle between my ribs into my chest cavity. They drew out a syringe full of pus and squirted the contents into the tub. Again and again they jabbed me in different spots until the syringe came up dry. Every day they repeated the procedure.

It was after one of those procedures, as I lay on my bed drifting in and out of consciousness that I realized I was about to die. Some of my roommates had already written me off. I could hear them debating who would get the meager lumps of uneaten bread lying on the windowsill above my head. Fear gripped my heart. I wasn't afraid of death per se. The war had made death a constant companion. I had witnessed countless men die. The pain couldn't get much worse. I was already fading. In many ways I would welcome an end to the suffering.

There was something else about death that disturbed me. It was the thought of meeting God. I started to recall a few Bible verses I'd learned as a kid. One in particular haunted me. It had to do with man being appointed once to die and after that to face judgement. Fear gripped my heart like I had never known. Crying out to God, another verse came: *The wages of sin is death, but the gift of God is eternal life through Jesus Christ*. I wanted that gift, wanted life, could hardly grasp all implications.

The words of our anthem, "*I will be free*" echoed in my thoughts as I drifted into unconsciousness. I don't know how many days or weeks passed. But I awoke with the unmistakable knowledge that I had made my peace with God.

Sistra (sister) Tatyana always comforted the seriously sick and dying. (Russians, like Germans, call their nurses "sisters.") Tatyana spoke German fluently. It was rumored that she had learned it while performing with a theater group that had entertained German officers. She was young, slender, and compassionate, with a lovely smile and a gentle way about her.

One day, Tatyana disappeared from work. She didn't return for days. When she came back, her smile and compassion were gone. She never spoke German again. Our captors obviously disapproved of Tatyana's kindness toward us. I shudder to think what they must have done to her.

There was one patient on my floor that I still remember with unease. He moved between rooms, befriending patients who were well enough to interact with him. As I started to recover, he came to visit me in my room, and invited me to come to his. His room was right next door, and was basically a mirror-image of mine. The guy told me that he came from the Königsberg area and had also served in the infantry. There was something disconcerting about the coincidence, and about the way this blond soldier asked questions. What's more, I was suspicious about his good physical condition. It became obvious to me that he was a planted spy informer. When he suddenly vanished, that seemed to be confirmed.

Though there were no surgical facilities in the hospital, Dr. B. taught surgical procedures in the morgue. The morgue was a primitive dirt-floored root cellar in the basement. The dingy space was lit by a few bare light bulbs hanging from the ceiling. The lights were concentrated above a large metal table near the entrance. The corpses were stacked along the far side.

Recovering POWs could volunteer to assist with the surgical demonstration and clean-up, for which they received an extra morsel of bread. I was chosen to help out twice. We moved the body Dr. B. selected onto the metal clad table. Then we waited in the shadows while he cut the body open and instructed the Russian residents in internal medicine and surgical techniques. On one of the days I volunteered, he cut open the body of a POW who had worked in a coal mine. He showed the residents the black coal dust filling his lungs. He also pulled out the organs and pointed out how the liver, kidneys, and other internal organs had been atrophied and damaged by malnutrition how the intestines were like parchment. He told them that all the prisoner's insides would look like that— even the ones who were still alive.

When the lesson was over, we replaced the corpse's organs or body parts, closed the incision with a kind of upholsterer's needle and coarse thread, cleaned up the blood and tissue, and moved the corpse back onto the pile to be disposed. At night two able-bodied POWs loaded the corpses on a cart. A peasant hitched up his horse to the cart and hauled them away under cover of darkness. There were countless men who died nameless and faceless, hauled off to the morgue and unmarked graves. Russians report that the numbers who died and were buried around Pakamony POW hospital is about 2,000. I suspect that the actual number was far greater.

After nine months in the hospital, the doctors determined that I was well enough to return to work in the labor camps. They must have specified that I couldn't yet do strenuous physical work, and that my condition was still fragile, because I was taken to a camp where the work was easier and the food better than any camp I had been in.

The camp was situated in a small village. Workers in that camp were assigned to help out with the agricultural industry in the area. I remember being marched out the gate, down one road, and then turning down another dusty road to get to our work site. My job was to paint large wooden vats with tar pitch. The vats were about four feet high and at least that much in diameter. I heard of one brigade over-achieving their quota by simply pouring the tar over the rim and letting it run down the walls instead of painting it on. The vats were used to process green tomatoes. It's no wonder that we found chunks of tar in our containers on the rare occasions we were served green tomato soup.

As I said, there were some remarkable differences between that camp and the others I had gone through. First of all, water was plenteous. That meant that we could drink as much as we wanted and could wash our hands. We were even afforded the privilege of a monthly communal "bath". On the appointed day we were marched to the bath facility. A matronly Russian woman, *Sistra Banya* (Sister Bath), was in charge. She marched us down to the bath room. It must have been an old laundry facility, because it contained a massive steel cauldron, built into the top of a wood-fired brick stove. There was a water pump on the concrete floor, and a trough and drain.

We were taken into an adjacent room and told to strip down. The room was empty except for a portable coat rack with wire hangers, on which we hung our threadbare clothes. A couple POWs were assigned to splash the floor with water to keep it clean. They then rolled the rack of smelly clothes down the corridor into the furnace chamber. We called it the '*Entlausungsofen*'. (de-lousing oven). As we received our bath, the high heat killed the lice and eggs hidden in our clothing, bringing a few days relief.

Naked we had to undergo a 'shave', where any trace of hair was removed from our bodies. The razor was crude. It consisted of a razor blade inserted into the slit of a thin stick. A man, who was designated as our barber, razed off traces of hair from any part of our bodies. Periodically he would sharpen the blade by rubbing it back and forth against the inside surface of a glass cup.

Because of the malnutrition, no one grew much hair. We were thankful that often there was nothing to shave from one month to the next. The barber was rough and unskilled. The procedure was bloody and painful. Given the tools, he had to work with, even the most skilled barber could not have done a decent job.

After the shave, we stood in line to step up to where Sistra Banya inspected us. If satisfied, she administered the bath. First, she splashed the POW with a pitcher full of warm water, quickly followed by a second pitcher of cold water. There was no time to rub down or turn around. Sistra Banya didn't care if we didn't get wet all over. And with no soap, there was little chance we'd actually get clean. But the splash of water felt like a luxury nonetheless. After our bath we sat on a wooden bench to dry off and wait for Sistra Banya to bathe the other prisoners. Our rack of clothing was then fetched from the furnace room. The last few prisoners didn't have the chance to dry off. They had to get into their hot clothes while their bodies were still wet.

  On the rare days off work, mostly when there was a political rally of some sort, we were also ordered to house-clean our dorms. Beside lice, there was an over-abundance of bedbugs to combat. Unlike lice, which spared no one, the bedbugs were selective in choosing their victims and usually only attacked in the dark. The lights in the hallway stayed on all night so the bedbugs congregated and hid in our sleeping quarters. The irony is, we never had any bedding—even in the hospital I slept on boards. We had no mattresses for the bedbugs to hide in. Our pillows were the tunics of the uniforms we had been captured in, which were filthy and tattered from wearing them every day. We must have received shirts at one point, because I can envision a memory of dashing out into the hallway during random night roll-calls, with my fellow POWs and me frantically trying to get the shirts over our heads. Those of us, who needed a pillow to sleep on, rolled our shirts and tunics around whatever we had for personal belongings. For most of us that was just a tin can and a makeshift spoon that we used for eating our daily rations.

  For house-cleaning we had to remove the boards, take the crosspieces off the back, disassemble the iron frame of the bunk beds and take everything down to the yard. Room by room we were called forward, were given a plumber's torch to go over every surface. We singed the metal bed frames. We also had to run the flame over every surface of every board, taking care not to set it on fire. The flame killed the bedbugs and their eggs. It made things a little more tolerable for a few days. But even with the baths and house-cleaning, the bedbugs and the lice always came back.

  Several times we had to stand in line for hours to receive injections from a doctor. We stripped down naked, shuffled past his table, and got an injection of some kind in the buttocks. For many of us, that was the only place fleshy enough to receive it. I have no idea what those injections were for. For all I know they may have been using us as guinea pigs to test some experimental drugs.

  The ration of soup I received each day was slightly more nutritious than I had gotten at the other camps. It contained nettle leaves and greenery which POWs had gathered from surrounding land. I remember getting an extra ladle of soup on my birthday. That was a perk unique to that camp. Another perk was that we occasionally got an anchovy—a small salted fish— along with our rations. A couple of times we even got some tobacco.

  Most of us still wore the uniforms we were captured in. I had been wearing the same military pants and tunic day and night for over a year. Needless to say, my uniform was in extremely bad condition. On certain days a supply room wicket was open where we could obtain some rudimentary supplies for mending our uniforms. When I went to the wicket and displayed the tear in my pants I was given a strip of tent fabric and a sewing needle for the repair. No thread. It was obvious that the fabric came from a German '*Zeltbahn*', and had been used before, because it was frayed on the edge. I carefully unraveled thread from the long edge of the strip and used that to stitch up the tear. The needle and remnant of tent fabric had to be returned to the wicket where I got it.

The rules in the camp were more lenient. Some of the guys were allowed to keep make-shift cigarette lighters, consisting of small pieces of steel, flint, and cotton stored in a piece of tubing, or in an empty rifle cartridge. If a POW had the good fortune to procure some paper, a knife blade without the handle, or the stub of a pencil, the officers wouldn't confiscate it. There were no prisoners publicly brutalized or stuck into a 'hole' to die—not that I witnessed, anyhow.

Best of all, the camp offered one highly prized reward to POWs who had met their quota and had regularly attended voluntary political indoctrination classes: to write a card to loved ones. A prisoner's entire brigade had to achieve their quota consistently for one month before its members qualified for this privilege.

I was finally given a postcard with printed lines for writing a personal note. I knew the cards would be screened, and that if I said anything negative, my postcard wouldn't be sent. So I tried to be as generic and positive as I could. I told my family that I was alive in a Russian POW camp, and that I was being treated well. I passed on my love and greetings and signed my name at the bottom. I addressed the letter to my Dad, Mom and sister—care of my uncle's address in Hermannsfeld. I had no idea if it would reach them, or if any of them were still alive.

A commission of 5 or 6 people periodically showed up at the camp to evaluate the physical status of the prisoners. They were likely from some official government agency. They never showed up at my previous camps, only at this one. It was their job to determine our work capacity—what type of work we were fit to do. We were given a classification, and based on this classification, were assigned to different brigades and types of work.

When a commission showed up, we had to strip down naked, line up, and march past the seated officials for evaluation. The evaluation was simple. One of the commission members pinched the skin on our upper arms or legs to check the extent of our muscle atrophy. Prisoners who had less wasting were assigned a higher classification, while those whose skin clung to their bones with little remaining flesh, were assigned a lower classification. D1 to D4 were designations for the weaker ones, D4 was the classification for the most emaciated.

Every time a commission showed up, rumors of imminent release circulated. It was said that these commissions had power to release prisoners to be sent back to Germany. Disappointment followed every new rumor. We dubbed these inspections: *'Fleischbewertung'* (meat inspection).

My health deteriorated rapidly. The guards had to assign other prisoners to help me to the workplace and back. My classification was abysmally low, but it declared me fit for that particular task, so I had to perform it. I was getting weaker and weaker by the day. My cough was getting worse, and my chest was rattling and giving me sharp pains when I breathed. I was certain that a final life-ending episode of pneumonia and pleurisy was in the making.

Again, one morning, as we were getting ready to line up at the gate, orders came to strip down and march past another commission. This time they were high ranking Russian Army officers in full regalia. Again, rumors of release started to fly. What was different about this commission was that none of the members pinched anybody. We just had to stand and parade in front of them. A few of us were asked to approach and were tapped on the back or the chest and examined with a stethoscope. The examiners exchanged a few words, one officer recorded names and classification as they were spelled out. One by one we were ordered back to our rooms to dress and line up at the gate in the usual formation. I had been given the D4-TB designation.

When assembled in the yard, they singled out about a dozen men, including me, to stay behind and remain in the camp while the rest of the group prepared for their daily work detail. With that order the rumors of release became so intense and convincing that we were showered with scraps of paper from fellow prisoners as they lined up in their brigades to go to work. They pressed scraps of paper with names and addresses of loved ones into our hands and begged us to notify them that they were alive.

The guards loaded the twelve of us on a truck and took us to another camp, where rumors of our impending release seemed to be confirmed, because, yet again, we had to go through a battery of intense questioning. Every scrap of paper was taken away from us during the frequent searches. A few of the guys from my camp must not have answered the questions to the interrogator's satisfaction, because they didn't make it to the next stage. It may have been that they asked to be released to West Germany. Prisoners were only allowed back into the DDR, communist East Germany at that time. I was fortunate that my uncle lived on the eastern side of the border dividing Germany.

What happened next is a blur, but somehow, I ended up sitting in the window seat of a passenger train headed for Germany. I remember catching a glimpse of the Black Sea and thinking about my childhood home. My thoughts were interrupted when the train ground to a halt. Peering out of the window I noticed a freight train standing on an adjacent set of tracks. Heavily armed Russian soldiers guarded the cargo. It took a moment for me to realize that the railcars were crammed full of humans—some screaming in obvious agony. Two years ago, I was held captive on such a train, squeezed and suffocating in the dark amidst the screams. I shrunk down in my seat. My palms were sweaty. My knuckles were white. My heart thrashed wildly against my ribs. I barely dared breathe. After what felt like an eternity, the freight train slowly pulled out of the station and headed east. And thankfully, my train resumed its journey west.

Everything Passes

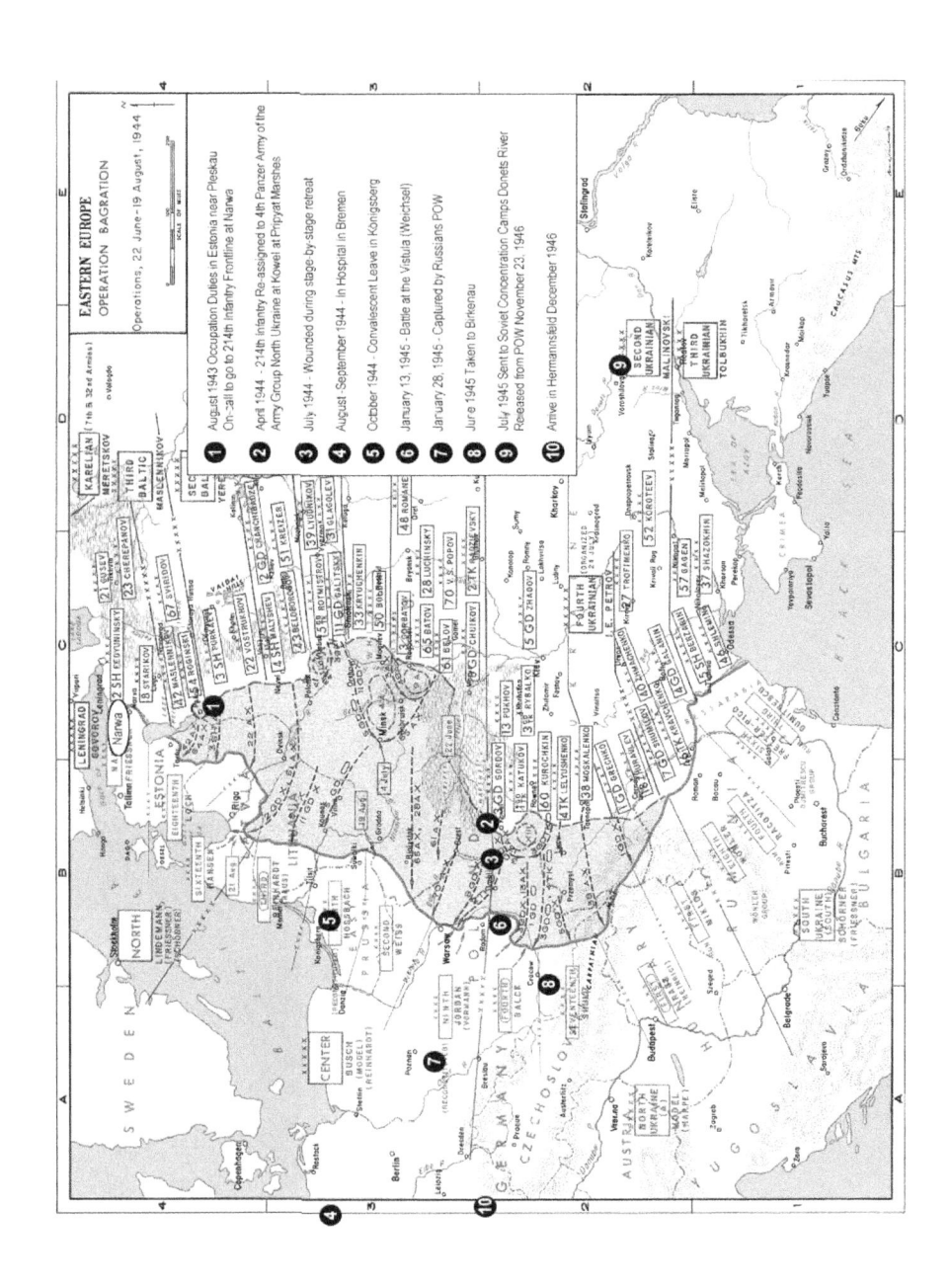

EASTERN EUROPE
OPERATION BAGRATION
Operations, 22 June–19 August, 1944

1. August 1943 Occupation Duties in Estonia near Pleskau On call to go to 214th Infantry Frontline at Narwa
2. April 1944 - 214th Infantry Re-assigned to 4th Panzer Army of the Army Group North Ukraine at Kowel at Pripyat Marshes
3. July 1944 - Wounded during stage by stage retreat
4. August-September 1944 - In Hospital in Bremen
5. October 1944 - Convalescent Leave in Königsberg
6. January 13, 1945 - Battle at the Vistula (Weichsel)
7. June 28, 1945 - Captured by Russians POW
8. July 1945 Sent to Soviet Concentration Camps Donets River
9. Released from POW November 23, 1946
10. Arrive in Hermannsfeld December 1946

174

10 | TO THE VICTOR GO THE SPOILS

The Russians handed me over to East German officials on October 23, 1946. I don't remember arriving at the POW transition camp near Frankfurt an der Oder. Nor do I remember the weeks I spent in quarantine. I was suffering from tuberculosis (TB), an infectious disease of the lungs. My prognosis was not good. I could barely breathe. I was coughing up bloody sputum and burning up with fever. TB was dreaded by the Russians because of their inability to properly diagnose and treat the disease, and because of their fear of catching it. Having been labeled as afflicted with TB was undoubtedly the reason I was among some of the first POWs repatriated.

The common term for TB was "consumption," because the disease seemed to "consume" its victims as they rapidly lost weight. Not that my 5'11" frame had any weight left to lose. By the time I was "well enough" to be discharged into my father's care, I was still at death's door, and literally nothing more than skin and bones. My father picked me up from the transition camp and took me by train to the village of Hermannsfeld. I weighed a mere 97 pounds.

Judging from my release paper, I was among the first hundred thousand POWs of the roughly 2.5 million German soldiers the Russians say they captured and the 2 million they say they repatriated. The Russians claim that only 20% of German POWs died in captivity.

But the official Russian figures can hardly be trusted. They're certainly not in line with what I witnessed. And, according to the Red Cross, 1.3 million German military personnel are still officially listed as missing and presumed to have died as POWs in the gulags. When representatives of the Red Cross came to visit and interview me in the spring of 1950, they told me that I was only one of 7 survivors they were able to locate of the estimated 11,000 prisoners that had gone through a particular camp. I'm sure that must have been the third camp I was in—the exceptionally brutal gulag where our captors withheld even water.

As I said, I don't recall anything about my time in quarantine, nor do I recall Dad picking me up, nor do I recall anything about my reunion with Dora or my mother. The only memory I have of that time is standing unsteadily at the foot of the long dark stairway leading up to where my family had found lodging. My dad must have helped me up, because there was no way I could have climbed those stairs on my own.

It was a miracle, really, that we'd all survived. Much later, I heard accounts of how my family made it there. My mother's story was the most dramatic. She escaped Königsberg during the "Bloody Winter of East Prussia"—one of the worst episodes of the war, and German genocide of which so few people in the world are aware. Mom hardly ever spoke of it, but from my sister's accounts and historical records I've pieced together what happened.

The Russian siege of Königsberg began in early 1945; just weeks after I had finished my convalescent leave and returned to the Eastern Front. By then, reports of the advancing Red Army's barbarism against German citizens had reached the populace. Particularly horrifying were the Soviet atrocities at Nemmersdorf. Young women and old ladies were gang raped and crucified naked on the doors of sheds. Children had their skulls smashed in. Old men were tortured and mutilated. Villagers were burned alive in their homes. Fleeing civilians were machine-gunned down or crushed under Russian tank treads.

Lev Kopelev, a Russian journalist who took part in the invasion of East Prussia, sharply criticized the atrocities. For this he was arrested and sentenced to a ten-year term in the Gulag or "bourgeois humanism" and for "pity for the enemy." Aleksandr Solzhenitsyn, a captain in the Soviet Red Army wrote a lengthy poem entitled "Prussian Nights." It described their 1945 march across East Prussia and the traumatic acts of rape and murder that Solzhenitsyn witnessed as a participant in that march.

The little daughter's on the mattress,
Dead. How many have been on it
A platoon, a company perhaps?
A girl's been turned into a woman,
A woman turned into a corpse.

Solzhenitsyn, too, was arrested and sent to the gulags because he dared to speak out against the Red Army's barbarism. Had a German soldier raped a Russian woman, he'd face certain military punishment if caught. Such behavior was against Wehrmacht regulations and was considered immoral and inhumane. But the Red Army had no such qualms. In fact, Stalin ordered his soldiers to rape Germans, and audaciously, even to keep log books of the number of "trophies" they'd managed to claim and humiliate. Russian soldiers had repeatedly taunted us POWs with their catch-phrase of vicious sexual retribution. It was a war-trophy to which they felt entitled. Even today, few are aware of the true scale of the atrocities that the Russians perpetrated on their way to Berlin. I hesitate to speak of it, and mention it only because that part of the war story is rarely told.

Mom was still there when the Red Army reached Königsberg and began to pepper it with artillery shells and tank grenades. The orders to evacuate didn't come until the city was under relentless siege and nearly completely surrounded. By then, Königsbergers were in a frenzied panic to leave, and by any means available. One rail line remained open. Refugees crammed into trains departing for the port of Pillau. Throngs of people fought to get on, with many getting trampled and injured in the process. January of 1945 was bitterly cold. Passengers—many of them children—froze to death in the icy temperatures. With no room for the living, let alone the dead, the bodies of those who had succumbed were thrown from the windows. Mom was among the last few people to evacuate by train on January 22, before the Russians bombed the track and cut off that route of escape.

As the Red Army took over East Prussia, multitudes of refugees were ferried across the Baltic Sea from Pillau to central and western Germany on every sea vessel available—ships, freighters, fishing boats, merchant vessels and naval craft. Icebreakers worked relentlessly to carve paths through the stubborn winter ice. Enemy planes often attacked the port, and sometimes shot at vessels in the open sea. As you can imagine, there was absolute panic in Pillau. Chaos reigned. Thousands fought for a place on vessels sailing to the West. Desperate refugees pushed, shoved, and screamed. Some slipped on ice and fell or were pushed into the frigid water. Boats were loaded beyond capacity. On the pier, mothers held out their children, and begged occupants of departing vessels to take them.

Mom managed to board a small fishing boat in Pillau sometime on January 30. We know the date because she told my sister that her fishing boat was one of the vessels that responded to the distress call of the *Wilhelm Gustloff*. The *Wilhelm Gustloff* was a passenger cruise vessel that had departed from the adjacent port of Gdynia, near Danzig, on January 30, filled over-capacity with more than 10,000 German refugees—wounded amputees from the military hospitals and pregnant women, for which the promenade deck was turned into a maternity ward. Other passengers included the elderly and women with children. It's estimated that at least forty percent of the passengers on board were children.

That night, the *Wilhelm Gustloff* was hit by three Soviet torpedoes fired at point blank range. The slogans decorated on the missiles announced that the German women and children on board were slaughtered "For Stalingrad!", "For the Motherland!", and "For the Soviet People." The cruise vessel full of civilians sank in less than an hour. The first German ship to respond to the distress call managed to pluck a few hundred survivors out of lifeboats and the water using nets. It was no easy task. Three minesweepers arrived on the scene to assist in the desperate race against time and the cold, saving dozens more. By the time two freighters and other smaller boats—including my mother's—arrived to assist, it was too late. All they could do was help pluck the frozen lifeless bodies of children from the water. It was the largest loss of life in maritime history, far eclipsing the death toll of the Titanic. Yet few have even heard of the *Wilhelm Gustloff*.

Mom was lucky to have made it out when she did. After the Red Army cut off the overland route out of the city, the only way to reach the port was to walk across the frozen waters of the Frisches Haff Lagoon. Out of desperation, thousands attempted to escape via that route. The bitter cold, blowing snow, and the icy surface made the trek extremely difficult. Some made it. But many of the women and children who fled were attacked by Soviet bombers and fighter aircraft and were blown to pieces, or died when their wagons broke through the bomb-riddled ice.

This photo was taken at the port of Pillau on January 26, 1945, just days before my mother managed to board a boat. Conceivably, she may have been standing in the throng of people crowding the docks

When the Russians claimed Konigsberg as their own, only about 120,000 German women, children and elderly remained in the ruins. The vast majority of these later died from disease, starvation, rape, and revenge-driven ethnic torture. The rest were held as slave laborers. In 1949, the Soviet government expelled the 20,000 who remained.

Just like that, the population of Germans in East Prussia was reduced from millions to zero. My people were forcibly expunged from ancient homelands and everything they owned. The extermination and ethnic cleansing of Germans from East Prussia was the largest exodus and displacement of people in human history. It was a genocide of Germans that, in an act of supreme hypocrisy, was endorsed by all of the Allied "big three"--the United States, Britain, and the Soviet Union. As Winston Churchill avowed: "Expulsion (of the Germans) is the method which . . . will be the most satisfactory and lasting. . . A clean sweep will be made."

A few days after the Wilhelm Gustloff slaughter, the fishing boat in which Mom escaped made it to a port near Stettin (Now the Polish city of Szczecin). From there, she headed southwest, walking mostly, and hitching rides whenever possible. She made it to Uncle's place in the village of Hermannsfeld—my family's agreed upon rendezvous-point—by the end of February 1945, shortly before the end of the war. She was one of the first refugees to trickle into that small village.

Hermannsfeld was a small farm community of about 100 inhabitants. It was situated at the foot of Dachsberg mountain, which is no more than a hill really, on the border between the German provinces of Thuringen and Bavaria. It was a picturesque village surrounded by rich flora and fauna, the deciduous forest of the Thuringian forest, and charming valleys and glens. Historical records date its existence to the seventh century. Notable buildings were the hunting lodge that belonged to Duke George I of Saxony-Meiningen, and a beautiful historic church.

Other than having men conscripted, Hermannsfeld had largely been untouched by the war. Tradition reigned, and life went on as normal for the inhabitants, who seemed almost oblivious to the horrors of the political drama being acted out in other parts of Europe. Uncle Gottlieb had been exempted from military service because of a deformed back. That, and the fact that he was the operator of the only carpentry business in the area. When Mom arrived in Hermannsfeld, Uncle Gottlieb introduced her to Ella—a woman he'd married after his first wife died. Ella and the other folks of the village were friendly enough, but Mom felt extremely lonely and had trouble coping with their general lack of understanding of the trauma she'd experienced. It wasn't long, though, until the quaint village was awakened to the new political reality.

Germany unconditionally surrendered in early May of 1945. A few weeks later, at the Potsdam Conference, the Allies divided the country into four military occupation zones—France in the southwest, Britain in the northwest, the United States in the south, and the Soviet Union in the east. Russian soldiers marched into Hermannsfeld to establish and enforce the border, whose lines had been drawn between Thuriga and Bavaria. Hermannsfeld, being situated along the east side of the border, came under Soviet control. True to the tenets of Communism, the Russian authorities began to monitor and control people's movements, and put guards in place to prevent anyone from leaving the East for the West.

My sister Dora arrived in Hermannsfeld in the late fall of that year, while the occupation was still being established. Prior to the Soviet advance she had been stationed with an anti-aircraft unit near Rastenburg, about 80 kilometers southeast of Königsberg. When the Russian Army advanced through East Prussia, she and her unit were re-stationed near Vienna. They were then ordered to move to Fürth, near Nürnberg in Bavaria, and finally, to move their base to the barracks in Kulmbach, Bavaria. By then, Germany was clearly losing the war and on the verge of surrender.

My sister and a friend were the only two anti-aircraft operators who reported to Kulmbach for duty. A kind sergeant advised them to change into civilian clothes and leave, and warned them not to disclose that they'd been involved in shooting down enemy aircraft. Somehow, Dora managed to secure a job and lodging with a baker's family in the area, who made her aware when a clothing depot was opened for people in need. She managed to get some undergarments, a coat and some blouses and skirts. After American troops occupied the area that summer, and Japan surrendered in early September, Dora decided that it was safe enough to make her way to the rendezvous point. Catching the odd ride here and there, but mostly on foot, she finally made it to Hermannsfeld.

Mom was obviously relieved to be reunited with her daughter. But they had no idea whether Dad and I were alive. And since returning to Konigsberg was out of the question, Dora decided that she needed to do what she could to establish Hermannsfeld as the family's new home. More and more refugees were arriving in the village and accommodation was getting scarce. So Dora approached the village mayor and petitioned him to help find a place for her and Mom to live. The fact that Hermannsfeld was her father's birthplace, and that her Uncle was a life-long resident, undoubtedly influenced the mayor to pull some strings. They were given a two-room suite on the upper floor of a farm house. It had accommodated foreign farm laborers. The farmer had died on the Eastern front, and the widow wanted to rent out the space, as she had a handicapped son to care for. Dora was also successful in getting some furniture from a nursery that was closing down.

Mom and Dora were elated when Dad arrived in the summer of 1946. His army unit had fought its way out of Königberg when the Russians besieged it. But unfortunately, he was captured during their retreat and taken as a prisoner of war in Czechoslovakia. Due to his expertise with horses he was assigned to help a local farmer. That farmer asked the POW camp commander to permanently assign Dad to the farm. It wasn't long before Dad managed to escape. At one point during his flight he was stopped by American patrols and questioned. But because of his age, they let him go with some kind of certificate of freedom. He went to stay with one of his sisters in Sondheim, which was in the American zone not far from Hermannsfeld. When he received word that Mom and Dora had made it to my uncle's farm, he crossed the border into the Russian zone.

A few weeks later my family received word that I was being released. I was turned over to the German authorities in October. My dad picked me up several weeks later. I arrived in Hermannsfeld on December 4, 1946 after 21 months in Russian captivity. I was 21 years old.

The first few months after being reunited with my family were difficult for me, and no doubt, for those around me. We did not talk much. I think we were all in shock, each one of us dealing with different demons of the war. My struggle was perhaps more physical. The first battle I had to face was that of not overeating and of avoiding all rich and heavy food. When Dad picked me up from quarantine, he was advised that I should drink whey, if possible, to ease into normal eating. Many POWs died when they got home because they ate the wrong foods, or consumed too much too quickly. Their starved and malnourished systems simply couldn't handle normal food. Whey, they said, was the perfect drink to prepare the body for regular food. So my family fed me whey. I shudder now, just thinking of it.

Even with all their efforts to ease me in, my body reacted. I retained water. My face and limbs swelled up. My skin broke out in boils. But slowly, as the weeks passed, I began to notice positive changes. I remember being astonished when I noticed that I needed to clip my nails. In prison camp, my hair and nails had thinned and totally stopped growing. I hadn't clipped them in years. Another sign that my body was regaining health was that I didn't lose any more teeth, and those that remained in my gums stopped wobbling around like drunken sailors. The boils on my skin dried up, and the open sores from lice bites closed over. (It took several years for the last sore to heal completely. It would close during the summer and start to itch and break open in late fall, even during my first few years in Canada.) Slowly, my body adjusted to a regular diet. But the mental scars of having nearly died of starvation remain. Even now, more than sixty years later, I have to battle feelings of anxiety and agitation whenever my stomach growls and I feel hungry.

I've been trying to recollect thoughts and feelings of those early days in Hermannsfeld. When, exactly, did I shake off the 'prisoner mentality'? When was it that I decided to think about the future rather than remain imprisoned by the horrors of the war? Was it when I finally managed to climb the stair to our apartment unaided? Was it when I could go out at night without someone guiding me like a blind man? Was it when my sister brought her friend, Loni, into our room and I saw the look of shock on her face at my emaciated condition? Truth is, I don't know. But perhaps the call for help from a local farming couple had something to do with it.

They asked my mother if I might visit their only son. He had returned from Russian POW camp shortly before I did. The parents were heartbroken because their boy just lay in bed staring at the ceiling with vacant eyes, not interested in anything. They hoped that talking to someone who had experienced what he did might help. I had to squeeze my feet into shoes two sizes too small in order to venture out. And the walk to their place was absolutely exhausting. But sadly, my efforts were in vain. There was nothing I could say or do to give the young man the will to live. He had come home to die. I can't tell you how many times during the war years, and especially during my time in hospital, I heard guys say "I want to go home to die." He reached his goal a short time after my visit.

Due to the influx of refugees and the arrival of Russian and German border guards, Hermannsfeld had doubled in size. The villagers resented the newcomers, but because my Dad had grown up in Hermannsfeld, I was welcomed and accepted with open arms. A young man from the village befriended me and invited me to join a small group who met regularly at the church for Bible study. That's how I became better acquainted with my future wife, Loni, my sister's friend. The meetings were held in the evenings and because I was night blind for the first few months, I couldn't venture out without escorts. I got to and from the meetings guided by my sister on one arm and her friend Loni on the other. Loni became my constant companion when my sister was not around, which led from dependency to friendship and ultimately blossomed into love.

With regained strength came clearer thoughts, acceptance of the new reality, and thoughts of the future. During my school years in Königsberg I dreamt of becoming a surveying engineer. My army training only intensified that desire. So I set out to the closest city, Meiningen, to try to find a job related to surveying. I hoped that such work would allow me to eventually enter technical school or university and become a surveyor.

In Germany, surveyors do not work independently, but are employees of the state, and work in State Land Title Offices. The State not only hires these engineers, but also hires and trains other surveying staff to assist with tasks such as cartography and maintaining survey markers. I hoped that my wartime surveying experience with the theodolite gun-sight would help me get my foot in the door in a lower level surveying position. But my career hopes were dashed when the employment office informed me, that as a former Wehrmacht soldier, I could give up the idea of ever being employed by the state in any capacity whatsoever. My best bet, they said, was to learn a trade and contribute to Germany's war debt as a blue collar worker. I felt crushed. I was not free to choose a career path. Government authorities would once again dictate the terms of my life.

I went home dejected. Only my mom shared my disappointment. Uncle Gottlieb was absolutely elated. As he had no children, he had high hopes of me taking over the family business. The Thomas farming and woodworking business had been passed down from father to son for a few generations. I assume that it was started by my great-great-grandfather, the Russian mercenary, in the early 1800s. The business was taken over by his son, my great-grandfather Johann, and after that by his son, my Opa Heinrich (Barbarossa). My dad was Barbarossa's oldest son, but wanted no part of farming and woodworking, so Uncle Gottlieb took over. Uncle was thrilled that I had ended up in Hermannsfeld and that his new heir-apparent could carry on the Thomas tradition.

Gottlieb was a craftsman, but didn't have master certification. That meant he wasn't qualified to train apprentices. However he had connections in the industry, and managed to find me a carpentry apprenticeship in Meiningen. He also insisted that I move to the family property to live with him and Tante Ella. There, I could more readily learn how to manage the carpentry workshop and the various pieces of farmland he owned.

Living with Onkle Gottlieb and Tante Ella meant that I was the beneficiary of regular sumptuous meals. Ella was an excellent cook. And since my uncle owned chickens, pigs, cows, goats, a sheep and several pieces of farmland, we didn't lack for sustenance—as was the case for most villagers and refugees. Food was extremely scarce. People, especially the refugees, were on a bare subsistence diet with the rations they were issued. In order to survive, Loni's family foraged for wild berries and greens to supplement their rations.

It's a little known fact that after the war, millions of Germans died as a result of deliberate Allied starvation policies. Eisenhower forbade international relief and food imports. Allied occupying forces were ordered to burn or discard excess food. Under threat of punishment, they were not to feed ethnic Germans. Women who tried to give starving German POWs food were shot at by Allied soldiers. The food situation became worst during the extremely cold winter of 1946–47, when German calorie intake ranged from 1,000 to 1,200 calories per day, a situation made worse by severe lack of fuel for heating. Average adult calorie intake in U.S was three times that amount—a U.S. soldier got four times as much. The Deputy to General Eisenhower went on record stating: "I feel that the Germans should suffer from hunger and from cold as I believe such suffering is necessary to make them realize the consequences of a war which they caused."

Asked if he wanted the German people to starve, Roosevelt's response was "Why not?"

Thomas Homestead and Workshop

Due to starvation and malnutrition, the German infant mortality rate was double that of other nations in Western Europe until well after 1948.

I made the 13 kilometer trip to Meiningen six days a week. Monday to Friday I worked under the tutelage of a master craftsman. Saturday morning I attended trade classes. For the first few months I walked back and forth every day, rain or shine. Then my uncle dug out a bicycle, which he had buried in his lumber storage shed. It was rusty and old and needed a few adjustments, but did I ever appreciate it! My travel time was reduced to less than half. There were three high hills on the road to Meiningen, so steep that one could not pedal uphill. But it sure was a joy to coast down! And it was especially fun when my girlfriend, Loni, rode with me every Friday, on her trip back to Hermannsfeld for the weekend, from her job in Meiningen.

My apprentice training was extensive, covering basics of furniture finishing, a broad spectrum of woodworking, tool care, and even basic training as a lock smith. Whenever possible, I helped Uncle in his shop or on the various pieces of land he farmed. Sometimes I put in several hours of work early in the morning before I left for Meiningen.

A special breed of cattle was used to do all the tilling and harvesting. It was quite the experience when I first had to take one to the local blacksmith for shoeing. Uncle told me that I would just have to hold the front hoof of the cow while the blacksmith was doing his work. That was easier said than done. The more I tried to lift the hoof, the more weight the cow put on it. The blacksmith got a kick out of watching me wrestle with the massive animal. Amused, he finally told me not to try to lift, but to just gently cradle and stabilize the hoof. Things went well after that.

I was equally inexperienced when it came to ploughing. But I learned how to thresh with a flail in sync with two or three other workers, and how to use the scythe and sharpen its edge. I also learned how to use all of Uncle's shop machinery, which was run by one motor through an array of overhead and under the floor pulleys with idlers to be engaged or disengaged for the different machines.

Onkle Gottlieb and Tante Ella

Things in the East zone were getting progressively worse. Store shelves were bare. Food and basic necessities were more difficult to obtain, even when one managed to wrangle a purchasing voucher out of the authorities. It was nearly impossible to find basic supplies for the shop, though Uncle Gottlieb was in the envious position of being able to barter with food or honey.

Government officials started making regular visits to shop and farm operations. They came around at feeding time to count the number of chickens, pigs and cows. They counted our livestock and how many hives were in our bee house. Based on their tallies, they calculated the quota of products we needed to hand over to the government. Failure to meet our quota would result in severe punishment, and perhaps even loss of our property.

Uncle outwitted the officials by hiding some hives in the lumber shed, but we lived under the constant threat of the "headhunter's" visits. The occupying government implemented Communist policies and introduced more and more restrictions. It made me nervous. I advised Uncle about the harsh and corrupt quota system I had witnessed in Russia. I warned him that under Communist rule, his private farm and business might be unilaterally collectivized —taken over by the government. He didn't believe me. He argued, "They can do that in Russia, but not in Germany!"

Onkle Gottlieb was proud of his bees

In the early days of the occupation, the Allies controlled traffic between the zones to manage the flow of refugees and prevent the escape of former Nazi officials and intelligence officers. These controls were gradually lifted in the Western zones, but were tightened between Western and Soviet zones to stem the flow of economic and political refugees from the Soviet zone. Hundreds of thousands of Germans were fleeing the Soviet zone and moving to the West. So the Communists imposed an increasingly strict regime on the eastern Soviet zone boundary. The number of Soviet soldiers on the boundary was increased and supplemented with border guards from the newly established East German *Volkspolizei* ("People's Police").

A ploughed strip 10 meters (33 feet) wide was created along the entire length of the inner German border. In Hermannsfeld, Soviet soldiers conscripted villagers and refugees to clear the forest and brush. Loni and her family had to help with this process. An adjoining "protective strip" (*Schutzstreifen*) 500 meters (1,640 feet) wide was placed under tight control. Later, a "restricted zone" (*Sperrzone*) a further 5 kilometers (3 miles) wide was created in which only those holding a special permit could live or work. Trees and brush were cut down along the border to clear lines of sight for the guards and to eliminate cover for would-be crossers. Guard towers were erected. Houses adjoining the border were torn down, bridges were closed and barbed-wire fencing was put up in many places. Farmers were permitted to work their fields along the border only in daylight hours and under the watch of armed guards, who were authorized to shoot if their orders were not obeyed.

When I first arrived in Hermannsfeld, it was possible to take a leisurely stroll across the border into the American zone. But as time passed, being caught near the border became increasingly risky. Generally, a person was just briefly detained and reprimanded for a first offence. For a second offence one might have to spend a few days in jail. But after repeatedly being caught in the border zone, an offender would almost certainly be shipped away on a train headed east, or would simply "disappear."

One evening, Loni and some other young people and I went to the Baptist Church in Meiningen for a youth rally. As we walked home singing, we were accosted by the Russian border patrol, who asked us for ID. They had been huddled by the side of the road watching for people who did not belong in the area. After checking to ensure we lived nearby, they let us go. Shortly after that run-in we encountered a couple of women coming from the direction of the border. We linked arms with them and persuaded them to walk with us so they could avoid being caught. But the patrols must have been watching. They came running and angrily started interrogating us as to why the two women had joined our group. The situation was getting heated, so I stepped up and took the blame for inviting the strangers. The guards dismissed the rest of the group, but put me and the two women under arrest, intending to take us to headquarters for questioning and punishment.

At that moment, the patrols spotted some other people in the border zone. As if to serve as a warning to behave, they pushed and hit us, roughing us up a bit. At that time I could still understand enough Russian to follow their conversation. One of the soldiers sprinted off to intercept another group and told the other to keep watch. It was an opportune moment! I told the two ladies to run for it, and I bolted away. It was a dark night, so it wasn't too difficult to elude them, and the Russians probably had their hands full with other captives. I eventually caught up with my friends. But I never did find out what happened to the two women.

The incident was unnerving, but it didn't deter me from sneaking across the border when the situation called for it. One circumstance that required a foray into the American zone was the constant shortage of supplies for Uncle's shop. It was impossible to buy nails, glue, and sandpaper in East Germany. But we came up with a solution. Uncle had friends across the border who manufactured wooden boxes for cheese. They paid their workers daily according to the number of pieces built. I took the liberty to take the occasional day off from my apprenticeship under the guise of "helping" my uncle with the family business. I couldn't let my master know what kind of help was required. I would steal across the border and spend the day building cheese boxes in order to earn enough West German money to buy shop supplies. After Loni left Hermannsfeld, the job provided money for postage, and later for my train ticket to freedom.

After one such trip I was caught by the East German Border Guards and put in jail in Hermannsfeld. I would have been in big trouble had they found West German currency wrapped around my leg under my sock. But thankfully they placed me in the cell without a thorough search. Fearing that a strip search might accompany my interrogation, I hid the money on a mattress slat on the upper bunk. After my release, I contacted the local lady, who I knew to be responsible for keeping the jail clean. She gladly obliged and retrieved the money for me without even accepting a reward.

It became a real challenge to keep my bicycle tires in repair. I constantly patched the tubes. But the ride seemed to get bumpier every day. It was impossible to get replacement bike tires anywhere in the East Zone. More days of building cheese boxes finally enabled me to purchase new ones. The trouble was, the Russian patrols caught me on my way back to Hermannsfeld. The tires were confiscated and I was put in jail again. A judge was hauled out from Meiningen for my trial. The evidence of the new bike tires was undeniable. A terrible crime had been exposed.

I was given a chance to address the judge. Thanks to the indoctrination attempts in POW camp, I knew just the right terminology to persuade the judge of my best intentions to exploit "the West" in order to better contribute to the success of the Communist state. New tires would allow me to arrive at work fresh, and not tired after a 13 kilometer walk each direction. I simply needed the tires for the good of all. Not only did I get my tires and tubes back, the judge praised me for my extraordinary efforts. No sentence. No jail time. Back to work the next day!

The apprentice shop in Meiningen was only a few blocks from the Russian headquarters. It still came as a surprise when a very agitated Russian soldier burst in. He wanted to drag my master away. I heard the commotion downstairs in the machine room and went to find out what was going on. I could still understand and speak enough Russian to communicate. It turned out that they needed some construction work done at their headquarters because of an upcoming inspection. My master was happy that he got off the hook, and sent me to do the work. He was not so happy when their demands for my services became more frequent and culminated in a mass effort to renovate a local movie house for the Russian troops. That was very likely close to the time I had to take my journeyman's exam and finish up my employment in Meiningen. At any rate, it was the last time I remember having to work for the Russians.

Life became more stressful as Communism became more and more entrenched. Hermannsfeld was in the Restricted Zone and had to cope with regular Russian border patrols, roving Russian patrols, around the clock manned guard towers, and German border guards.

At 23 years old I was the oldest apprentice in the entire school. One day each week was classroom time for all apprentices. My teacher was not much older than I. I don't remember exactly how or when my teacher approached me to get his wife across the border. I met with him and his wife a few times in their home to work on the plan. Everything had to be prepared in secrecy.

I don't remember all the details. I just recall my apprehension about the whole thing. It was getting increasingly dangerous to assist people across. A few other guys from my Bible Study and I had smuggled individuals over the border, but the patrols were on the alert, and the tap on the window at night might be a Communist spy rather than a legitimate request for help. It was difficult to know who to trust. Thankfully everything went well. I got my teacher's wife across and he followed a short time later. The white shirt I wore at my wedding was a gift from them before they left.

To my surprise, the next person who asked for my help crossing the border was my own girlfriend! Her brother Kurt had convinced their family to flee. He'd been a POW in Britain. In the spring of 1948, Kurt got a government permit to travel from East to West Germany on a temporary visit. He entered the East-Zone with fear and trepidation. He could not believe how emaciated and malnourished everyone looked. Loni's mom weighed only 90 pounds! Kurt was absolutely appalled at their appearance and impoverished circumstances. And he got sick trying to eat the wild spinach and forest pickings with which they supplemented their rations. Kurt urged his family to leave East-Germany while it was still possible. Border security was becoming increasingly strict, and so were the penalties for those caught crossing. He and Loni's father agreed that the family would escape East-Germany, and then find a way to leave Germany altogether, and hopefully immigrate to America.

I felt conflicted. I didn't want Loni to leave, but I cared so much for her that I would do anything to ensure her safety and happiness. I knew that living under Communism would become increasingly difficult and oppressive. So that summer, when Loni's Father was home on summer break from his teaching job, I helped them put their plan into effect.

Little by little, I helped them smuggle their meager belongings over the border under the cover of night. It was too dangerous for Loni's Dad to help. He had to stay out of it. Due to his position as a Russian language teacher, he could not afford to be caught. If Loni or her mom or I were caught, we would have probably been jailed. But for him, the consequences would have been much more severe. The three of us crossed the border about ten times. Possessions were few and precious, so trip after trip we carried across all their clothing, bedding, tools, utensils, pots and pans . . . and even their encyclopedia set.

On Sundays, Loni and I would go for a stroll to investigate and decide on that week's route. We took a different route through the forest every time we crossed the border. The process took several hours, and I had to be at work in Meiningen the next morning by 8 o'clock. We usually started out at dusk. Often it was so dark in the dense forest that we could hardly see where we were going. But then we had to cross the clear-cut. The hundred meter wide clear-cut between the East and West zones was maintained by the Russians, and later fortified with a barbed wire fence. It was extremely dangerous because it was so open and vigorously patrolled. After crossing the clear-cut, there was lots of underbrush on the American side, so we had to move slowly and try to stay on established paths.

The closest town in West Germany was Ostheim. There, it was easy to move around. Nobody would stop or bother us. We'd go directly to the rail station and ship our belongings to Kurt. Getting back was less dangerous since we had no baggage and were heading from West to East. We could easily pose as farm workers returning from the fields. I always parted with Loni and her mom in Ostheim, so I could quickly cross the border and make my way straight to work. Each trip meant staying up all night, but we had to carry on with our normal activities for the rest of the day in order to avoid arousing suspicion.

We experienced some extremely close calls on our trips across. Once, the border patrols spotted us and took up chase. Carrying heavy burdens through the drizzling rain we couldn't move quickly. The only option was to jump into a small thicket in the middle of a forked path. The path joined together again at the other end of the thicket. I held my breath and prayed as the guards passed right beside and around us. We could see the beam of their flashlight passing through the darkness over our heads. Agitated, one hollered, "They must be here somewhere!" We stayed huddled there for quite some time. Humanly speaking, it seemed impossible that they didn't find us. But I think my prayers had something to do with that. Due to that delay, I couldn't continue on. Arriving late to work the next morning would endanger the whole plan.

On another occasion, I was returning by myself, on a narrow forest path bordered by a steep embankment. There was no way to avoid using that path. As I approached the narrow spot, which was just wide enough for one person, I heard footsteps and voices coming towards me. I froze in my tracks. I was trapped! I couldn't jump down the cliff, and I couldn't climb up the rock. There was nowhere to go! In desperation, I covered my face with my hands and pressed my body tightly against the rock, hoping my dark clothes would help me blend in. Two American border guards approached, engaged in deep conversation. They had their rifles slung over their shoulders. They passed by so close that that the butt of one guard's rifle hit me on the back end as he walked past. But miraculously, they didn't notice me wedged against the rock.

The final crossing involved the three of us plus Loni's Dad, younger sister, and disabled brother. It was by far the most dangerous. In order to pull it off, we engaged in some careful planning and serious scouting. At the fire patrol station, I managed to talk to the German border guards on duty to glean information about their routes and schedules for the week. On the designated night, I stole out of my room and met up with the family at their place.

Nothing but large furniture remained. We had managed to get everything else across. That night, we only had to take the bulky handcart along for Loni's brother Hans to ride in. He had muscular dystrophy and his ability to walk had deteriorated. We took a route past the "Gasthaus" on the edge of the village. I carried the handcart and Loni's Dad carried Hans until we were well into the forest. The moon periodically broke through the clouds, bathing the countryside with light. We had to wait for the moon to tuck behind the clouds so we could bolt across the clear cut area. Thankfully, everything went as planned. I accompanied Loni's family to the train station in Ostheim and said good-bye as they boarded the train to Cologne.

Saying good-bye was difficult. That whole year was difficult. Several months earlier, my mother became ill. At first, she was diagnosed with the prevalent ailment, "swelling of the liver." Even the simple medical diagnostic tools of those days had been confiscated and shipped to Russia, so doctors were mostly limited to guesswork. When Mom didn't get better at home, she was admitted to the hospital where Dora worked as a nurse. Initially, her condition seemed to stabilize, but as time progressed, she started acting strange—wandering off, not eating, and becoming less cooperative. Dora accompanied Mom when she was moved to a care home in Hildburghausen. We had a harder time to visit her as it required a ride by train.

Maria Marquardt Thomas
1892-1948

Mom became more and more confused and deteriorated to the point where she didn't even recognize us. The doctors assumed that she had a brain tumor or an aneurysm. But as all the medical equipment had been stripped from Germany, they were unable to do the necessary tests to confirm this diagnosis.

Mom's illness was one of the major reasons I chose to stay in East Germany—that, my apprenticeship, and the obligation I felt toward my Uncle Gottlieb and the family business. Loni and I had wanted to get engaged, but because the future was uncertain, her father advised against it. After I escorted Loni and the Pokrandt family across the border, Mom's condition rapidly deteriorated. She died about a week later, on August 29, 1948. My Dad hired a farmer with a horse and wagon and we brought Mom's body home. Uncle built a coffin. We buried her in the community cemetery. Dad hewed a gravestone out of a large rock, and hand carved the inscription into the smoothed face.

I missed my mother. I missed Loni. An embargo on mail going to West Germany brought more tension. People desperate to stay in touch with relatives on the other side tried to smuggle mail to the nearest post office in West Germany, which resulted in increased vigilance and more frequent patrols around the village. Several times I snuck across the border to mail my letters. To pass censure with delicate messages, when I did not want to risk the crossing, I would write on a picture post card and paste another one over top of it, applying glue only to the edges. I proposed to Loni in one of my letters, and promised her that I would join her as soon as I was able. It would take a while. I had to periodically sneak across to Ostheim and build cheese boxes to save up enough West German money for the train fare to Cologne.

One day, a stranger showed up at our house. Her sister had learned from my uncle Paul's family that I was living in Hermannsfeld, close to the border. Her sister had told her to contact me and ask for my help crossing the border. Her name was Erna Barth. Prior to the war, her family had operated a bed and breakfast home in Cranz, a resort paradise along the Baltic coast, east of where we had spent our summer holidays. During the war, Erna worked as a typist in Rotenstein, near Königsberg. When the Russians invaded, they sent her to a labor camp. She had been released, and wanted to be reunited with her sisters in West Germany.

The reason for not immediately taking her across the border alludes me now, but it took several days before I could manage the trip. I stayed at Dad's place at night while she slept in my bedroom at Uncle's house. During the day, while Dad was at work, she kept hidden and busy at his place. She prepared meals, mended things and attended to the needs of a somewhat neglected household. Dad started to correspond with Erna after I got her across the border. She returned to Hermannsfeld several months later, when they decided to get married. Dad and "Omi" (as she liked to be called) lived in Hermannsfeld for several years until dad was no longer able to work. They got permission to go to West Germany, where they had many happy years together in Hemer until Dad died in December 1968. Omi then moved to Dillenburg to be near my sister Dora, who looked after her until Omi died.

Loni's uncle, Paul, wanted to cross the border to be reunited with his family. He had been released to Hermannsfeld from a Polish labor camp. But his family, who'd been released from a different camp, had settled in West Germany. Loni's cousin asked me if I could help him across.

I decided to volunteer as a night fire patrol so that I could determine the time and patterns of the border guards' movements. The German border guards frequently stopped at the fire patrol's guard house for a chat. It was more difficult to determine the routine of the Russian guards. Nevertheless, being a volunteer gave me an excuse to be out at night. I also made sure I knew which farmers had dogs. Not many of them did. But I wanted to avoid them, as their barking would alert the patrols.

In the forest one could not help causing a racket when coming near wild boars, but that was not a give-away as they were easily startled by other wildlife. After some careful planning with Uncle Paul, I put the plan into motion. I have vivid memories of that night. It was exceptionally dark and stormy when I entered the forest after I had bid goodbye to him at the train station on the American side. I still feel the fear of getting lost in the woods because of the storm and not making it back to work in time.

I finished my carpentry apprenticeship with honors and started to work full-time with Uzaaaaaancle Gottlieb. I had already learned how to handle most of the chores involved in farming his widely scattered small parcels of land. The biggest challenge was a piece on a hill, around the Russian guard tower, where the 'Peace Cross" now stands. Only a thin layer of soil covered the slate-like bedrock. Barley was about the only crop with any hope of growing there. In the best of years there wasn't much to harvest. Thankfully, we also had a lush meadow in the valley beside a stream. That supplied us with enough hay to feed the animals for the year. All the farming had to be done by hand, as no commercial farming equipment was available in East Germany. Early in the morning we cut the crop with a scythe. Depending on the weather, we had to turn the swath over once or twice a day until it dried. When it was ready, we harnessed a cow to our wagon and brought the hay home to store in the barn. Work in the shop was reserved for inclement weather or during the winter when the crops and the bee hives didn't demand attention.

One of our sections of land was located around the Russian border guard tower

Out of the blue and to my complete bewilderment came a letter from the government addressed to "The Journeyman Ulrich Thomas." It was an official notice to appear at a set time and day, about two weeks from then, at the Employment Office in Meiningen. Was it for a job? Had the employment office changed its stance on me becoming an engineer? I decided that I'd better wear my best clothes and try to forego the long walk or bike ride. A truck travelled to the city twice each day to transport milk and to bring goods back to the village. For a bribe, the driver would allow people to catch a ride. Since I was going on 'official business' I made arrangements with him for the early run. He dropped me off at the edge of Meiningen. It was officially '*VERBOTEN*' (forbidden) for him to transport people.

There were several young men in the waiting room when I got there. A uniformed official stood at the door to another room. In silence he collected our summons and compared them to the names on his list. "Wait till your name is called" was the terse order. No one spoke a word. Most guys just puffed nervously on cigarettes. Smoke and tension filled the air.

When my name was called I entered the room, where I met an official who verified my name and entered it on a form, which he handed to me without explanation. He then motioned me out another door. The form turned out to be a detailed checklist with appointments for staggered times in various rooms scheduled for the better part of the day. In some rooms, they questioned me about my childhood and my involvement in the war. The same questions were asked in another room. One stop was for a physical checkup. Obligingly, I stripped down. A man in a white coat tapped here and there, and recorded my medical history. He seemed genuinely concerned that my assessment as D4 in POW camp and my TB diagnosis and subsequent quarantine in Frankfurt/Oder had not been followed up on. With the paperwork from his room I had to go to another room, and from there to the final place on my checklist. I still had no idea why I was there.

The last scheduled appointment turned out to be a wicket, where I was asked to sign for money, extra ration cards, vouchers for work clothing, and a train ticket. This gave me the clue I needed. I had heard rumors about young men being conscripted to work in a uranium mine close to the border of Czechoslovakia. The work clothes and train ticket appeared to confirm the rumors. My heart started beating wildly. They were trying to send me to the uranium mines! I prayed that the Lord would help me avoid this. I refused to accept the offer of money and vouchers or to sign for anything. The man at the wicket insisted that I had no choice in the matter. I argued and argued with him, and refused to cooperate. In frustration, he sent me to go see the chief administrator.

With trepidation, I climbed the broad flight of stairs to the administrator's office and knocked on the heavy wood door. The administrator sat behind a massive desk. He asked me to take a seat and inquired why I had been sent up. I told him that I had no intention of accepting the money, vouchers, train ticket or job offer. I worked with my Uncle Gottlieb and wasn't looking for any other employment. The administrator claimed that I had committed a criminal offence by leaving my employment in Meiningen to work for my uncle. It would be entirely to my advantage to go to the uranium mine, earn good money and work for reparation. When I replied that my two years in Russian POW camps more than paid for the crime he was accusing me of, he lost his temper. He shouted that the only option open to me was going to the mine or to jail. I hollered back that he'd have to throw me in jail . . . there was no way I was going to work in the mine! And the God who brought me through the war and out of POW camp would surely also rescue me from prison!

At that, the administrator jumped up from his chair, menacingly leaned into my face, and threatened that he could have me arrested on the spot. I didn't budge. After a few moments he seemed to calm down a little. He must have seen that threats weren't going to work, because then he tried a "nice guy" approach. He offered me a cigarette (which I declined, being a non-smoker), sat down in his chair, and again tried to persuade me to take the lesser of the two evils—to accept the offer to work in the mines rather than rot in jail. Not getting anywhere, he finally dismissed me with a threat. He warned me, that I'd better not think that because my home was close to the border, I could escape. What's more, sooner or later the government would catch up with me and force me to repay them for my crime of working for my uncle rather than them. Shaken, I got out of there as fast as I could. It was obvious to me that the man didn't have the authority to throw me in jail, as he claimed he did, but I was worried that he would report me to someone who could.

Uncle anxiously awaited my return. I relayed my experience and told him of my resolve to leave for the West to be with Loni as soon as possible. He was not too surprised, but expressed his disappointment, and showed me his notarized will, which appointed me heir of his estate. If I stayed, I would inherit the family business and all his land. I tried to convince him of my fears about the future of East Germany under Communism. He maintained his opinion that the drastic measures to force communism in Russia couldn't be implemented in Germany.

I'm sorry to say that my predictions came true. Uncle wrote to tell me that even worse things had happened. His land was taken away. He lost ownership of his shop, and had to work in it with his own tools for employee wages when the government made it part of the village "co-operative." At least they didn't throw him in jail or forcibly "re-settle" him. That's what happened to numerous village acquaintances. Not long after I left, the Communists implemented "*Operation Ungeziefer*," which means vermin or pests. People whom the state deemed politically unreliable were removed from the village by force and re-settled in places farther East and/or conscripted to forced labor. Citizens with Western contacts, churchgoers, former members of the NSDAP, farmers who failed to meet their delivery quotas, and anyone who expressed any negative sentiment toward Communism were "cleaned out" of the restricted zone. There's no doubt in my mind that I would have been classified as vermin during that operation, and forced to go work in the deadly uranium mine.

The Baptist church in Meiningen fell under extreme government harassment and persecution for accepting international clothing donations for refugees. The church officials were accused of spreading American propaganda. For this crime, the Pastor and deacons were imprisoned. Even the pastor's pregnant wife, who distributed clothing and food to the poor, was jailed. Her baby was born in prison. I have no idea what eventually happened to all of them. I shudder to think of it.

I kept my plans to escape East Germany from everyone but uncle Gottlieb for fear that someone might inadvertently drop a word. After my encounter at the Employment Office, I was worried that even the slightest suspicion or misstep would land me in jail. It was bad enough that I had to cross the border several times before my final departure to work to save up for the train fare. East German money had been devalued and wasn't accepted in the West.

I don't know if I expressed my gratitude to uncle Gottlieb enough when I said good bye to him on December 13, 1949. I could only ask him to relay my best wishes and thanks to Aunt Ella. She didn't know that I was leaving, nor did my father. That last evening, on my way to the border, I stopped at his home to say good bye. Of course my dad was shocked. Saying good-bye was hard and awkward at the same time. I think he must have been hurt that I hadn't confided in him. But he wished me all the best, and said he wanted to give me a parting gift. Looking around at his meagre possessions, he chose a creamy white, lightweight raincoat. A tailor had made it for him from army surplus material. I tried to refuse, but he insisted. Since my small suitcase was packed tight, I wore the coat as dad accompanied me to the edge of the village. Little did we know how important this gift would turn out to be.

The clouds hung low. There'd been a light sprinkling of snow earlier that day. Under the cover of night, I planned to zigzag across the open field, slip across a high gravel road, and into the forest on the other side. But when I was half-way across the field, I heard Russian voices coming from the direction of the road. I was out in the open. There was nowhere to hide! Desperate, I sprawled out on top of my suitcase. The creamy white raincoat must have served as camouflage against the snowy ground. The patrols, who were less than 100 feet away, didn't see me. I'm so thankful that God put it into my dad's mind to give me that coat!

The shock and tension of that close-call didn't wear off until I was well past the clear cut into the American zone. Relieved, I guess I let my guard down a bit too much. Yes, I had escaped the Russian border guards. But I had not been vigilant about the American ones. Coming out of the forest I ran smack into them. The American Border Guards marched me back to their station. From there, I was taken to a school building they used to house, question, and process illegals. I'd never been caught in the West before, so from their viewpoint, I'd be a first-time offender. I suspected that they'd only keep me overnight and long enough for questioning. My biggest fear was that they'd take me back to East Germany and turn me over to the Russians. I'd end up in the uranium mine for sure.

During questioning I was asked if I had any valuables. My suitcase had already been confiscated and placed in storage. The money was wrapped around my leg under my sock. If they took that, I wouldn't have a hope of catching a train to Cologne. When my answer was negative, I was led to my room, which turned out to be holding about a dozen people. Seeing the motley crowd, and re-thinking my decision to lie about the money, I asked the guard for permission to see the judge again. The guard, of course, wanted to know the reason. When I told him that I had been untruthful and had hidden money, he said that he would take it for safekeeping and that I would receive it upon my release. He appeared amused when I rolled down my socks and handed him the few bills I had risked so much to earn. I began to worry—not so much about the money—but about the timing of my release. I prayed that when the time came, I might be the only one released. The Americans customarily loaded illegals into a jeep to take back to the border and turn them over to the Russians. But they wouldn't bother making the trip to deport only one illegal.

Again, God answered my prayers. My name was called, and I alone was taken to a clerk's office, where I was asked to sign a return receipt for my possessions, and sign a declaration that I would leave the American Zone within 24 hours. I got the suitcase back and amazingly also got all my money back. I left that place with great trepidation and fear that I would be followed or detected by the border patrols. On the alert for anyone trailing me, I carefully made my way to the train station and purchased a ticket. Nervously, I hid in a washroom stall until the departure time. Determined not to let my guard down again, I boarded the train at the very last minute.

It wasn't until I arrived in Rheidt that the tension started to lift. I had made it to the West. I was going to be reunited with the woman who would soon be my wife. Together we would leave behind our war-torn pasts, immigrate to a new country, and start a new life. Loni and I announced our engagement at her parent's 25th wedding anniversary celebration a few days later, just before Christmas 1949.

Because of my carpentry skills I was soon able to secure a job at a woodworking shop. But before I could start work, I had to legalize my stay in West Germany by going through a camp for refugees. I spent a few days at that camp and after lengthy and thorough interrogation finally was granted refugee status. That qualified me to start work, and also entitled me to food ration stamps. The Pokrandts had some anxious days, waiting and praying that I would not be sent back to the Communist Zone

When we found out that if we were married, Loni and I could apply for a small development grant to renovate a neighbor's attic, and have a place to rent, we decided to get married fast. We posted the required three week public notice and planned to wed on the next day we'd both have off work. On Monday, April 17, 1950, we were married at the Justice of the Peace. We built the suite, saved up money for wedding rings, a wedding dress, a suit, a photographer, and a formal church wedding. There were 13 people at our wedding celebration dinner in her parent's living room.

Loni finished her three-year dressmaking apprenticeship later that year. I took the train to work at seven each morning and usually didn't make it home till eight each evening. On Saturdays we both worked half-days. Loni was pregnant. We were dirt poor. We were treated like second-class citizens because we were refugees. But we were safe and we were happy.

Loni's cousin Elimar Weidner had immigrated to Canada. We were interested in going to either Australia or New Zealand, but neither country was accepting German refugees. When Loni's brother, Kurt, got word from the Canadian immigration office that he was accepted, we decided to follow suit and also apply for Canadian immigration. In the summer of 1953 we packed up our two children, all our possessions, my tools and my box of salvaged nails, and made the train trip to Bremen to board a ship for Canada. For months I had picked up and saved every nail I could find, thinking that I could use them at the farmer's place when we got to Canada, and perhaps even build some furniture for us. Elimar had secured a farmer's signature, guaranteeing me a job. Without that, I wouldn't have been able to immigrate.

Saying good-bye to Loni's parents, sister and disabled brother was heart-wrenching. It was only made easier with her Dad's insistence that the Germany we once knew was gone, that it was the right decision to leave, and that they would follow when they could.

In Bremen, we stayed at a camp and were screened for immigration. Those were anxious days. Not only was I a former Nazi soldier, but the physical exams showed shadows on my lungs. More testing and x-rays were required. I was interrogated and re-interrogated about my background and political involvement. I lost count of the number of times I had to tell my war and prisoner-of-war story. But finally, we got the required permission from the officials.

Our ship was scheduled to leave on the 24th of June 1953. Before we boarded Dieter spent our last German coins at a candy store. I held Dieter's hand and Loni held the baby as we watched from the rail on the deck of the ship. There was a brass band playing on the pier: "Nun ade Du mein lieb Heimatland, lieb Heimatland ade! Jezt geht es nun zum fremden Strand, lieb' Heimatland ade!" *"Adios my beloved homeland, beloved homeland adios. Now we leave for an unfamiliar shore, beloved homeland adios."*

I hoped we had made a good decision. I hoped we would land in a country whose government didn't dictate people's ideas and what they could say and do. I hoped we'd be able to make our own choices and with God's help, work hard and chart the course of our own lives. I hoped that the ocean would take me and my young children far away from all the danger, destruction, pain, loss, and hardship caused by arrogant dictators and Communist and socialist regimes. The hope of the captive still resonated in my heart: *"Everything passes, all things will flee, three years in Russia and we will be free."*

The band played the "Adios" song over and over. Festive streamers exploded into the air as the ship pulled away from its moorings and slipped into the vast grey waters. Such a mix of bitter-sweet emotions! We gripped the rails, cried, smiled, blew kisses, and waved to the people on shore until they were merely specks and we could no longer hear the music. "*Adios beloved homeland Adios!*"

EPILOGUE

History is written by the victors. The losers are shamed into silence and their perspective collectively omitted from the official storyline. The winners are lauded as the "good guys." *They're* the ones who fought and vanquished evil! Even if their actions were just as heinous, ignoble and deplorable, those deeds are whitewashed, overlooked, or shrugged off as necessary, or at very least justified. Any grade school child will tell you that when it came to World War 2, the Allies were in the right, and the Axis in the wrong. Allies were the good guys. Axis were the bad.

My experience indicates that the lines are not so clear or simple. I hope that my story has shed some light on the pain, suffering and loss of the German people. Most of them were innocent bystanders—a school boy with dreams of becoming an engineer, a young girl playing hopscotch down the lane, fisher-women bartering over the price of eels, young lovers feeding the swans at the lake, two old men exchanging stories at the local pub.

Canada has been good to me and my family. It's provided political opportunities and freedoms that I did not have under Hitler's dictatorship or East Germany's Communist regime. For that I am grateful. I am ever so thankful that my children, grandchildren, and great-grandchildren live in a democratic country where they can think for themselves, speak up for what they believe, and pursue their dreams—a country where diligence and hard work is rewarded. I hope that they'll never take these freedoms for granted.

War is horrible. But despite its atrocities, I maintain that there are some things that are worth fighting for, and also worth dying for . . . freedom is one of those things. But I would be remiss to note that ideological and political freedom—as important and valuable as it is—isn't the ultimate or highest freedom.

The ultimate freedom does not depend on politicians. It can be experienced in the darkest jail or most inhumane gulag. It's the freedom I found when my life hung by a thread over the brink of death in that POW hospital in Pakamony. The ultimate freedom is the freedom of the soul. I have found the words of Scripture to be true: "Therefore if the Son makes you free, you shall be free indeed!" (John 8:36)

This month I will celebrate my 90th birthday. I know that the story of my life will soon reach its final chapter. Soon, I will see God wipe away every tear from the eyes; no more death, nor sorrow, nor crying, no more pain." (Revelation 21:4). Then will I echo the epitaph of Dr. Martin Luther King:

"Free at last, free at last,
thank God,
we are free at last!

Heimweh
U. K. Thomas

Es kam ganz plötzlich in der Nacht,
kam auf mich zu mit aller Macht.
Selbst träumend hätt' ich nie gedacht
welch Herzensqual es mit sich bracht',
das Heimweh.

Wie Nebel überm Meere wallt
sich das Gefühl im Herzen ballt
und furchterregend, mit Gewalt
sich tiefer in die Seele krallt;
das Heimweh.

Jedoch die Heimat ist nicht mehr.
Geraubt von einem fremden Heer
belastet es das Herz gar sehr,
zieht es zurück zum fernen Meer;
das Heimweh.

Und immer mehr greift es mich an,
daß ich mir garnicht helfen kann.
Reißt mit sich auf die steile Bahn
erbarmungslos der mächt'ge Wahn;
das Heimweh.

Nur langsam wird es in mir still.
Wallt in mir auf ein Freudgefühl,
daß mir durch Gottes Gnadenfüll'
gegeben ist ein ew'ges Ziel,
statt Pein mir Frieden geben will.
Das wahre Heimweh

The Longing
for Home (Heimweh)
U. K. Thomas

It came suddenly at night,
Confronting me with all its might.
My wildest dreams could not foresee
The agony this brought to me.
The Longing

As fog upon the water hovers
The feeling all the senses covers
And frightening, with full control
Grips deeper yet into the soul.
The Longing

Alas, that home no more exists,
Fell prey to foreign soldier's fists.
But even harder draws it more
The thinking back to distant shore.
The Longing

And ever stronger gets its hold,
Sucks helpless me into its fold
And takes me down the slipp'ry slope
Merciless, without all hope.
The Longing

But bit by bit returns the peace
Replaced by joy's reflective bliss
For God in His abundant grace
Stores up for me a better place
That, still restrained by time and space,
Gives members of the human race
True Longing

ABOUT THE AUTHOR

Ulrich Karl Thomas was born in 1925 in the East Prussian City of Königsberg, near the Baltic Sea. He was a young boy when Hitler came to power. Caught up in political events beyond his control, he was conscripted to serve on the Eastern Front as a Nazi soldier. He was wounded in battle, convalesced, sent back to the front, captured by the Russians, and taken as POW to slave in the gulags. Eventually, he was released to a border town in the restricted zone between East and West Germany. He helped smuggle people across the border, fled as a refugee, and finally immigrated to Canada in 1953, where he worked in the construction industry until his retirement in 1990. Karl and his wife Eleonore have been married for 65 years. They have 6 children, 12 grandchildren & 8 great-grandchildren (and counting).

Made in the USA
Monee, IL
12 December 2022